W9-ASG-980

欢迎:中学汉语课本

HUANYING

An Invitation to Chinese

JIAYING HOWARD AND LANTING XU

VOLUME
1

Cheng & Tsui Company
Boston

Copyright © 2009 Cheng & Tsui Company, Inc.

All rights reserved. No part of this publication may be reproduced or transmitted in any form or by any means, electronic or mechanical, including photocopying, recording, scanning, or any information storage or retrieval system, without written permission from the publisher.

20 19 18 17 16 15   5 6 7 8 9 10

First edition 2009

Published by
Cheng & Tsui Company, Inc.
25 West Street
Boston, MA 02111-1213 USA
Fax (617) 426-3669
www.cheng-tsui.com
"Bringing Asia to the World"™

Hardcover edition:
ISBN 978-0-88727-662-0

Paperback edition:
ISBN 978-0-88727-615-6

Library of Congress Cataloging-in-Publication Data

Howard, Jiaying.
    Huanying : an invitation to Chinese = [Huan ying : Zhong xue Han yu ke ben] / by Jiaying Howard and Lanting Xu.
        p. cm.
    Chinese and English.
    Includes index.
    Parallel title in Chinese characters.
    ISBN 978-0-88727-662-0 (v. 1) — ISBN 978-0-88727-615-6 (v. 1 : pbk.) 1. Chinese language—Textbooks for foreign speakers—English. I. Xu, Lanting, 1963 Jan. 28- II. Title. III. Title: An invitation to Chinese. IV. Title: Huan ying : Zhong xue Han yu ke ben.

    PL1129.E5H67 2008
    495.1'82421--dc22

                                        2008062314

Illustrations by Landong Xu, Qiguang Xu and Augustine Liu
Photos by Peizhi Bai, Junye Bai, Lanting Xu, Jiaying Howard and Bob Phelan
Textbook design by Linda Robertson
Chinese text editor: Jing Wu

Because this page cannot accommodate all copyright notices, credits are listed after the index and constitute an extension of this copyright page.

All logos and references mentioned in this textbook are used for identification purposes only and are the property of their respective owners.

Printed in Canada

PUBLISHER'S NOTE

Demand for Chinese curricular materials at the secondary school level has never been greater, and Cheng & Tsui is pleased to offer *Huanying* — the first comprehensive secondary-school series written by experienced Chinese teachers in North American schools and based on ACTFL National Content Standards for Foreign Language Learning. Designed specifically for the North American classroom, *Huanying* offers a learner-centered communicative approach, a great variety of engaging activities, contemporary topics that appeal to secondary school students, a full-color textbook design, and additional resources that will reduce teacher preparation time and allow teachers to focus on teaching.

The Cheng & Tsui Chinese Language Series is designed to publish and widely distribute quality language learning materials created by leading instructors from around the world. We welcome readers' comments and suggestions concerning the publications in this series. Please contact the following members of our Editorial Board, in care of our Editorial Department (e-mail: **editor@ cheng-tsui.com**).

- Professor Shou-hsin Teng, *Chief Editor*
  Graduate Institute of Teaching Chinese as a Second Language
  National Taiwan Normal University

- Professor Dana Scott Bourgerie
  Department of Asian and Near Eastern Languages
  Brigham Young University

- Professor Samuel Cheung
  Department of Chinese
  Chinese University of Hong Kong

- Professor Ying-che Li
  Department of East Asian Languages and Literatures
  University of Hawaii

- Professor Timothy Light
  Department of Comparative Religion
  Western Michigan University

AUDIO DOWNLOADS

Users of this textbook have access to free, downloadable audio files that correspond to both the text-book and workbook for *Huanying* Volume 1. The sections in your textbook and workbook that have corresponding audio files are marked with an audio CD icon: ⊙. To download the audio files, you simply need to register your product key on our website.

Your Product Key: B54C-82J5

Instructions for Downloading Audio Files:

1. Visit the Cheng & Tsui Download Center at http://www.cheng-tsui.com/downloads and follow the instructions for creating a Cheng-Tsui.com user account.

2. Register your product key.

3. Download the audio files.

4. For technical support, please contact support@cheng-tsui.com or call 1-800-554-1963.

Textbook Audio Content:

- Audio recordings for sounds introduced in Unit 1.1, "A Brief Introduction to Chinese Pinyin"
- Dialogues
- New Words
- Pronunciation Practice
- A Glimpse into Chinese Culture
- Extend Your Knowledge

Workbook Audio Content:

- Listening Practice

CONTENTS

PREFACE

Huanying: An Invitation to Chinese (欢迎：中学汉语课本) is a series of textbooks designed for secondary school students who are non-native speakers of Chinese with minimal or no background in Mandarin Chinese. Following the *Standards for Foreign Language Learning* developed by the American Council on the Teaching of Foreign Languages, *Huanying* will offer four volumes covering four years of study at the secondary school level and taking students to an intermediate-high level of language proficiency, or the equivalent of two years of college Chinese. Each volume includes a textbook, a student workbook (in two parts, one for each semester), a teacher's book (also in two parts, one for each semester), and free downloadable audio recordings.

Huanying is organized around thematic units that are essential to everyday communication. All material in each unit — vocabulary, grammar, idiomatic expressions, culture — is carefully developed with learners' interests and real-life uses in mind, starting from self-introductions and the student's immediate surroundings, such as family, school, and daily life, and eventually extending to the bigger world. Students learn the vocabulary related to the theme, the grammar and idiomatic expressions they need to communicate about the theme, and the cultural information that helps to contextualize the language use. Language practice focuses on authentic communicative tasks that integrate several modalities of language skills and are intellectually engaging. Individual, pair and group activities are rooted in meaningful contexts that appeal to the interests of students and allow students to present, interpret and negotiate meanings through active communication.

Each volume of *Huanying* is designed for an entire school year, with the assumption that there are 180 instructional hours, or one hour of language class, per day. There are six units in each volume. Each unit includes five lessons and one unit review lesson. Teachers may plan to use a week to study one lesson. After the unit review lesson, a unit test can be given to students to assess their learning. The pre-prepared unit tests are in the *Huanying Teacher's Book*.

What Is the Pedagogical Philosophy Behind *Huanying?*

Our Goal: Communication

Huanying is developed based on the belief that the purpose of learning Chinese is to communicate in Chinese accurately and appropriately. *Huanying* is designed to help students achieve this goal through monitored language input via sequenced and organized instruction; vigorous language practice via performance-based communicative tasks and constant reinforcement of language skills; and systematic evaluation via quizzes, unit tests, and student self-assessment. All of the above serve the purpose of helping students communicate in Chinese from the very first day of class.

Our Content: Incorporating the "5 C's"

Huanying reflects the philosophy outlined by the *Standards for Foreign Language Learning* developed by the American Council on the Teaching of Foreign Languages (ACTFL). It strives to provide students with the necessary knowledge and skills that will enable them to be "linguistically and culturally equipped to communicate successfully in a pluralistic American society and abroad." *Huanying's* primary focus is on meaningfulness, which is the core of communication. By imbedding language input and output in communicative tasks set in a broader socio-cultural context, *Huanying* requires students to draw from other academic disciplines and the knowledge of their own cultures to facilitate their understanding of Chinese language and culture. *Huanying* also provides students with opportunities to extend their knowledge in Chinese by exploring the Chinese-speaking communities around them. The ultimate goal of *Huanying* is for students to become more aware of themselves, as well as their own language and culture, through the study of Chinese.

Our Approach: Teaching for Understanding

Different from traditional Chinese language instructional approaches, *Huanying* adopts an integrated approach that promotes teaching for understanding. Instead of teaching discrete bits and pieces of language (vocabulary, sentence structures and idiomatic expressions) through repetitive drills without any meaningful context, *Huanying* takes a real-life communication task as its starting point. This holistic approach allows *Huanying* to teach vocabulary, grammar and cultural information not in isolation, but in context. In order to enhance accuracy in language use, language points are practiced in context. Practice of form, meaning, and function are always interwoven in the communication tasks. Through varied forms of learning tasks, students learn to comprehend, use, and analyze the Chinese language. In brief, *Huanying's* approach affords students with the opportunity to construct their own understanding of new concepts and therefore become more effective learners. Based on our belief in teaching for understanding, *Huanying* pays particular attention to topics and situations that are authentic and that appeal to students. Authenticity and relevance are motivational tools for students to become life-long learners.

Our Strategy for Success: Negotiate Meaning in Context

Successful language learners know how to negotiate meaning by relying on their previous knowledge, and by analyzing and discovering cues from the communicative context. The activities in *Huanying* are designed to stimulate students' schemata, or schemes of how one perceives the world, to aid students in comprehension — getting both the main ideas and specific information — and to guide students step by step through some challenging tasks. *Huanying* also tries to convey the idea that language proficiency cannot be achieved from word-by-word translation. Effective learners approach language learning by looking at the context and structure, not by putting together dictionary definitions.

Huanying involves students in every step of the learning process. Students not only actively participate in learning activities, but also make decisions about using appropriate strategies to accomplish tasks. To help students build a tolerance for some ambiguity and risk as they explore a new language, we have purposefully made some pedagogical decisions while writing this book: 1) we do not provide English translations for the dialogues and texts in the textbook and workbook, 2) we include in the texts and activities some new words which do not interfere with students' overall comprehension of the text/task and which are not glossed, 3) we gradually decrease the use of pinyin as learning progresses, and 4) we ask students to assess, periodically, their own learning.

How Is *Huanying* Structured?

The structure of *Huanying* can be best described by using the "3 P's" (Presentation, Practice, Production) language instruction model as an analogy. The textbook focuses on presentation, and the student workbook on practice and production.

As many teachers still rely on textbooks as the starting point for class organization and planning, we want to assist teachers to achieve success in their teaching. The textbook and workbook are derived from a carefully planned communicative curriculum, with corresponding goals and tasks. The teacher's book is intended to make lesson preparation more efficient for busy teachers; it contains workbook activities, answer keys, suggestions on how to facilitate a learner-centered classroom, and quizzes and unit tests.

Textbooks

Volume 1 of *Huanying* includes six units. Each unit focuses on one theme. There are five lessons and a review lesson in each unit, so that three units are typically covered per semester. Learning goals are clearly stated at the beginning of each unit, and students can check their progress by taking a self-assessment questionnaire at the end of the unit. A typical lesson consists of two dialogues or texts, a new word list (with simplified and traditional characters, pinyin, parts of speech, and English explanations), language notes, pronunciation practice, information about Chinese culture and some knowledge-related language activities ("Extend Your Knowledge"). Units 1–3 focus on helping students master the pinyin pronunciation system and learn the basics of Chinese character writing. Each lesson in Units 1–3 contains a special pronunciation practice section, which is phased out in Units 4–6 and replaced with "A Glimpse into Chinese Culture," containing Chinese poems, idioms, proverbs, stories, and other cultural material, both classical and contemporary. Although the material in this section continues to serve the purpose on pronunciation practice, it is also intended to expose students to Chinese culture. We have intentionally narrowed the depth and breadth of exposure at this stage of learning due to students' limited language skills. The scope of cultural exposure will expand as students advance in their language proficiency.

At the end of the textbook, three indexes are provided: vocabulary, proper nouns, and language notes. Three helpful appendixes are included for students' easy reference: an appendix of strokes, stroke order, and radicals; an appendix of pinyin tone changes and spelling rules; and an appendix of dialogues and texts in traditional characters, designed for students who would like to learn traditional Chinese characters alongside simplified ones.

Workbooks

The workbook contains a wealth of communicative, ready-to use language activities and is divided into two parts: Volume 1 Part 1 for the first semester, and Volume 1 Part 2 for the second semester. For each lesson, the workbook has two types of language practice: listening practice and integrated language practice. The *Huanying Volume 1 Workbook* for first-year students contains an additional third section, Chinese character practice, designed to help students master the writing of Chinese characters.

Listening Practice involves two or more skills — usually listening/reading, listening/writing, listening/speaking, etc. It is separated from Integrated Language Practice because students will need the audio recordings (free as downloads from **www.cheng-tsui.com/downloads**) to complete these activities. Language practice comes in a variety of communicative activities, such as interviews, bingo, board games, role-play, and more. Students will benefit from this hands-on format that lets them use different language skills simultaneously (for example, interviewing a classmate while taking notes and filling out a chart in the workbook). Teachers will benefit because all of the activities are presented in a convenient, ready-to-use format — students do all activities directly in their workbooks and no photocopying of other materials is needed.

Teacher's Books

The Teacher's Books include copies of all the student workbook activities with answer keys, together with "Notes to the Teacher" in both simplified Chinese and English that help teachers effectively conduct the activities and facilitate a communicative classroom environment. Additional information at the front of the book includes general tips on lesson planning and classroom management, and an overview chart of content covered in the course. The appendix contains quizzes and unit tests (with keys). Two quizzes are provided for every lesson: one is a vocabulary quiz that can be given at the beginning of the lesson and the other is a general quiz that can be given at the end of the lesson. Preparing for quizzes and tests is made simple for teachers — just photocopy them.

We hope that *Huanying* will introduce secondary school students to Chinese language and culture. Learning a foreign language opens up a new world for exploration, and the new world welcomes (*huanying*) young adventurers.

Acknowledgments

First of all, we would like to thank Ron and Ken for their support and understanding when we spend more time with *Huanying* than with them. Without them, *Huanying* would be impossible.

We wish to thank our illustrators Qiguang Xu, Landong Xu and Augustine Liu for creating wonderful line art to suit our special instructional needs. Many thanks also go to Peizhi Bai and Bob Phelan for giving us the permission to use their photographs.

We would also like to thank the foreign language teachers at Bellarmine College Preparatory for sharing their best practices over the years. Their professional support and encouragement are invaluable to the compilation of this textbook series. Our gratitude also goes to the Chinese language students at Bellarmine College Preparatory and La Jolla Country Day School. Their unique perspectives and insightful comments serve as a constant reminder that this textbook series are designed for them and that the successful implementation of the curriculum relies by and large on their involvements.

Last, but not least, we would like to thank Ms. Jill Cheng and the editors at Cheng & Tsui for their meticulous reading of our manuscripts and the suggestions and comments they made to make *Huanying* a better series.

ABBREVIATIONS OF PARTS OF SPEECH

Abbreviation	Part of speech
abbr.	abbreviation
adj.	adjective
adv.	adverb
aux.w.	auxiliary word
conj.	conjunction
excl.	exclamation
m.w.	measure word
n.	noun
num.	number
o.v.	optative verb
part.	particle word
p.n.	proper noun
prep.	preposition
pron.	pronoun
s.p.	set phrase
v.	verb
v.c.	verb plus complement
v.o.	verb plus object

第一单元：同学们和我

UNIT 1 My Classmates and I

LEARNING GOALS OF UNIT 1

By the end of this unit, you will learn:

- The Chinese sound system – Hanyu Pinyin
- The rules for writing Chinese characters
- How to read and write 80 commonly used Chinese characters
- Some basic Chinese grammar structures used to form simple sentences (word order, positive statements, negative statements, tag questions, yes/no questions, questions with interrogative pronouns, possessive pronouns)
- Some set phrases for everyday communication
- Numbers 0–10

Your knowledge will enable you to:

- Pronounce Chinese words using pinyin
- Write Chinese characters by following the basic rules of stroke order
- Greet people
- Introduce yourself briefly to other people
- Exchange simple personal information, such as the place where you live, your telephone number and email address

1.1 汉语拼音简介
A Brief Introduction to Chinese Pinyin

In this book we introduce the Hanyu Pinyin (汉语拼音) romanization system as a method for pronouncing Chinese characters. Pinyin is a way to transliterate the pronunciation of Chinese characters using Latin letters. We will be teaching modern Mandarin Chinese, which is the official language spoken in the People's Republic of China, Taiwan, Malaysia and Singapore.

The first recorded attempt of using the Latin letters to denote the sound of Mandarin was made by Matteo Ricci and his fellow Jesuit Nicolas Trigault in the seventeenth century.[1] Since then several romanization systems for Chinese characters have been developed; among which the most popular are the Wade-Giles system, the Yale system, Phonetic Symbols 注音符号, also called BoPoMoFo) and Hanyu Pinyin.

The Hanyu Pinyin system was first adopted by the government of the People's Republic of China in 1958. In 1982, the International Organization for Standardization also adopted Hanyu Pinyin as the standard romanization system for modern Chinese. In recent years the Pinyin system has gained popularity among students and scholars who study the Chinese language, thanks to the convenience of pinyin as an input method for Chinese word-processing. Currently, besides the People's Republic of China, the Pinyin system is also used by Singapore, the Library of Congress, the American Library Association, and most international institutions.

How to Pronounce Chinese Using Pinyin

In the Pinyin system, the pronunciation of each Chinese character in Mandarin is transliterated into a pinyin syllable, which contains a combination of consonants and vowels using the 26 most common letters in the Latin alphabet. For example, the character 中, meaning "center," is transliterated into "zhong." Since this character is pronounced in the first tone, a

---

[1] Matteo Ricci (1552–1610), an Italian Jesuit and the founder of the Jesuit mission to China. In his 1605 publication entitled 《西字奇迹》 (*The Wonders of the Western Words*) he introduced a system of denoting Chinese pronunciation using the Latin alphabet. This system was further improved by the French Jesuit Nicolas Trigault (1577–1629) and was published in 1626 in his 《西儒耳目资》 (*Aid to the Eyes and Ears of Western Literati*).

horizontal tone mark is also added on top of the vowel "o" to indicate the tone of this syllable: "zhōng."

A pinyin syllable for each character, therefore, consists of three elements: a consonant called the "initial," a vowel or a combination of vowels and other elements called the "final," and a tone mark. The tone mark is placed over the vowel. For example:

hàn yǔ   pīn yīn

汉   语   拼   音

1. 声母 Initials

There are 21 initials in Pinyin, not including **y** and **w**. The letters y and w are placed in parentheses in the table below, because they function as initials when the finals **i**, **u**, and **ü** do not have any initial before them. For example, **iě** becomes **yě**, **ú** becomes **wú**, and **ǘ** becomes **yú**.

 Chinese Initials

b	d	g	j	zh	z	(y)
p	t	k	q	ch	c	(w)
m	n	h	x	sh	s	
f	l			r		

2. 韵母 Finals

Pinyin has 36 finals. The finals take one of three forms: (1) a simple final (such as **à** in **pà**), (2) a compound final (such as **ǎo** in **hǎo**), or (3) a vowel and an ending (such as **ān** in **pān**). The simple finals are spelled the same as the five vowels in the English alphabet (**a, e, i, o, u**) plus **ü**. The compound finals consist of two or more vowels. The finals that have ending consonants consist of one or two vowels plus **n**, **ng**, or **r**. In the table below, the finals are arranged into rows depending on whether the first (or only) sound in the final is **i**, **u**, or **ü**.

Chinese Finals

	i (y)*	u (w)*	ü
a	ia	ua	
o		uo	
e (–e)*	ie		üe
ai		uai	
ei		ui (uei)*	
ao	iao		
ou	iu (iou)*		
an	ian	uan	üan
en	in	un	ün
ang	iang	uang	
eng	ing	ueng	
ong	iong		
er			

*The finals in parentheses indicate the actual pronunciation.

3. 拼音拼写规则 Pinyin Spelling Rules

While most Mandarin words can be simply spelled out by combining an initial, a final, and a tone mark, there are some special cases where minor changes to the spelling of either the initial or the final must be made. When you compare the chart of Chinese finals above with pinyin words in print, you will see that their spellings sometimes differ; this is the result of special spelling rules at work. These special cases are outlined as follows:

- When **i** appears at the beginning of a syllable, **i** is written as **y**. For example: **ya**, **yao**, **ye**, **you**, **yan**, **yin**, **yang**, **ying**, **yong**.
- When **u** appears at the beginning of a syllable, **u** is written as **w**. For example: **wa**, **wo**, **wai**, **wei**, **wan**, **wen**, **wang**, and **weng**.
- When **ü** appears at the beginning of a syllable, a **y** is added before **ü**, and **ü** is written as a regular **u**.
- When **j**, **q**, and **x** are followed by **ü**, **üe**, **üan**, and **ün**, the **ü** is written as a regular **u** so that there will not be ambiguities in pronunciation.
- When **b**, **p**, **m**, and **f** are combined with the final **uo**, the **u** is dropped. For example: **bo**, **po**, **mo**, and **fo**.

By now it might seem that there are too many rules to remember in using pinyin. Don't be discouraged! These rules will quickly become second nature as you learn the pinyin system, and you don't need to commit all the rules to memory right now.

4. 声调和声调符号 Tones and Tone Marks

There are five basic tones in modern Mandarin, namely, the first tone (the flat tone), the second tone (the rising tone), the third tone (the dip and rise tone), the fourth tone (the down tone) and the neutral tone. When a syllable is not stressed and does not have a tone mark above the final, it is known as the neutral tone. For example: bà**ba**, mā**ma**, hái**zi**. The neutral tone cannot be pronounced alone and always follows a stressed tone. The tones are indicated by these four different tone marks:

Tone name	Tone mark	Example
1st tone	–	mā, yī, fēi, tāng
2nd tone	´	má, yí, féi, táng
3rd tone	ˇ	mǎ, yǐ, fěi, tǎng
4th tone	`	mà, yì, fèi, tàng
neutral tone	none	māma, nǎinai, jiějie, mèimei

The following diagram shows the pitch ranges of the four tones: 1st tone uses a high pitch, 2nd tone starts with a middle pitch and ends with a high pitch, 3rd tone starts with a lower-middle pitch and ends with a mid-high pitch, and 4th tone travels from a high pitch to a low pitch.

Tones and Their Pitch Ranges

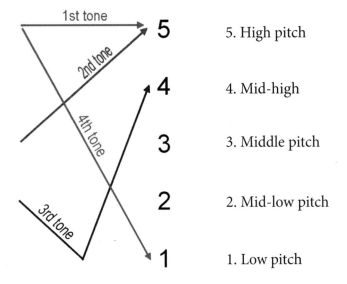

The tone mark is always placed above a vowel. The rules for determining on which vowel the tone mark appears are as follows:

- If there is more than one vowel and the first vowel is **i, u,** or **ü,** then the tone mark appears on the second vowel. For example: **huà, jiē, niú.**
- In all other cases, the tone mark appears on the first vowel. For example: **hǎo, bèi, lóu.**
- These rules do not apply to **y** and **w,** which are not considered vowels. For example: **yuè, wǒ, yǔ.**

你知道吗？ **Did you know?**

Mandarin is referred to as 普通话 (Pǔtōnghuà, "Common Language") in the People's Republic of China, 国语 (Guóyǔ, "National Language") in Taiwan, 华语 (Huáyǔ, the Language of the Cultural China) in many overseas Chinese communities, and Mandarin in the West. It is the official spoken language in the People's Republic of China, the Republic of China (Taiwan), Malaysia, and Singapore. Chinese is spoken by one-quarter of the world's population, and in the United States, it is the language of the second-largest group of non-English speakers, after only Spanish. Because of the increasing popularity of Chinese as a foreign language, in 2007 Mandarin Chinese was offered for the first time as an Advanced Placement (AP®) course by the College Board in the United States. The Advanced Placement course in Mandarin is called "the AP® Chinese Language and Culture" course, and leads up to an exam that, if you pass, will allow you to place out of beginning college-level Chinese.

 课堂用语 **Classroom Expressions**

听我说。	Tīng wǒ shuō.	Listen to me.
跟我说。	Gēn wǒ shuō.	Repeat after me.
请你说。	Qǐng nǐ shuō.	You say it, please.

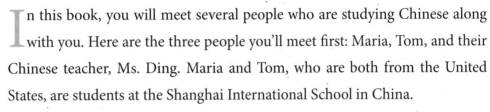

1.2 丁老师
Our Teacher

Dīng Lǎoshī
丁老师

In this book, you will meet several people who are studying Chinese along with you. Here are the three people you'll meet first: Maria, Tom, and their Chinese teacher, Ms. Ding. Maria and Tom, who are both from the United States, are students at the Shanghai International School in China.

 对话一 **Dialogue 1**

(It is the first day of school. Maria Rossini goes to her Chinese class.)

Dīng Lǎoshī: Nǐ hǎo! Wǒ shì Dīng Lǎoshī. Nǐ ne?
丁老师： 你 好！ 我 是 丁 老师。 你 呢？

Mǎlìyà: Nín hǎo! Wǒ shì Mǎlìyà.
玛丽娅： 您 好！ 我 是 玛丽娅。

Dīng Lǎoshī: Nǐ hǎo! Wǒ shì Dīng Lǎoshī.
丁老师： 你 好！ 我 是 丁 老师。

Mǎlìyà
玛丽娅

Tāngmǔ: Nín hǎo! Wǒ shì Tāngmǔ.
汤姆： 您 好！ 我 是 汤姆。

对话二 **Dialogue 2**

(The class is over.)

Dīng Lǎoshī: Zàijiàn.
丁老师： 再见。

Mǎlìyà: Zàijiàn.
玛丽娅： 再见。

Tāngmǔ
汤姆

 生词 **New Words**

	Simplified	Traditional	Pinyin	Part of Speech	English
1.	你		nǐ	*pron.*	you
2.	好		hǎo	*adj.*	well, good, fine
3.	我		wǒ	*pron.*	I, me
4.	是		shì	*v.*	am, are, is (to be)
5.	老师	老師*	lǎoshī	*n.*	teacher
6.	呢		ne	*aux.w.*	a modal particle used in a tag question (see Language Note 2)
7.	您		nín	*pron.*	you (respectful form)
8.	再见	再見	zàijiàn	*s.p.*	good bye

Proper Nouns

9.	丁		Dīng	*p.n.*	a Chinese surname
10.	玛丽娅	瑪麗婭	Mǎlìyà	*p.n.*	Maria
11.	汤姆	湯姆	Tāngmǔ	*p.n.*	Tom

语言注释 Language Notes

1. Basic word order of a Chinese sentence

The word order of modern Chinese is rather fixed. A sentence usually begins with a noun or pronoun as the "subject," followed by a predicate, which can be in the form of a verb, a verbal phrase or an adjective.

*There are two forms of characters in written Chinese—simplified form and traditional form. In this book, we primarily use simplified characters. Most of the simplified and traditional characters are the same. If there is a difference, the traditional version is shown in the second column. See p. 14 for more information about the differences between simplified and traditional characters.

Subject (Noun/Pronoun)	Predicate (Adjective/Verb/Verbal phrase)
你	好!
您	好!
我	是　丁老师。

2. Tag questions using 呢？ (how/what about …?)

呢 can be used to form a special type of question called a "tag question." It is usually used when the second speaker asks the same question that the first speaker has just asked. It is similar to saying "What about you" or "And you?" in English.

汤姆： 你好！我是汤姆。你呢？
　　　　Hi, I'm Tom. What about you?

玛丽娅： 你好！我是玛丽娅。
　　　　Hi, I'm Maria.

3. How to address someone in Chinese

The Chinese address each other much more formally than in the West. It is customary in China to address people whom you've just met using their formal titles, such as "Director Li" or "Professor Wang." If a professional title isn't known, people address each other using a generic title such as "Mr. Wang" (王先生 Wáng Xiānsheng) or "Ms. Li" (李小姐, Lǐ Xiǎojiě). Children are never allowed to address adults by their first name. Instead, they will call the adults of their parent's age "Uncle Li" (李叔叔, Lǐ Shūshu) or "Auntie Wang" (王阿姨, Wáng Āyí), etc. To address someone in Chinese, add the person's title after his/her last name. For example:

Surname	Title	English meaning
丁	老师	Teacher Ding
汤	叔叔	Uncle Tang
王	阿姨	Auntie Wang

4. Grouping pinyin syllables into words

In Dialogues 1 and 2, did you notice that some pinyin words like "Dīng" contain one syllable, while other pinyin words like "Lǎoshī" contain two or more syllables? The *Basic Rules for Hanyu Pinyin Orthography* 《汉语拼音正词法基本规则 》[2] published by the Chinese government specifies 36 rules regarding the standards in pinyin spelling. In general, when a Chinese word (词) that represents an independent meaning contains more than one character, this word should be transliterated as one multi-syllable word in pinyin. For example, the word 学生, meaning "student," should be written in pinyin as "xuésheng," instead of "xué sheng." In the Pinyin system, proper nouns are capitalized, and the first letter of the first word in a sentence should be capitalized.

5. Special tone rules

There are some special rules for pronouncing Chinese words. In our text, 你好 is written as "nǐ hǎo" but pronounced as "ní hǎo." This is because when two or more 3rd tones come one after another, the first 3rd tone will be pronounced as a 2nd tone. The last 3rd tone will always be pronounced as a 3rd tone. For example:

nǐ hǎo   (pronounced as **ní hǎo**)

yě hěn hǎo   (pronounced as **yé hén hǎo**)

When you listen to the audio recording of the text, pay attention to the tone change when the speaker pronounces 你好. In this textbook, we will write these words with their proper tone marks; you should be sure to adjust your pronunciation when you see two third tones in a row.

---

[2] 《中文拼音正词法基本规则 》 (*Basic Rules for Hanyu Pinyin Orthography*), published and adopted by the Bureau of National Standardization of the People's Republic of China, 1996. See http://www.pinyin.info/ for more information.

An Introduction to Chinese Characters (Part 1)

1. The Evolution of the Chinese Written Script

The Chinese written script, also known as "Chinese characters," has enjoyed a long and continuous history of evolution. The earliest examples of Chinese writing consist of inscriptions on oracle bones, often made of turtle shells or cow's shoulder blades. These inscriptions, dated to the late Shang Dynasty (ca. 1700–1027 BC), are called Oracle Bone Inscriptions (甲骨文, jiǎgǔwén) and were used for divination. The second stage of the evolution of Chinese characters is represented by the inscriptions on ritual bronze vessels, dated from late Shang to Western Zhou Dynasty (ca. 1027–771 BC).

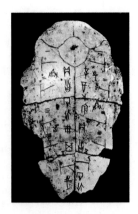

Oracle bone inscriptions.

The standardized Chinese writing script, the modern form of which is still in use today, evolved during the Qin Dynasty (221–207 BC) as the first Emperor of China, Qin Shihuang, attempted to establish the first unified empire. Since then many calligraphic styles for writing Chinese characters have been developed. Indeed, these styles have become an art in itself, practiced by the educated class. Here are some of the most popular calligraphic styles, used to write the character 马 (mǎ, horse).

oracle bone script	small seal script	clerical script	standard script	grass script	simplified script
ca. 1400–1200BC	221–207BC		|_____207BC–220AD		_____| 1958

2. Strokes of a Character

Chinese characters are written following certain rules and in a certain order. Each Chinese character consists of one or more strokes. A few characters can contain as many as 30 strokes, but most contain fewer than 15 strokes. A stroke can be defined as a line/dot that you write in a single brush movement. The following is a list of the basic character strokes:

丶 一 丨 丿 乀 亅 乛 ⺄ 亅 乚 乚 乁

Examples:

认 不 中 人 大 冰 口 了 刻 饭 也 我

3. Stroke Order[3]

The strokes of Chinese characters must be written in a certain order. Here are the basic rules for writing characters in the correct order.

Rule	Example
Left before right	一
Top before bottom	三
Top to down	川
Horizontal stroke before intersecting vertical stroke	十
Left-slanted stroke before right-slanted stroke	八
Left vertical stroke (usually) before top horizontal stroke	口
Horizontal "support stroke" last	生
Center stroke before wings	水
Left-falling stroke before right-falling stroke (Diagonal right-to-left before left-to-right)	文
Outside before inside	向
Bottom enclosing strokes last	国
Minor strokes (often) last	戈

4. Character Simplification

There are two character sets, or ways to write Chinese characters, in use today. One is called "simplified characters" and the other is called "traditional characters." In an attempt to eradicate illiteracy, the government of the People's Republic of China began to develop the simplified character set in the 1950s. The first list of standard simplified characters was

---

[3] For an animated illustration of the stroke orders in Chinese, please go to the following web link: http://en.wikipedia.org/wiki/Stroke_order#Basic_rules_of_stroke_order. If you would like to see the stroke orders of each character that you are learning, here's a fantastic website: http://online.eon.com.hk/.

announced in 1956. This list was later revised and expanded into a total of over 2,000 simplified characters. Characters can be simplified in a number of ways. One way to simplify a character is to abbreviate some or all of the strokes (these abbreviations were often used in different calligraphic styles of handwriting prior to the development of simplified characters):

馬　马

見　见

Another way to simplify a character is to retain only one part of the traditional character:

開　开

號　号

There are other ways to simplify characters, many of which are a continuation of a simplification process that has been present throughout China's literary history. Today, the People's Republic of China, along with Singapore and Malaysia, use simplified Chinese characters, while Hong Kong, Macau, and Taiwan continue to use traditional Chinese characters.

你知道吗? Did you know?

There are about 3,500 most commonly used characters in Chinese.[4] As for total number of characters, 《康熙辞典》 (Kāngxī Cídiǎn, *The Kangxi Dictionary*), one of the most authoritative Chinese dictionaries published in the Qing Dynasty (1644–1911), collected 46,964 characters; while 《汉语大字典》 (Hànyǔ Dàzìdiǎn, *The Dictionary of Chinese Characters*) published during the 1980s in the People's Republic of China listed over 56,000 individual characters. In general, upon completion of nine years of compulsory education in China, a Chinese student should know all 3,500 of the most commonly used characters, and a graduate of a four-year university should know about 4,000–5,000 characters. Students of Chinese as a foreign language can begin to read Chinese newspapers, with the help of a dictionary, if they know about 1,200–1,500 of the most commonly used characters.

[4] 《现代汉语常用字表》 (Xiàndài Hànyǔ Chángyòngzì Biǎo, *The Most Commonly Used Characters in Modern Chinese*), compiled by the National Language Committee and the National Education Committee of the People's Republic of China, 1987.

发音练习 **PRONUNCIATION PRACTICE**

1. **Read aloud the following syllables after your teacher and concentrate on pronouncing each of the four tones correctly.**

First tone: Imagine that you are tuning your music instrument to the A note ("la" on the "do-re-mi" scale). What sound do you hear? Keep that sound in mind when you pronounce the first tone.

bō	bān	bāng	bēn	mēng	miē	mī	miāo
zhī	zhā	zhē	zhūn	chāng	chōng	chuāi	chōu

Second tone: Try to say "What?" in English. What would you do? Most likely you would raise the pitch. Now keep that sound in mind as you pronounce the second tone in Chinese.

wó	hú	háo	wén	wánr	shéi	shén	zán
bó	páng	mián	néng	wán	cóng	sú	zháo

Third tone: Try to produce the third tone by lowering your head. The pressure on the vocal cord will force you to produce a perfect third tone in Chinese.

sǎn	sǒng	sǔn	shǎng	chǎng	chǒng	chǔn	chuǎi
wǒ	wěn	wǎn	wǎng	yǐng	yǎn	xǐng	yǒng

Fourth tone: Some people call it the "angry tone," because the fourth tone in Chinese, in terms of the intonation, is similar to "No!" in English.

pàn	pàng	pò	pèng	nòng	niàng	nàn	nù
lù	luò	luàn	liàn	ràng	rèn	ròu	rù

 课堂用语 **Classroom Expressions**

汉语怎么说…?	Hànyǔ zěnme shuō …?	How do you say … in Chinese?
对不对?	Duì bù duì?	Is it correct?
对了。	Duì le.	Correct.
不对。	Bù duì.	Incorrect.

1.3 大卫
David

Dàwèi
大卫

🔘 对话一 Dialogue 1

(Maria greets Tom.)

Mǎlìyà: Nǐ   hǎo   ma,   Tāngmǔ?
玛丽娅：   你   好   吗，汤姆？

Tāngmǔ: Hěn   hǎo,   xièxie.   Nǐ   ne?
汤姆：   很   好，谢谢。你   呢？

                    Nǐ   zěnmeyàng?
                    你   怎么样？

Mǎlìyà: Wǒ   yě   tǐnghǎode.
玛丽娅：   我   也   挺好的。

🔘 对话二 Dialogue 2

(Tom introduces David to Maria. David is an international student who comes from France.)

Tāngmǔ: *(To Maria)* Āi,   Mǎlìyà,   nǐmen   rènshi   ma?
汤姆：   唉，玛丽娅，你们   认识   吗？

                    Zhè shì Dàwèi.   Tā yě shì wǒmen bān de xuésheng.
                    这是大卫。他也是我们班的学生。

                    (To David) Zhè   shì   wǒ   de   péngyou Mǎlìyà …
                    这   是   我   的   朋友   玛丽娅。

Mǎlìyà: Nǐ   hǎo,   Dàwèi!
玛丽娅：   你   好，大卫！

Dàwèi: Nǐ   hǎo,   Malìyà!
大卫：   你   好，玛丽娅！

生词 **New Words**

	Simplified	Traditional	Pinyin	Part of Speech	English
1.	吗	嗎	ma	aux.w.	a modal particle used in a question (see Language Note 1)
2.	很		hěn	adv.	very
3.	谢谢	謝謝	xièxie	s.p.	thank you, thanks
4.	怎么样	怎麼樣	zěnmeyàng	s.p.	how (is it?)
5.	也		yě	adv.	also
6.	挺…的		tǐng…de	s.p.	quite…
7.	唉		āi	aux.w.	hey
8.	你们	你們	nǐmen	pron.	you (plural)
9.	认识	認識	rènshi	v.	know (to recognize)
10.	这	這	zhè	pron.	this
11.	他		tā	pron.	he/him
12.	我们	我們	wǒmen	pron.	we, us
13.	班		bān	n.	class (a group of students meeting regularly in a course)
14.	的		de	aux.w.	a possessive particle (see Language Note 3)
15.	学生	學生	xuésheng	n.	student
16.	朋友		péngyou	n.	friend
18.	还不错		hái bu cuò		not bad/okay/fine

Proper Noun

17.	大卫	大衛	Dàwèi	p.n.	David

语言注释 Language Notes

1. Asking a yes/no question

To form a yes/no question, simply add 吗 to the end of a sentence. For example:

我是丁老师。	I am Teacher Ding.
⟶ 你是丁老师吗?	Are you Teacher Ding?
他是大卫。	He is David.
⟶ 他是大卫吗?	Is he David?

2. Basic word order of a Chinese sentence (continued from 1.2)

When the predicate—either a verb or an adjective—of a sentence takes a modifier such as an adverb, a time word, or a place word, the modifier should precede the verb or the adjective. See the examples below:

Subject (Noun/pronoun)	Predicate (Modifiers+Adj./verb/verbal phrase)	
我	也	挺好的。
这		是我的朋友，玛丽娅。

3. Personal pronouns and possessive pronouns

Personal pronouns in Chinese do not vary between subject and object forms, as is the case in English where you say "I" as a subject but "me" as an object. For example, you can use the same word 我 as both the subject ("I") and as the object ("me") of a sentence.

The possessive pronouns in Chinese can be formed simply by adding the possessive particle 的 after the pronoun. Following is a table that lists all the personal pronouns and possessive pronouns:

	Singular			Plural		
	Subject form	Object form	Possessive pronoun	Subject form	Object form	Possessive pronoun
	我	我	我的	我们	我们	我们的
	你	你	你的	你们	你们	你们的
	您	您	您的	你们	你们	你们的
	他	他	他的	他们	他们	他们的
	她	她	她的	她们	她们	她们的

When a possessive pronoun (我的、你的、他的···) is used to modify a noun that indicates a close personal relationship, the 的 in the possessive pronoun can be dropped. For example:

我的朋友　　⟶　我朋友　　　　(my friend)

你的爸爸　　⟶　你爸爸　　　　(your dad)

他们的老师　⟶　他们老师　　　(their teacher)

4. Sentences used in introductions

When introducing somebody to others, use "这是 ……" instead of "他是……":

玛丽娅，这是大卫。

大卫，这是我的朋友，汤姆。

When introducing somebody to others in a more formal setting, use "这位是……" (zhè wèi shì…)

玛丽娅，这位是丁老师。

5. The use of 你好 and 谢谢

In the past, many Chinese lived in the same village or neighborhood for many years or even generations. People knew each other very well and their relationships were quite close. Since everyone was living in an extended "family," their interactions were quite informal. Greetings and niceties like 你好 (hello) and 谢谢 (thank you) were considered too formal among family members, releatives, friends and close neighbors. The Chinese would often greet each other with phrases like 吃了吗？ (chī le ma, Have you eaten?); 去哪儿？ (qù nǎr, Where are you going?); 出去啊？ (chū qù a, Are you going out?); and 下班啦？ (xià bān la, You're off work?). When they received a favor from their friends or neighbors, they didn't need to say 谢谢, as they often helped their friends as well. As an old Chinese saying goes, 朋友之间不言谢 (péngyǒu zhījiān bù yán xiè, "There is no need to say thank you among friends").

This old custom, however, is fast becoming a thing of the past. Due to large-scale urbanization, people from different regions are now living in the same city and working together. Their relationships have also become more distant and formal. These days, it is very common to greet other people by saying 你好. When you help a stranger, you are likely to hear 谢谢. 你好 has become the most prevalent greeting in Chinese cities. Casual acquaintances may greet each other by saying 你好. If you call a business, you are most likely to be greeted by 你好. 你好 is now widely used even among good friends, particularly among the younger generation. There are hundreds and thousands of ways to greet in China, and 你好 is the most appropriate way.

An Introduction to Chinese Characters (Part 2)

Radicals of Chinese Characters

A radical is the semantic element (the part bearing the meaning) of a Chinese character. Most Chinese characters are composed of several parts, with one or more parts indicating meaning, and one or more parts indicating sound. The word "radical" (bùshǒu, 部首) literally means "section header." In a Chinese dictionary, all characters that are associated with a given "radical" are listed under it. Therefore, studying radicals will not only help you to understand the meaning of characters, but also help you to use Chinese dictionaries.

For example, in the character 妈, the left part 女 (woman) gives a clue as to the character's meaning and the right portion 马 (mǎ) bears the approximate pronunciation. When using a dictionary to look up the character 妈, we have to start with the radical 女.

The following are some frequently-used radicals from characters that we have learned so far. See Appendix 2 for a complete list of Chinese radicals.

Radical	Meaning	Example
亻	people	你，他，们 you, he, plural (for people)
口	mouth	吗，呢，吃，喝 (modal particle) , (modal particle), eat, drink
女	woman	妈，好 mother, good
宀	house	家 family/home
足	foot	路 road
讠	language/talk	请，谢，认识，语 invite, thanks, know, language
氵	water	海，港，汤 ocean, seaport, soup

你知道吗？   **Did you know?**

About 90 percent of characters used in modern Chinese can be described as "phono-semantic," which means that one part of a character indicates its meaning, and another part indicates its sound. The method of categorizing Chinese characters was developed by Xu Shen (许慎, 59-147 AD). In his 《说文解字》 (shuōwén jiězì, *The Lexicography of Chinese Characters*), he lists Chinese characters in six categories:

1. Pictographs (象形 xiàngxíng), as in the character 日 (rì) meaning "sun." The character ☉ (日) visually resembles the sun.

2. Simple indicatives (指事 zhǐshì), as in the character 上 (shàng) meaning "up" or "top." The character ⟂ (上) itself indicates the idea of "up."

3. Compound indicatives (会意 huìyì), as in the character 林 (lín) meaning "forest." In the character 𣝣 (林), two trees are joined to indicate a forest.

4. Phono-semantic compound characters (形声 xíngshēng), as in the character 提 (tí) meaning, among other things, to carry, lift, raise, promote, or bring up [an issue]. The left part of this character (扌, the hand radical) indicates the meaning, while the right part (是) indicates the pronunciation.

5. Borrowed characters (假借 jiǎjiè), as in the character 東 (dōng) meaning "east." 東 originally depicted a bundle tied on both ends but was borrowed to refer to "east."

6. Derived characters (转注 zhuǎnzhù), as in the characters 老 (lǎo) and 考 (kǎo). These two characters have a similar etymological root but different pronunciations and different meanings.

Learning to write Chinese characters.

发音练习 PRONUNCIATION PRACTICE

1. Read the following names of major Chinese cities after your teacher. How many can you identify on the map?

Běijīng	Shànghǎi	Guìyáng	Kūnmíng
Chóngqìng	Guǎngzhōu	Lāsà	Xiānggǎng
Dàlián	Qūfù	Shěnyáng	Hā'ěrbīn
Xī'ān	Luòyáng	Hūhéhàotè	Wūlǔmùqí
Dàtóng	Nánjīng	Lánzhōu	Xīníng
Sūzhōu	Hángzhōu	Nánníng	Guìlín
Wǔhàn	Chángshā	Hǎikǒu	Nánchāng

2. **Read the names of the provinces and autonomous regions in China after your teacher. How many can you locate on the map?**

Běijīng	Shànghǎi	Jiāngsū	Ānhuī
Chóngqìng	Tiānjīn	Zhèjiāng	Jiāngxī
Hēilóngjiāng	Nèiměnggǔ	Fújiàn	Guǎngdōng
Jílín	Liáoníng	Guǎngxī	Hǎinán
Héběi	Hénán	Guìzhōu	Yúnnán
Shāndōng	Shānxī	Sìchuān	Xīzàng
Qīnghǎi	Gānsù	Níngxià	Táiwān
Shǎnxī	Xīnjiāng	Àomén	Xiānggǎng
Húnán	Húběi		

学无止境 EXTEND YOUR KNOWLEDGE

Choose one of the two research topics below.

1. **Research one of the cities listed on page 24 and find out what famous historical or scenic sites are located in this city. Share the results with your classmates.**

2. **Research the administrative structure of the People's Republic of China and write down the answers to the following questions:**

   A. How many provinces, autonomous regions, municipalities and special administrative districts are there in China?

   B. Use different colors to indicate on the map on page 25 the municipalities, special administrative districts and the autonomous regions in China.

   C. Discuss your results with your classmates.

你知道吗？ Did you know?

There is no strict gender etiquette in China when it comes to introductions. One does not need to introduce a woman before a man. However, there is a rather strict rule that, in a formal social setting, one should first introduce the person who holds a position of seniority, either in social status or in age.

When the Chinese meet each other for the first time in business settings or on relatively formal social occasions, it is customary for people to exchange business cards. When presenting or receiving a business card, one should hold the card with both hands. After receiving a business card, one should put the card carefully in a business card holder. It is considered impolite to casually stuff the card into one's wallet or pocket.

 课堂用语 Classroom Expressions

懂了吗？	Dǒng le ma?	(Do you) understand?
懂了。	Dǒng le.	(I) understand.
不懂。	Bù dǒng.	(I) don't understand.

1.4 自我介绍
Introducing Myself

Kǎilì
凯丽

对话一 Dialogue 1

(Maria meets Kelly at a lunch table. Kelly is an international student who comes from the United States.)

Mǎlìyà:	Nǐ	hǎo!	Wǒ	jiào	Mǎlìyà.
玛丽娅:	你	好！	我	叫	玛丽娅。
	Nǐ	jiào	shénme	míngzi?	
	你	叫	什么	名字？	
Kǎilì:	Nǐ	hǎo!	Wǒ	jiào	Kǎilì,
凯丽:	你	好！	我	叫	凯丽，
	wǒ	xìng	Sītǎnnà.		
	我	姓	斯坦纳。		
Mǎlìyà:	Nǐ	jiā	zhù	zài	Shànghǎi ma?
玛丽娅:	你	家	住	在	上海 吗？
Kǎilì:	Bù,	wǒ	jiā	zhù	zài Hángzhōu.
凯丽:	不，	我	家	住	在 杭州。
	Nǐ	jiā	zhù	zài	nǎr?
	你	家	住	在	哪儿？
Mǎlìyà:	Wǒ	jiā	zhù	zài	Shànghǎi.
玛丽娅:	我	家	住	在	上海。

杭州

上海

 对话二 **Dialogue 2**

(The people in Maria's class are introducing themselves.)

Mǎlìyà:
Nǐmen hǎo! Wǒ jiào Mǎlìyà, xìng Luóxīní.
玛丽娅： 你们 好！ 我 叫 玛丽娅， 姓 罗西尼。

Wǒ jiā zhù zài Shànghǎi. Wǒ xuéxí Hànyǔ.
我 家 住 在 上海。 我 学习 汉语。

Tāngmǔ:
Dàjiā hǎo! Wǒ xìng Wáng, jiào Tāngmǔ. Wǒ jiā
汤姆： 大家 好！ 我 姓 王， 叫 汤姆。 我 家

yě zhù zài Shànghǎi.
也 住 在 上海。

Dàwèi:
Wǒ jiào Dàwèi Gélín. Wǒ jiā bù zhù
大卫： 我 叫 大卫 格林。 我 家 不 住

zài Shànghǎi. Wǒ jiā zhù zài Xiānggǎng. Wǒ
在 上海。 我 家 住 在 香港。 我

yě xuéxí Hànyǔ.
也 学习 汉语。

生词 **New Words**

	Simplified	Traditional	Pinyin	Part of Speech	English
1.	叫		jiào	*v.*	given name is, full name is
2.	什么	甚麼	shénme	*pron.*	what
3.	名字		míngzi	*n.*	name
4.	姓		xìng	*n./v.*	*n.* surname; *v.* surname is
5.	家		jiā	*n.*	family
6.	住		zhù	*v.*	live
7.	在		zài	*prep.*	in, at
8.	不		bù	*adv.*	no, not
9.	哪儿	哪兒	nǎr	*pron.*	where
10.	学习	學習	xuéxí	*v.*	study, learn
11.	汉语	漢語	Hànyǔ	*p.n.*	Chinese (language)
12.	大家		dàjiā	*n.*	everybody, everyone

Proper Nouns

	Simplified	Traditional	Pinyin	Part of Speech	English
13.	凯丽	凱麗	Kǎilì	*p.n.*	Kelly
14.	斯坦纳	斯坦納	Sītǎnnà	*p.n.*	Steiner
15.	上海		Shànghǎi	*p.n.*	Shanghai
16.	杭州		Hángzhōu	*p.n.*	Hangzhou (a city near Shanghai)
17.	罗西尼	羅西尼	Luóxīní	*p.n.*	Rossini
18.	王		Wáng	*p.n.*	a Chinese surname
19.	格林		Gélín	*p.n.*	Green
20.	香港		Xiānggǎng	*p.n.*	Hong Kong

13. zì jǐ
自己
= self

14.
自我介绍
= self introduction

15. 会
huì
1. be able to
2. can
3. will, be likely to

16. 说
shuō
to speak or say

17. 一点儿
yì diǎn er
a little / not many

18. 太 = too
tài
Ex: bu tai
hao
不太好

19. 明国人
guó rén.
citizenship

语言注释 Language Notes

1. Chinese names

First name only: 我叫玛丽娅。

My first name is Maria. / I am Maria.

Last name only: 我姓罗西尼。

My last name is Rossini.

Full name: (1) 我姓王，叫王丽娅。

My surname is Wang, I'm Wang Liya.

(2) 我叫玛丽娅·罗西尼。

I am Maria Rossini.

Unlike European names, the order of Chinese name is "last name (surname) + first name (given name)". When the Chinese introduce themselves, they usually tell people their family names first, followed by their full name. For example:

我姓林，我叫林大卫。

我姓王，叫王丽。

It is not very common for people in China to call each other by their given names, unless they are close friends. Usually colleagues and acquaintances address each other by their surnames, with a prefix such as 老 (lǎo) for older people or 小 (xiǎo) for younger people.

2. Negating a present tense statement

To negate a statement in present tense, simply add the adverb 不 before the verb.

Subject	Adverb	Verbal phrase	English meaning
我	不	住在上海	I don't live in Shanghai.
我	不	住在杭州。	I don't live in Hangzhou.
他	不	是大卫。	He is not David..
他	不	学习汉语。	He doesn't study Chinese.
丁老师	不	认识他。	Teacher Ding doesn't know him.

3. Formulating a question using interrogative pronouns

When formulating a question using interrogative pronouns such as 什么 and 哪儿, simply insert the interrogative pronoun at the place where the answer would normally appear. In terms of the sentence word order, a question keeps the word order of a normal sentence, that is: Subject-Predicate. There is no need to change the word order. In addition, an interrogative sentence does not need the question particle 吗. For example:

他叫什么？　　⟶　他叫<u>大卫</u>。

他姓什么？　　⟶　他姓<u>林</u>。

他住在哪儿？　⟶　他住在<u>上海</u>。

Below is a list of interrogative pronouns:

Chinese	*Pinyin*	*English*
谁	shéi / shuí	who/whom
谁的	shéide / shuíde	whose
什么	shénme	what
哪儿/哪里	nǎr / nǎlǐ	where
哪 + measure word	nǎ	which
为什么	wèishénme	why
怎么	zěnme	how

4. The Chinese language

There are several terms that are commonly used to refer to "Chinese language." They include 汉语, 中文 (Zhōngwén), 华语 (Huáyǔ), etc. In general, 汉语 refers to the Chinese language as a whole (both spoken and written), while 中文 the written form. 华语 is mainly used in Singapore, Malaysia and overseas Chinese communities.

5. Special tone rules for 不

In Dialogue 2, 大卫 says, "我家不住在上海." When you listened to this sentence, did you hear that 不 is pronounced differently than usual? When 不 is followed by a 4th tone syllable, it is pronounced as a 2nd tone (**bú**) instead of as a 4th tone (**bù**). For example:

不是 **bù shì** is changed to **bú shì**

不对 **bù duì** is changed to **bú duì**

6. 儿 as a suffix

儿 (ér), meaning "son," is commonly used as a familiar suffix for nouns in northern Chinese dialects and is incorporated into Standard Mandarin. In terms of pronunciation, the **er** sound merges with the syllable preceding it. Therefore, 哪儿 is pronounced as **năr** instead of **nă ér**.

The suffix 儿 is prevalent in Beijing dialect; its use extends to other parts of speech, such as place words and time words, and it is even used for verbs. In other parts in China – this is particularly true in southern China – other suffixes are used. A good example would be the two words meaning "where" introduced in this lesson: 哪儿 and 哪里. In Beijing you will most likely hear 哪儿, whereas in Shanghai 哪里 is the word that gets you to places. Througout this book you will learn more words with 儿 suffix.

学无止境 EXTEND YOUR KNOWLEDGE

What other languages can you speak? Below is a list of Chinese words for foreign languages. Tell the class what languages you are studying by using the sentence 我学习 ...

Spoken language	Written language	Pinyin	English
日语	日文	Rìyǔ/Rìwén	Japanese
英语	英文	Yīngyǔ/Yīngwén	English
法语	法文	Fǎyǔ/Fǎwén	French
德语	德文	Déyǔ/Déwén	German
俄语	俄文	Éyǔ/Éwén	Russian
拉丁语	拉丁文	Lādīngyǔ/Lādīngwén	Latin
西班牙语	西班牙文	Xībānyáyǔ/Xībānyáwén	Spanish
意大利语	意大利文	Yìdàlìyǔ/Yìdàlìwén	Italian
汉语	中文	Hànyǔ/Zhōngwén	Chinese

中国
měi 美国
韩国 or 文 or 语

An Introduction to Chinese Characters (Part 3)

The Structure of a Chinese Character

Each Chinese character can be considered a single unit that is made up of one, two, or three parts. These parts, or components, of characters are generally arranged in several common patterns:

Structure	Name	Examples
□	Single structure	丁, 一, 上
□	Left and right structure	好, 妈, 你
□	Top and bottom structure	是, 老, 看
□	Left, middle, and right structure	哪, 谢, 挺
□	Top, middle, and bottom structure	桌, 墨, 黄
□	Semi-encircle structure	房, 病, 虎
□	Enclosed structure	国, 回, 四

Thinking of characters in this way—as made up of different components that are arranged into common patterns—will make it easier for you to recognize how they are composed and remember how to write them correctly, than thinking of them simply as a bunch of strokes to be memorized.

 发音练习 **PRONUNCIATION PRACTICE**

1. **Read the following names of popular dim sum dishes after your teacher.**

点心 **Dim Sum**

Dim sum (点心, pronounced "diǎn xin" in Mandarin and "dim sum" in Cantonese) refers to a special kind of Cantonese cuisine that comes with a wide variety of dumplings, pastries and other Cantonese delicacies, served with tea. It is a delightful way to get together with family and friends, drinking tea and tasting the dumplings while chatting away on a Sunday morning. The commonly served dim sum items include:

虾饺	xiājiǎo	steamed shrimp dumplings wrapped in thin, transparent rice flour wrappers
烧麦	shāomài	(siu maai in Cantonese) steamed meat dumplings wrapped in thin wheat flour wrappers
肠粉	chángfěn	steamed rice noodle rolls stuffed with shrimp or beef
粉果	fěnguǒ	steamed dumplings stuffed with pork, peanuts, dried shrimp and other spices
叉烧包	chāshāobāo	steamed barbecued pork buns
叉烧酥	chāshāosū	pastry filled with barbecued pork
糯米鸡	nuòmǐjī	sweet rice wrapped in lotus leaves, stuffed with dried shrimp, chicken and shiitake mushrooms
麻团	mátuán	deep-fried sweet pastry filled with red bean paste and rolled in sesame seeds
蛋挞	dàntǎ	egg custard tart
油条	yóutiáo	fried dough usually eaten with soy milk or rice porridge
豆浆	dòujiāng	soy milk
粥	zhōu	rice porridge that can be plain or flavored with seafood or meat, among other things
小笼包	xiǎolóngbāo	Shanghai-style steamed pork buns known for their small size and rich broth inside
锅贴	guōtiē	(pot stickers) pan-fried meat or vegetable dumplings
春卷	chūnjuǎn	(spring rolls) deep fried roll consisting of vegetables, meat, and eggs

2. Read the following names of popular Chinese dishes after your teacher.

gōng bǎo jī dīng 宫保鸡丁 *Kung Pao Chicken*	má pó dòu fù 麻婆豆腐 *Mapo Tofu*	jiè lán niú ròu 芥兰牛肉 *Beef and Broccoli*
yú xiāng ròu sī 鱼香肉丝 *Fish-Flavored Pork*	běi jīng kǎo yā 北京烤鸭 *Peking Duck*	méng gǔ niú ròu 蒙古牛肉 *Mongolian Beef*
yāo guǒ xiā qiú 腰果虾球 *Prawn and Cashew Nuts*	shuāng dōng niú ròu 双冬牛肉 *Beef with Mushroom*	gǔ lǎo ròu 古老肉 *Sweet & Sour Pork and Bamboo Shoots*
táng cù yú 糖醋鱼 *Sweet & Sour Fish*	jī dàn chǎo fàn 鸡蛋炒饭 *Egg-Fried Rice*	xiā rén chǎo miàn 虾仁炒面 *Shrimp-Fried Noodles*

学无止境 EXTEND YOUR KNOWLEDGE

Go out with your family or friends and have dim sum, lunch, or dinner at a Chinese restaurant – yes, those Chinese fast food counters in your local shopping malls also count. Try to order your dishes in Chinese. Reflect on your experience and share it with your classmates.

你知道吗？ Did you know?

As in the West, Chinese children generally take their father's surname. In the past, women in China changed their surname to their husband's after marriage. But this custom is no longer practiced in Mainland China. Women now keep their maiden names after marriage.

There are many different ways of asking a person's name in China, depending on how formal the occasion is. In informal settings, "你叫什么名字？" would be sufficient. However, in formal settings, one should use "您怎么称呼？" (Nín zěnme chēnghū?) or "您贵姓？" (Nín guìxìng?)

课堂用语 **Classroom Expressions**

请再说一遍。	Qǐng zài shuō yī biàn.*	Please say it again.
第一声	dì yī shēng	first tone
第二声	dì èr shēng	second tone
第三声	dì sān shēng	third tone
第四声	dì sì shēng	fourth tone
轻声	qīng shēng	neutral tone

*When yī (一) is used to indicate amount (one of something), its pronunciation changes according to the syllable that follows it: yī (一) is pronounced as a 4th tone (yì) instead of a 1st tone when followed by 1st, 2nd, and 3rd tone syllables and as a 2nd tone when followed by a 4th tone syllable. For example:

yī tiān   (pronounced as **yì tiān**)

yī nián   (pronounced as **yì nián**)

yī diǎn   (pronounced as **yì diǎn**)

yī biàn   (pronounced as **yí biàn**)

1.5 电话和电子邮件
Telephone and Email

0	1		2	3	4	5	6	7	8	9	10
零	一		二	三	四	五	六	七	八	九	十
líng	yī (also yāo)[5]		èr	sān	sì	wǔ	liù	qī	bā	jiǔ	shí

 对话一 **Dialogue 1**

(Maria and Tom exchange their contact information.)

Mǎlìyà: Wǒ jiā de diànhuà hàomǎ shì: liù sān wǔ yāo-yāo èr sān bā.
玛丽娅： 我 家 的 电话 号码 是：6351-1238。

Nǐ jiā de diànhuà hàomǎ shì duōshao?
你 家 的 电话 号码 是 多少？

Tāngmǔ: Wǒ jiā de diànhuà hàomǎ shì: sān qī bā jiǔ-liù wǔ wǔ yāo.
汤姆： 我 家 的 电话 号码 是：3789-6551。

Mǎlìyà: Nǐ de diànzi yóujiàn ne?
玛丽娅： 你 的 电子 邮件 呢？

Tāngmǔ: Wǒ de shì: tom@hotmail.com.
汤姆： 我 的 是：tom@hotmail.com.

Mǎlìyà: Xièxie.
玛丽娅： 谢谢。

[5] See Language Note 2.

对话二 **Dialogue 2**

(Tom meets Kelly in the school's cafeteria.)

Tāngmǔ: Qǐng wèn, nǐ shì Dài'ān ma?
汤姆： 请 问，你 是 黛安 吗？

Kǎilì: Bù shì, wǒ shì Kǎilì.
凯丽： 不 是，我 是 凯丽。

Tāngmǔ: Duìbùqǐ.
汤姆： 对不起。

Kǎilì: Méiguānxi. Nǐ rènshí Dàwèi ma?
凯丽： 没关系。你 认识 大卫 吗？

Tāngmǔ: Rènshí. Tā shì wǒ péngyou. Wǒ jiào Tāngmǔ.
汤姆： 认识。他 是 我 朋友。我 叫 汤姆。

Kǎilì: Rènshí nǐ hěn gāoxìng. Nǐ zhīdào Dàwèi de
凯丽： 认识 你 很 高兴。你 知道 大卫 的

shǒujī hàomǎ ma?
手机 号码 吗？

Tāngmǔ: Zhīdào. Yāo sān yāo èr-èr wǔ sì-sān sān liù liù.
汤姆： 知道。1312–254–3366。

Kǎilì: Xièxie.
凯丽： 谢谢。

Tāngmǔ: Bù kèqi.
汤姆： 不 客气。

 生词 **New Words**

	Simplified	Traditional	Pinyin	Part of Speech	English
1.	电话	電話	diànhuà	*n.*	telephone
2.	号码	號碼	hàomǎ	*n.*	(telephone or street) number
3.	多少		duōshao	*s.p.*	how many/what's the number
4.	电子邮件	電子郵件	diànzi yóujiàn	*n.*	e-mail address (see Language Note 4)
5.	请问	請問	qǐngwèn	*s.p.*	excuse me
6.	对不起	對不起	duìbùqǐ	*s.p.*	I am sorry
7.	没关系	沒關係	méiguānxi	*s.p.*	that's all right, no problem
8.	高兴	高興	gāoxìng	*adj.*	glad
9.	知道		zhīdào	*v.*	to know (a fact)
10.	手机	手機	shǒujī	*n.*	cell phone
11.	不客气		bù kèqi	*s.p.*	don't be polite, you are welcome

Proper Noun

12.	黛安		Dài'ān	*p.n.*	Diane

语言注释 Language Notes

1. How to read a Chinese telephone number

There are eight digits in a telephone number in China. For cell phones the number of digits rises to 11. When reading out a Chinese telephone number, group every four digits together. For example, if a phone number is 87658972, read it as 8765-8972. For cell phone numbers, the grouping pattern is usually 4-3-4. That is: 1315-788-8890.

2. 1 (yī) or 1 (yāo)

It is common for Chinese people to read the number one as "yāo" instead of "yī" when giving out phone numbers. This may be due to the fact that the sound "yī" can be mistakenly heard as "qī."

3. The possessive particle 的

The possessive particle 的 is roughly equivalent to the function of 's (apostrophe + s) or the "of" in the phrase "the president of our class" (following the grammatical structure "Noun 1 of Noun 2") in English.

Noun/Pronoun	的	Noun	English meaning
我	的	电话号码	My phone number
大卫	的	朋友	David's friend
你们	的	老师	Your teacher

Sometimes when the object under discussion has been mentioned in the previous sentences, the noun after 的 can be omitted.

我的电话号码是8244-5667,你的(电话号码)呢?

(My phone number is 8244-5667, what is yours?)

When a possessive pronoun (我、你、他...) is used to modify a noun, the possessive particle 的 can be omitted if a close personal relationship exists between the pronoun and the noun.

我(的)朋友   my friend

他(的)朋友   his friend

你(的)爸爸(bàba)   your father

4. 电子邮件 (email)

电子邮件 is also abbreviated as 电邮. The longer form is more often used in formal expressions. In daily communication, it has become more and more common for the Chinese to simply use English words such as "email," "CD," and "iPod™" without translating them into Chinese.

我的email是 xiaowang@163.com, 你的呢?

这是我的CD。

Cultural Notes

Below is a list of polite expressions commonly used in China:

⊕ *Apologies:*

   To apologize: 对不起。 (Response: 没关系。)

⊕ *For minor errors or for disturbing others:*

   不好意思 (bù hǎo yìsi) It's embarrassing. (Response: 没关系。)

⊕ *Thank you:*   谢谢！ (Response: 不客气。   (bù kèqi) No need to be so polite.

   不谢！   (bù xiè) No need to thank me.

⊕ *Meeting someone for the first time (after introducing yourself or being introduced to somebody):*

   认识你很高兴。   (rènshí nǐ hěn gāoxìng) I'm happy to meet you.

   幸会，幸会！   (xìnghuì, xìnghuì) Pleased to meet you. (polite, formal expression)

⊕ *If the person you've just met is famous or you've heard a lot about him or her, then you'd say:*

   久仰，久仰！   (jiǔyǎng, jiǔyǎng) I've been admiring you for a long time.

⊕ *When asking for help or interrupting others:*

   请问······ (qǐngwèn...)   May I ask …?

   对不起，请问······   (duìbùqǐ, qǐngwèn) Excuse me, may I ask …?

发音练习 **PRONUNCIATION PRACTICE**

The Neutral Tone

A syllable with no tone mark is pronounced in the neutral tone. The neutral tone usually occurs: 1) as the last syllable in a multi-syllable word, or 2) as a question or mood particle at the end of a sentence. You can produce a neutral tone by slightly prolonging the sound of the syllable prior to it.

1. Read the following syllables after your teacher and pay attention to the neutral tones.

wǒ de	nǐ de	gēge	jiějie	mèimei
wǎnshang	xiàlai	zǒuzhe	shàngqu	fàngxia
màn mān de	hóng hóng de	kào biān qu	lái wǎn le	chī fàn le

2. Read the following sentences after your teacher and pay attention to the syllables with neutral tones.

A. Jiějie de míngzi jiào Lìli.

(My elder sister is called Lili.)

B. Wǒ de yì jiā zhù zài Běijīng.

(My family lives in Beijing.)

C. Tā de dìdi hěn cōngming.

(His younger brother is very smart.)

D. Wǒmen jiā yǒu sān gè rén: bàba, māma, hé wǒ.

(There are three people in my family: dad, mom and I.)

E. Nǐmen rènshi ma?

(Do you know each other?)

F. Máomao yě zhù zài Jiùjīnshān ba?

(Maomao also lives in San Francisco, right?)

3. Try to say the following tongue twister.

Pèng Peng Chē

碰　碰　车

Pèng	peng	chē,	chē	pèng	peng,
碰	碰	车，	车	碰	碰，

Zuò	zhe	Péng	peng	hé	Píng	ping.
坐	着	朋	朋	和	平	平。

Píng	ping	kāi	chē	pèng	Péng	peng,
平	平	开	车	碰	朋	朋，

Péng	peng	kāi	chē	pèng	Píng	ping.
朋	朋	开	车	碰	平	平。

Bumper Cars

Bumper cars bump against each other,

In the bumper cars are Pengpeng and Pingping.

Pingping drives the bumper car to bump against Pengpeng,

Pengpeng drives the bumper car to bump against Pingping.

4. Try to say the following children's rhyme.

Shù Zì Gē

数　字　歌

Yī	èr	sān,	sān	èr	yī,
一	二	三，	三	二	一，

Yī	èr	sān	sì	wǔ	liù	qī,
一	二	三	四	五	六	七，

Qī	liù	wǔ,	wǔ	qī	liù,
七	六	五，	五	七	六，

Qī	liù	wǔ	sì	sān	èr	yī.
七	六	五	四	三	二	一。

A Rhyme of Numbers

One, two, three, three, two, one,

One, two, three, four, five, six, seven,

Seven, six, five, five, seven, six,

Seven, six, five, four, three, two, one.

你知道吗? **Did you know?**

Telephone did not become popular in China until the late 1980s. Since the telephone is a relatively new phenomenon, telephone etiquette in China is basically imported from the West. For example, one should make phone calls during normal business hours; one should answer the phone promptly after two or three rings; and one should sit up straight and smile when answering the telephone, etc.

The use of mobile phones in China has a rather interesting history. The first mobile phone service was established in China in 1987. At the time the mobile phones were usually bulky, the service expensive, and those who could afford them rather elaborate in their manners. Owning a mobile phone then was a symbol of power and wealth – indeed the mobile phones were nicknamed "大哥大" (dàgēdà, literally "Big Brother is Great"). In recent years, the number of mobile phone subscribers has increased dramatically, thanks to rapid economic expansion in China. According to the statistics published by the Ministry of Information Industry of the People's Republic of China, as of April 2007, there were more than 487 million cell phone subscribers in China.

 课堂用语 **Classroom Expressions**

请打开课本。	Qǐng dǎkāi kèběn.	Please open your textbook.
请打开练习本。	Qǐng dǎkāi liànxíběn.	Please open your workbook.
第 X 页。	Dì X yè.	Page X.
请看第一课。	Qǐng kàn dì yī kè.	Please look at Lesson 1.

1.6 第一单元复习
Unit 1 Review

Read the following dialogues and the text. There are a few words in color; please guess the meaning of the new words from the context.

对话 一 **Dialogue 1**

玛丽娅：	你 好!
汤姆：	你 好!
玛丽娅：	我 是 玛丽娅。你 呢?
汤姆：	我 姓 王，叫 汤姆。
大卫：	你们 好! 我 叫 大卫 格林。你们 认识 她 (tā) 吗? 她 是 我 朋友 凯丽。
凯丽：	你们 好! 认识 你们 很 高兴。

What is the meaning of 她?

It is "she/her". Pay attention to the radical on the left: 女 (woman).

对话 二 **Dialogue 2**

丁老师：	请问，你 叫 什么 名字?
凯丽：	老师 好! 我 叫 凯丽。
丁老师：	你 家 住在 哪儿?
凯丽：	我 家 住在 杭州。
丁老师：	你 家 的 电话 号码 是 多少?
凯丽：	三七二五–六七一九。
丁老师：	谢谢! 你 的 电子 邮件 是 什么?
凯丽：	是 kaili@sohu.com

课文 Text

你们 好！我 姓 丁，叫 丁明 (míng)。我 是 你们 的 汉语 老师。认识 你们 很 高兴。

我 住 在 上海。我 的 电话 号码 是 六三四五–八 八九零。我 的 电子邮件 是 ding@sohu.com.

Do you know the meaning of 汉语老师?

You guessed it. It is "Chinese language teacher."

生词 New Words

	Chinese	Pinyin	Part of Speech	English
1.	零	líng	*num.*	zero
2.	一	yī/ yāo	*num.*	one
3.	二	èr	*num.*	two
4.	三	sān	*num.*	three
5.	四	sì	*num.*	four
6.	五	wǔ	*num.*	five
7.	六	liù	*num.*	six
8.	七	qī	*num.*	seven
9.	八	bā	*num.*	eight
10.	九	jiǔ	*num.*	nine
11.	十	shí	*num.*	ten

发音练习 **PRONUNCIATION PRACTICE**

The Pronunciation of 一 and 不[6]

The tones of "一" and "不" change according to the tone of the syllable that follows. The character 一 is pronounced in the fourth tone (**yì**) when followed by 1st, 2nd and 3rd tones, and the second tone (**yí**) when followed by a 4th tone. Similarly, when 不 is followed by 1st, 2nd and 3rd tones, it is pronounced in the fourth tone (**bù**). When it is followed by a 4th tone, it is pronounced in the second tone (**bú**).

1. Read aloud the following syllables after your teacher, paying attention to the tone changes for 一.

yì tiān	yì zhāng	yì duān	yì zhuāng
yì nián	yì yuán	yì chuán	yì tiáo
yì dǐng	yì liǎng	yì kuǎn	yì liǎn
yí jiàn	yí gòng	yí dìng	yí lǜ
bù tīng	bù hē	bù chī	bù ān
bù máng	bù xíng	bù tíng	bù lái
bù mǎn	bù lǎn	bù gěi	bù xiǎng
bú yòng	bú kàn	bú jiàn	bú dìng

2. Read aloud the following phrases after your teacher.

yì	xīn	yí	yì		yì	qián	yí	hòu
一	心	一	意		一	前	一	后

yì	zhēn	yí	xiàn		yì	liǎng	yì	qián
一	针	一	线		一	两	一	钱

bù	sān	bú	sì		bù	huāng	bù	máng
不	三	不	四		不	慌	不	忙

bù	jǐn	bú	màn		bú	jìn	bú	tuì
不	紧	不	慢		不	进	不	退

[6] In the pronunciation exercises, we show tone changes for the purpose of teaching correct pronunciation. Elsewhere, we write pinyin words with their base tones.

3. Read aloud the following children's rhyme about a little mouse, paying attention to the tone changes for 不.

		Xiǎo	Lǎo	Shǔ	
		小	老	鼠	

Xiǎo	lǎo	shǔ,	shàng	dēng	tái,
小	老	鼠，	上	灯	台，
Tōu	chī	yóu,	xià	bù	lái.
偷	吃	油，	下	不	来。
Jiào	mā	ma,	mā	bù	lái,
叫	妈	妈，	妈	不	来，
Jī	li	gū	lu	gǔn	xià	lái.
叽	里	咕	噜	滚	下	来。

A Little Mouse

A little mouse got up onto the lampstand,
To steal some oil to eat, but could not get down again,
Called for his mom, but mom didn't come,
So he rolled and tumbled down to the ground.

4. Read aloud the following children's rhyme about a morning glory.

	Qiān	Niú	Huā		
	牵	牛	花		

Qiān	niú	huā,	xiàng	lǎ	bā,
牵	牛	花，	象	喇	叭，
Tā	bù	qiān	niú,	zhǐ	kāi	huā.
它	不	牵	牛	只	开	花。

Qiān   niú   huā,   dào   chù   pá,
牵   牛   花，   到   处   爬，

Pá   mǎn   wǒ   jiā   zhú   lí   bā.
爬   满   我   家   竹   篱   笆。

Morning Glory

The morning glory looks like a loudspeaker,

It does nothing but bloom.

The morning glory spreads everywhere,

Covers my house's bamboo fence.

5. Read the following children's rhyme.

Xiǎo Bǎn Dèng

小   板   凳

Xiǎo   bǎn   dèng,   nǐ   bié   wāi,
小   板   凳，   你   别   歪，

Ràng   wǒ   diē   die   zuò   xià   lái.
让   我   爹   爹   坐   下   来。

Wǒ   gěi   diē   die   chuí   chuí   bèi,
我   给   爹   爹   捶   捶   背，

Diē   die   kuā   wǒ   guāi   bǎo   bèi.
爹   爹   夸   我   乖   宝   贝。

A Small Bench

Small bench, don't tilt,

Let my dad sit down.

*I tap on my dad's back,**

Dad says I am a good kid.

*Tapping on someone's back is a form of massage in China.

SELF-ASSESSMENT

In Unit 1 you learned how to introduce yourself to your classmates and use Chinese to find out some information about your classmates. Have you reached the learning goals of Unit 1?

After completing the exercises for Unit 1 in your Workbook, fill out the following self-assessment sheet.

Yes/No	*Can you say these things in Chinese?*
	Greetings
	Your name
	Where you live
	Your telephone number
	Ask someone else their name, where they live, and their telephone number.

Yes/No	*Do you know how to do these things?*
	Count from 0–10.
	Pronounce pinyin when you see it.
	Know when to change the tones of 一 and 不.
	Know the stroke order for writing Chinese characters.
	Identify the radical of a character.

8–9   yes   excellent
5–7   yes   good
1–4   yes   need some work

第二单元：我的家

UNIT 2　My Family

By the end of this unit, you will learn:

- How to read and write 87 commonly used Chinese characters
- How to ask someone's age and state your age
- How to ask for someone's address and state your address
- How to ask someone's profession and place of work
- How to give a simple description of a person or object
- How to indicate likes and dislikes
- Numbers 1–99
- Names of some countries and languages
- Some common occupations
- Some set phrases for social interaction

Your knowledge will enable you to:

- Talk about your family (such as the number of people in your family, your family members' relationship to you, their ages, occupations, likes/dislikes and a simple description of them)
- Talk about your country of origin, nationality and language
- Talk about where you live
- Count in Chinese from 1 to 99
- Ask some "WH" questions (where, who, what, etc.)
- Describe where an action takes place

2.1 我家有五个人
There are Five People in my Family

对话一 **Dialogue 1**

(In Maria's Chinese class, students are taking turns to tell each other about their families.)

Mǎlìyà: Nǐ   hǎo,   Tāngmǔ!   Zhè   shì   wǒ   de   yī   jiā.
玛丽娅： 你 好，汤姆！ 这 是 我 的 一 家。

　　　　Wǒ jiā yǒu wǔgè rén, bàba, māma,
　　　　我 家 有 五个 人，爸爸、妈妈、

　　　　gēge, mèimei hé wǒ. Wǒ jiā zhù zài Shànghǎi.
　　　　哥哥、妹妹 和 我。 我 家 住 在 上海。

　　　　Wǒ bàba māma dōu zài Shànghǎi gōngzuò.
　　　　我 爸爸 妈妈 都 在 上海 工作。

　　　　Nǐ jiā ne?
　　　　你 家 呢？

Tāngmǔ: Wǒ jiā yǒu sì gè rén, bàba, māma,
汤姆：   我 家 有 四 个 人，爸爸、妈妈、

dìdi hé wǒ. Wǒ dìdi jiào Jiémǐ.
弟弟 和 我。我 弟弟 叫 杰米。

Wǒ māma zài Shànghǎi gōngzuò, wǒ bàba
我 妈妈 在 上海 工作，我 爸爸

zài Jiùjīnshān hé Shànghǎi gōngzuò.
在 旧金山 和 上海 工作。

对话二 Dialogue 2

(David and Kelly are chatting about their families.)

Dàwèi: Kǎilì, nǐ jiā yǒu jǐ gè rén?
大卫：   凯丽， 你 家 有 几 个 人？

Kǎilì: Wǒ jiā yǒu wǔ gè rén: bàba, māma,
凯丽：   我 家 有 五 个 人：爸爸、 妈妈、

liǎng gè jiějie hé wǒ.
两 个 姐姐 和 我。

Dàwèi: Nǐ méi yǒu gēge hé dìdi ma?
大卫：   你 没 有 哥哥 和 弟弟 吗？

Kǎilì: Méi yǒu. Nǐ ne?
凯丽：   没 有。 你 呢？

Dàwèi: Wǒ yǒu yī gè gēge hé yī gè mèimei.
大卫：   我 有 一 个 哥哥 和 一 个 妹妹。

Tāmen hé wǒ bàba, māma dōu zhù zài Xiānggǎng.
他们 和 我 爸爸、妈妈 都 住 在 香港。

生词 New Words

	Simplified	Traditional	Pinyin	Part of Speech	English
1.	有		yǒu	*v.*	*have, there is, there are (see Language Note 1)*
2.	个	個	gè	*m.w.*	a measure word for people and some other nouns (see Language Note 5)
3.	人		rén	*n.*	people, person
4.	爸爸		bàba	*n.*	dad, father
5.	妈妈	媽媽	māma	*n.*	mom, mother
6.	哥哥		gēge	*n.*	elder brother
7.	妹妹		mèimei	*n.*	younger sister
8.	和		hé	*conj.*	and (only used to link two nouns or noun phrases; see Language Note 6)
9.	都		dōu	*adv.*	all (see Language Note 7)
10.	工作		gōngzuò	*v.*	work
11.	弟弟		dìdi	*n.*	younger brother
12.	几	幾	jǐ	*pron.*	how many (for a number less than 10; see Language Note 2)
13.	两	兩	liǎng	*num.*	two (as in "two of something"; see Language Note 8)

| 14. | 姐姐 | jiějie | n. | elder sister |
| 15. | 没 | méi | adv. | do not (have) |

Proper Nouns

| 16. | 杰米 傑米 | Jiémǐ | p.n. | Jimmy |
| 17. | 旧金山 舊金山* | Jiùjīnshān | p.n. | San Francisco |

语言注释 Language Notes

1. 有 (to have, there is/are)

有 is used to indicate possession. Its negative form is 没有, or simply 没.

Subject	(Adverb)	有 (Verb)	Object	English meaning
我		有	妹妹。	I have a younger sister.
我	没	有	弟弟。	I don't have a younger brother.
我	没		姐姐。	I don't have an elder sister.
上海		有	很多人。	There are a lot of people in Shanghai.

2. 几 (how many)

几 in Chinese means "how many," but it is used when asking about a number that the speaker assumes to be less than 10. When using 几 to form a question, a measure word (see Language Note 5) must be inserted between 几 and the noun that follows. For example:

你有几个姐姐？   How many elder sisters do you have?

他们有几个汉语老师？   How many Chinese teachers do they have?

---

*Another Chinese name for San Francisco is 三藩市 (Sānfānshì).

3. How to address siblings in Chinese

If you have more than one elder brother or sister, or more than one younger brother or sister, you would differentiate them by adding a prefix before the 哥、弟、姐 or 妹. For example:

大哥 (dàgē, eldest brother); 二哥 (second elder brother);

三哥 (third elder brother), etc.

4. The adverbial of place

The "adverbial of place" is a phrase which indicates where an event takes place. It functions as an adverbial phrase that modifies the verb in a sentence, and hence is called "adverbial of place." The adverbial of place is always placed before the verbal phrase.

Subject	Adverbial of place	Verb	English meaning
他	在 旧金山	工作。	He works in San Francisco.
她	在 上海	学习。	She studies in Shanghai.

5. Measure words

Measure words in modern Chinese are similar to the English expressions such as "a piece of...", "a glass of...", "three pairs of..." etc. Like these English expressions, the Chinese measure words, to a certain degree, describe the shape or special characteristics of the nouns they accompany.

You should use a measure word whenever you want to indicate the quantity of a noun. Place the number and the measure word before the noun. There are many different measure words in Chinese, and 个 is one of the most commonly used ones.

Number	Measure word	Noun	English meaning
三	个	朋友	three friends
四	个	人	four people
五	个	老师	five teachers

f Pronouns

6. 和 (and)

The Chinese 和 is not the same as "and" in English. 和 is usually used to connect nouns, not other parts of speech and never whole clauses or sentences. In a sentence where several nouns are listed in a series, 和 is used to connect only the last two nouns in the series.

我家有爸爸、妈妈、弟弟和我。
In my family, there is my father, mother, younger brother and I.

他们是大卫、凯丽和汤姆。
They are David, Kelly and Tom.

我爸爸在旧金山和上海工作。
My father works in San Francisco and Shanghai.

7. 都 (all)

It is difficult to find an exact English translation for 都. The closest English meaning is "all." 都 in Chinese is an adverb that can only be used before a verb, an adjective or another adverb. It often follows a plural noun/pronoun, a collective noun, or a series of nouns/ pronouns.

Subject (plural)	都 (Adverb)	Verb/ Adjective	(Object)	English meaning
我们	都	学习	汉语。	We all study Chinese.
爸爸、妈妈	都 很	忙。		Both of my parents are busy.

8. 二 and 两

In modern Chinese, 二 is an ordinal number that is used only in counting. When talking about "two of something," you should use 两 instead of 二, followed by a measure word. For example: "两个朋友"、"两个老师".

发音练习 **PRONUNCIATION PRACTICE**

1. **Read aloud the following syllables, focusing on the correct pronunciation of j, q and x.**

jiā	jīng	jiǎng	jiàn	juān	jué	jùn
qī	qián	què	quǎn	qióng	qún	qiè
xuān	xú	xiè	xīng	xióng	xuě	xí

2. **Read aloud the following sentences, focusing on the correct pronunciation of j, q and x.**

A.   Nǐ jiào shénme míngzi?

Wǒ jiào Xiè Xiǎolán.

B.   Tā zài Jiùjīnshān gōngzuò ma?

Bù, tā zài Běijīng gōngzuò.

C.   Nǐ xuéxí jīngjì ma?

Duì, wǒ xuéxí Zhōngguó jīngjì.

3. **See who can say the following tongue twister fastest without any mistakes.**

Qī   Jiā   Yī

七   加   一

Qī   jiā   yī,   qī   jiǎn   yī,

七   加   一,   七   减   一,

Jiā   wán   jiǎn   wán   děng   yú   jǐ?

加   完   减   完   等   于   几?

Qī   jiā   yī,   qī   jiǎn   yī,

七   加   一,   七   减   一,

Jiā   wán   jiǎn   wán   hái   shì   qī.

加   完   减   完   还   是   七。

Seven Plus One

Seven plus one and minus one
Equals what?
Seven plus one and minus one,
Still equals seven.

4. Read aloud the following children's rhyme.

Bǐ
笔

Gē	ge	ná	zhe	yī	zhī	bǐ.
哥	哥	拿	着	一	支	笔。

Shén	me	bǐ?	Máo	bǐ.
什	么	笔?	毛	笔。

Shén	me	máo?	Yáng	máo.
什	么	毛?	羊	毛。

Shén	me	yáng?	Shān	yáng.
什	么	羊?	山	羊。

Shén	me	shān?	Gāo	shān.
什	么	山?	高	山。

Gāo	gāo	shān	shàng	shān	yáng	pǎo,
高	高	山	上	山	羊	跑,

Shān	yáng	shēn	shàng	yǒu	yáng	máo.
山	羊	身	上	有	羊	毛。

Jiǎn	luò	yáng	máo	zuò	máo	bǐ,
剪	落	羊	毛	作	毛	笔,

Máo	bǐ	xì,	máo	bǐ	hǎo.
毛	笔	细,	毛	笔	好。

A Writing Brush

My brother is holding a writing brush.

What brush?

A writing brush made of hair.

What (kind of) hair?

Sheep hair.

What (kind of) sheep?

A mountain goat.

What (kind of) mountain?

A high mountain.

Goats walk on high mountains,

Goats are covered with hair,

When hair is cut to make writing brushes,

The brushes are fine,

The brushes are good.

你知道吗？ Did you know?

The Chinese language has many specific terms to describe relationships within a family. The English word "sister" refers to an elder or a younger sister. In comparison, the Chinese language uses two words 姐姐 and 妹妹 to differentiate an elder sister from a younger sister. Likewise, an "uncle" in English refers to a brother or brother-in-law of either parent, while Chinese has different terms for paternal and maternal uncles. There are 200–300 words that are exclusively used to describe family relationships. In fact, there is a familial title for everyone. For instance, you would call the wife of your cousin (on your mother's side) either 表嫂 (biǎosǎo) or 表弟媳妇 (biǎodì xífù) depending on whether the cousin is older or younger than you. But if the cousin is on your father's side and is older than you, you will have to use a completely different title 堂嫂 (tángsǎo). It is a challenge to learn all the titles, but the beauty of this system is once you say a familial title, people know exactly how you and the other person are related. For example, when a Chinese hears 姨婆 (yí pó), she knows the woman is the sister of the maternal grandmother, whereas 姨奶奶 (yí nǎinai) is the sister of the paternal grandmother.

课堂用语

我们学习课文。	Wǒmen xuéxí kèwén.	Let's study the text.
我们学习生词。	Wǒmen xuéxí shēngcí.	Let's study the new words.
我们学习语法。	Wǒmen xuéxí yǔfǎ.	Let's study the grammar.

2.2 爸爸妈妈
Dad and Mom

🔘 课文 Text

(Maria is talking about her parents.)

Wǒ	bàba	sìshí	suì.	Tā	zài	yī	gè	gōngsī	gōngzuò.
我	爸爸	四十	岁。	他	在	一	个	公司	工作。

Tā	shì	jīnglǐ.	Tā	xǐhuān	yùndòng.
他	是	经理。	他	喜欢	运动。

Wǒ	māma	sìshíwǔ	suì.	Tā	shì	hùshì.
我	妈妈	四十五	岁。	她	是	护士。

Tā	xǐhuān	tīng	yīnyuè.	Tāmen	dōu	hěn	máng.
她	喜欢	听	音乐。	他们	都	很	忙。

🔘 对话 Dialogue

(Maria is looking at a picture of her Chinese friend Xiao Li's family.)

Mǎlìyà:

Zhè	shì	nǐ	bàba	ba?
玛丽娅: 这	是	你	爸爸	吧?

Xiǎolì:

Duì.
小丽: 对。

Mǎlìyà:

Nǐ	bàba	duō	dà	la?
玛丽娅: 你	爸爸	多	大	啦?

Xiǎolì:

Tā	sìshíliù	suì.
小丽: 他	四十六	岁。

Mǎlìyà:

Tā	zài	nǎr	gōngzuò?
玛丽娅: 他	在	哪儿	工作?

Xiǎolì:
小丽： Tā zài Běijīng de yī gè diànnǎo gōngsī gōngzuò.
他 在 北京 的 一 个 电脑 公司 工作。

Tā shì diànnǎo gōngchéngshī.
他 是 电脑 工程师。

Mǎlìyà:
玛丽娅： Nǐ māma zuò shénme gōngzuò?
你 妈妈 做 什么 工作?

Xiǎolì:
小丽： Tā shì Shànghǎi dì yī zhōngxué de lǎoshī.
她 是 上海 第 一 中学 的 老师。

生词 New Words

	Simplified	Traditional	Pinyin	Part of Speech	English
1.	岁	歲	suì	n.	years old (in age)
2.	公司		gōngsī	n.	company
3.	经理	經理	jīnglǐ	n.	manager
4.	喜欢	喜歡	xǐhuān	v.	like
5.	运动	運動	yùndòng	n.	sports
6.	护士	護士	hùshì	n.	nurse
7.	听	聽	tīng	v.	listen
8.	音乐	音樂	yīnyuè	n.	music
9.	忙		máng	adj.	busy
10.	吧		ba	par.	a modal particle (see Language Note 5)
11.	对	對	duì	adj.	right, correct
12.	多大		duō dà	s.p.	how old …
13.	啦		la	aux.w.	a particle to indicate a change of situation or state (see Language Note 3)

14.	电脑	電腦	diànnǎo	*n.*	computer
15.	工程师	工程師	gōngchéngshī	*n.*	engineer
16.	做		zuò	*v.*	do, work
17.	第		dì	*pref.*	prefix for ordinal numbers
18.	中学	中學	zhōngxué	*n.*	middle school

Proper Nouns

19.	小丽	小麗	Xiǎolì	*p.n.*	a person's name
20.	北京		Běijīng	*p.n.*	Beijing

语言注释 Language Notes

1. Counting in Chinese

After you know how to count from 1–10 in Chinese, it is easy to count from 1–99.

11 = 10 + 1	十一
15 = 10 + 5	十五
20 = two 10s	二十
70 = seven 10s	七十
33 = three 10s + 3	三十三
86 = eight 10s + 6	八十六
95 = nine 10s + 5	九十五

2. Asking someone's age

"How old are you?" is a common question in informal conversation in China. You may often be asked your age in Chinese, and you may want to ask others their age. It's important to ask this question in a culturally appropriate way. Depending on the age of the person whom you are addressing, you must phrase this question in one of the following three ways:

- To children under the age of 10:

你几岁? or 你几岁啦（了）?

- To people over the age of 10:

你多大? 你多大啦（了）?

您多大年纪? 您多大年纪啦（了）?

- To the elderly:

您老高寿 (gāoshòu)?

您多大岁数 (sùishù) 啦（了）?

您多大年纪 (niánjì) 啦（了）?

3. 啦

啦, often used in informal conversation, is a variation of the particle 了, which indicates a change of situation or a a completed event. Further explanation of the use of 了 as a completion particle will be given in Unit 6.

4. Stating your age

No verb is needed when you state your age or someone else's age. However, if you want to say you are not a certain age, you must use a verb.

Positive

Subject	Numeral	岁	English meaning
她	六	岁。	She is six years old.
我	三十	岁。	I am thirty years old.

Negative

Subject	不是	Numeral	岁	English meaning
他	不是	十八	岁。	He is not eighteen.
我	不是	十二	岁。	I am not twelve years old.

5. Questions using 吧

The model particle 吧 can be used at the end of a statement to form a question. In terms of meaning, the 吧 questions are similar to tag questions such as "isn't it?" and "aren't you?" in English. Different from the 吗 question, which you have learned in Unit 1, the 吧 question indicates that the speaker has an assumption about the situation under question and expects it to be confirmed.

Compare the following two sentences:

你是玛丽娅吗？ (Are you Maria?) The speaker does not know if you are Maria and would like to find out. The answer to this question can be either 是 or 不是.

你是玛丽娅吧？ (You are Maria, aren't you?) The speaker thinks that you must be Maria and expects a "yes" answer. The answer to this question has to confirm or negate the accuracy of the assumption, and therefore requires 对 or 不对.

学无止境 EXTEND YOUR KNOWLEDGE

By now you have learned how to say some names of professions in Chinese, such as 经理，工程师，老师，护士. Below is a list of some other professions:

yīshēng	shāngrén	lǜshī	fǎguān
医生	商人	律师	法官
doctor	*businessperson*	*lawyer*	*judge*
jǐngchá	fúwùyuán	shòuhuòyuán	tuīxiāoyuán
警察	服务员	售货员	推销员
police officer	*waiter/waitress /service person*	*store clerk*	*salesperson (for products)*
fángdìchǎn shāng	gōngsī zhíyuán	jīngjì fēnxīyuán	yǎnyuán
房地产商	公司职员	经济分析员	演员
real estate agent	*office worker*	*financial analyst*	*actor*

发音练习 **PRONUNCIATION PRACTICE**

1. **Read aloud the following words, paying special attention to the Chinese initials z, c and s.**

zá	zāi	zòng	zēng	zǒu	zú	zuì
cā	cuì	cǎo	céng	cù	cóng	cè
sān	suǒ	sēng	suì	sū	sǎng	sǒng

2. **Read aloud the following sentences, concentrating on the correct pronunciation of z, c and s.**

   A. Nǐ jiā yǒu sān gè rén háishi sì gè rén?

   Wǒ jiā yǒu sì gè rén.

   B. Nǐ yǒu dìdi ma?

   Yǒu. Wǒ dìdi jiào Sījié. Tā hěn cōngmíng.

   C. Nǐ zhīdào tā de diànhuà hàomǎ ma?

   Zhīdào. Liù sān wǔ jiǔ – sì sān sì liù.

3. **See who can say the following tongue-twister fastest without any mistakes.**

Sì Shí Sì Zhī Shí Shī Zi
四 十 四 只 石 狮 子

Sì   shì   sì,
四 是 四,

Shí   shì   shí,
十 是 十,

Shí   sì   shì   shí   sì,
十 四 是 十 四,

Sì   shí   shì   sì   shí,
四 十 是 四 十,

Sì   shí   sì   shì   sì   shí   sì,
四 十 四 是 四 十 四,

Sì   shí   sì   zhī   shí   shī   zi   shì   sǐ   de.
四 十 四 只 石 狮 子 是 死 的。

Forty-Four Stone Lions

Four is four,

Ten is ten,

Fourteen is fourteen,

Forty is forty,

Forty-four is forty-four,

Forty-four stone lions are dead.

你知道吗？ **Did you know?**

Family is the most important social and economic unit among the Chinese. In today's China, the number of small families living together with only two generations is increasing. However, it is still very common for three generations to live under one roof (三代同堂 sān dài tóng táng). The fact that the Chinese language has a special term to describe more than two generations living together shows how much value the traditional culture places on a big family. The word 三代同堂 (three generations under one roof) can be changed to 四代同堂 (four generations under one roof) or 五代同堂 (five generations under one roof), depending on the situation.

Parents are the highest authority in the family. Today, most Chinese women as well as men work outside the home. In a three-generation family, the grandparents usually take care of the children. When the grandparents become very old, they are often cared for by their family members. Chinese are raised to remain an integral part of their families throughout their lives.

Following cultural tradition, many Chinese are expected to sacrifice for family members. For instance, if the family doesn't have enough money to send two children to college, one child may give up the opportunity and let the other child go. In return, the child who goes to college has a responsibility to help his family members throughout his life after college graduation. If necessary, many Chinese parents would take several jobs so that they can pay for their children's education. Because of the traditionally strong emphasis placed on family, the Chinese tend to seek help from immediate and extended family when in need, before turning to neighbors, communities or professionals.

 课堂用语

我们复习第一课。	Wǒmen fùxí dì yī kè.	Let's review Lesson 1.
我们练习。	Wǒmen liànxí.	Let's practice.
我们做练习。	Wǒmen zuò liànxí.	Let's do exercises.

2.3 兄弟姐妹
Siblings

💿 课文 Text

(Maria talks about her siblings.)

Āndōngní
安东尼

Wǒ gēge jiào Āndōngní. Tā shì xuésheng.
我 哥哥 叫 安东尼。 他 是 学生。

Tā shàng gāozhōng. Āndōngní hěn cōngmíng.
他 上 高中。 安东尼 很 聪明。

Tā xuéxí hěn yònggōng. Tā yě hěn xǐhuān yùndòng.
他 学习 很 用功。 他 也 很 喜欢 运动。

Tā yǒu xǔduō péngyǒu. Wǒ mèimei jiào Nínà.
他 有 许多 朋友。 我 妹妹 叫 妮娜。

Tā shàng yòu'éryuán. Tā hěn kě'ài. Tā yǎng
她 上 幼儿园。 她 很 可爱。 她 养

yī zhī xiǎo māo hé yī zhī xiǎo gǒu.
一 只 小 猫 和 一 只 小 狗。

💿 对话 Dialogue

Jiémǐ
杰米

Mǎlìyà: Nǐ yǒu xiōngdì jiěmèi ma?
玛丽娅: 你 有 兄弟 姐妹 吗?

Tāngmǔ: Wǒ yǒu yī gè dìdi, jiào Jiémǐ.
汤姆: 我 有 一 个 弟弟, 叫 杰米。

Mǎlìyà: Jiémǐ duō dà la?
玛丽娅: 杰米 多 大 啦?

Tāngmǔ: Shí   suì.

汤姆：   十 岁。

Mǎlìyà: Tā   xǐhuān   zuò   shénme?

玛丽娅：   他 喜欢 做 什么？

Tāngmǔ: Tā   xǐhuān   yùndòng,   xǐhuān   wán   diànnǎo   yóuxì,

汤姆：   他 喜欢 运动， 喜欢 玩 电脑 游戏，

yě   xǐhuān   gēn   "Lǎohǔ"   wán.

也 喜欢 跟 "老虎" 玩。

Mǎlìyà: Lǎohǔ?

玛丽娅：   老虎？

Tāngmǔ: Jiémǐ   de   gǒu   jiào   "Lǎohǔ."

汤姆：   杰米 的 狗 叫 "老虎"。

生词 New Words

	Simplified	Traditional	Pinyin	Part of Speech	English
1.	兄弟姐妹		xiōngdì jiěmèi	*n.*	siblings, brothers and sisters
2.	上		shàng	*v.*	attend (school)
3.	高中		gāozhōng	*n.*	high school
4.	聪明	聰明	cōngmíng →míng *no tone*	*adj.*	intelligent, clever
5.	用功		yònggōng	*adj.*	diligent, hard-working
6.	许多	許多	xǔduō	*adj.*	many
7.	幼儿园	幼兒園	yòu'éryuán	*n.*	kindergarten
8.	可爱	可愛	kě'ài	*adj.*	lovely, cute
9.	养	養	yǎng	*v.*	raise, nurture

10.	只	隻	zhī	m.w.	measure word for certain animals such as dogs and cats (see Language Note 4)
11.	小		xiǎo	adj.	young, small
12.	猫	貓	māo	n.	cat
13.	狗		gǒu	n.	dog
14.	玩		wán	v.	play
15.	游戏	遊戲	yóuxì	n.	game
16.	跟		gēn	prep.	together with, with
17.	老虎		lǎohǔ	n.	tiger

Proper Noun

| 18. | 妮娜 | | Nínà | p.n. | Nina |

语言注释 Language Notes

1. Asking "WH" questions (interrogative pronoun questions)

To ask a question in Chinese, simply start with a basic sentence and place an interrogative pronoun (what, who, whom, where, why, etc.) at the place in the sentence where the answer would be expected. Unlike in English where the "WH" words are often placed at the beginning of the sentence, Chinese "WH" questions require no change of sentence order.

他喜欢电脑游戏。　　　　(He likes computer games.)

──→ 他喜欢什么？　　　　(What does he like?)

他的狗叫八弟。　　　　(His dog's name is Buddy.)

──→ 他的狗叫什么？　　　　(What is his dog's name?)

Interrogative pronouns

谁	shéi, shuí	who/whom
谁的	shéide / shuíde	whose
什么	shénme	what
哪儿/哪里	nǎr / nǎlǐ	where
哪 + MW	nǎ	which
为什么	wèishénme	why
怎么	zěnme	how

2. Using a noun to modify another noun

The first noun modifies the second noun. For example, the noun 电脑 modifies 游戏.

电脑游戏	(computer games)
公司经理	(company manager)
汉语老师	(Chinese language teacher)

3. Using an adjective to modify a noun

The adjective is placed before the noun it modifies. For example, the adjective 小 modifies 猫.

小猫	(kitten, small cat)
小狗	(puppy, small dog)
好朋友	(good friend)

4. Measure words for animals

Different animals have different measure words in Chinese. In general, the choice of measure word is connected with the special characteristics of the animal. Most mammals, anthropods and birds use the measure word 只, whereas fish and many types of reptiles use 条 (tiáo). 条 is also a measure word for other nouns that are long, narrow, or thin.

Domestic animals are a little different. For example, 马 (horse) uses the measure word 匹 (pǐ), and 牛 (ox) and 猪 (pig) use the measure word 头 (tóu).

学无止境 EXTEND YOUR KNOWLEDGE

In recent years, raising pets has become increasingly popular in China. People commonly raise 猫, 狗, 鸟 and 金鱼. Below is a list of popular pets and their measure words.

Chinese	Pinyin	English	Measure word
狗	gǒu	dog	只
猫	māo	cat	只
羊	yáng	sheep	只
仓鼠	cāngshǔ	hamster	只
鸟	niǎo	bird	只
乌龟	wūguī	turtle	只
青蛙	qīngwā	frog	只
金鱼	jīnyú	goldfish	条 (tiáo)
蛇	shé	snake	条
蜥蜴	xīyì	lizard	条
马	mǎ	horse	匹 (pǐ)

发音练习 **PRONOUNCIATION PRACTICE**

1. Read aloud the following words that contain the Chinese initials zh, ch and sh.

zhōng	zhá	zhuō	zhé	zhāi	zhèn	zhù
chē	chán	chǔ	chén	chōu	chǎng	chōng
shé	shéi	shù	shuò	shǎo	shěng	shān

2. Read aloud the following sentences, concentrating on the correct pronunciation of zh, ch and sh.

A. Āndōngní shì shéi?

Tā shì wǒ gēge.

B. Nǐ xué Zhōngwén ma?

Bù xué. Wǒ huì shuō Zhōngwén.

C. Nǐ de péngyǒu jiào shénme míngzi?

Tā jiào Chén Chāng Shuò.

3. See who can say the following tongue twister fastest without any mistakes.

Niǎo Dǎo

鸟 岛

| Niǎo | Dǎo | shì | dǎo, | niǎo | dǎo | yǒu | niǎo, |
| 鸟 | 岛 | 是 | 岛， | 鸟 | 岛 | 有 | 鸟， |

| Niǎo | Dǎo | de | niǎo | duō | dé | shǔ | bù | liǎo. |
| 鸟 | 岛 | 的 | 鸟 | 多 | 得 | 数 | 不 | 了。 |

| Yào | xiǎng | dào | Niǎo | Dǎo, | yī | dìng | yào | ài | niǎo, |
| 要 | 想 | 到 | 鸟 | 岛， | 一 | 定 | 要 | 爱 | 鸟， |

| Nǐ | bù | ài | xiǎo | niǎo, | jiù | bié | dào | Niǎo | Dǎo. |
| 你 | 不 | 爱 | 小 | 鸟， | 就 | 别 | 到 | 鸟 | 岛。 |

Bird Island

Bird Island is an island with birds,
There are countless birds on Bird Island.
If you want to go to Bird Island, you have to love birds,
If you don't love birds, don't go to Bird Island.

4. Try to say the following children's rhyme.

Yī	Èr	Sān	Sì	Wǔ
一	二	三	四	五
Yī	èr	sān	sì	wǔ,
一	二	三	四	五，
Shàng	shān	zhǎo	lǎo	hǔ.
上	山	找	老	虎。
Lǎo	hǔ	méi	zhǎo	dào,
老	虎	没	找	到，
Kàn	jiàn	xiǎo	sōng	shǔ.
看	见	小	松	鼠。
Sōng	shǔ	yǒu	jǐ	gè?
松	鼠	有	几	个？
Yī	èr	sān	sì	wǔ.
一	二	三	四	五。

One, Two, Three, Four, Five

One, two, three, four, five (footsteps),
(I) climbed the mountain to look for a tiger.
(I) didn't find a tiger,
(But I) saw several squirrels.
How many squirrels?
One, two, three, four, five.

5. Can you say the multiplication table in Chinese?

First, review your multiplication skills:

X	1	2	3	4	5	6	7	8	9	10
1	1	2	3	4	5	6	7	8	9	10
2	2	4	6	8	10	12	14	16	18	20
3	3	6	9	12	15	18	21	24	27	30
4	4	8	12	16	20	24	28	32	36	40
5	5	10	15	20	25	30	35	40	45	50
6	6	12	18	24	30	36	42	48	54	60
7	7	14	21	28	35	42	49	56	63	70
8	8	16	24	32	40	48	56	64	72	80
9	9	18	27	36	45	54	63	72	81	90

Next, let's try the multiplication of 1 in Chinese. The word 得 (dé) means "equals."

yī yī dé yī	一 一 得 一	1 x 1 = 1
yī èr dé èr	一 二 得 二	1 x 2 = 2
yī sān dé sān	一 三 得 三	1 x 3 = 3
yī sì dé sì	一 四 得 四	1 x 4 = 4
yī wǔ dé wǔ	一 五 得 五	1 x 5 = 5
yī liù dé liù	一 六 得 六	1 x 6 = 6
yī qī dé qī	一 七 得 七	1 x 7 = 7
yī bā dé bā	一 八 得 八	1 x 8 = 8
yī jiǔ dé jiǔ	一 九 得 九	1 x 9 = 9
yī shí dé shí	一 十 得 十	1 x 10 = 10

Now let's try the multiplication of 2 in Chinese. The word 得 (dé) means "equals." In the multiplication table, if the number is more than 10, 得 is omitted.

yī èr dé èr	一 二 得 二	1 x 2 = 2
èr èr dé sì	二 二 得 四	2 x 2 = 4
sān èr dé liù	三 二 得 六	3 x 2 = 6
sì èr dé bā	四 二 得 八	4 x 2 = 8
wǔ èr yī shí	五 二 一 十	5 x 2 = 10
liù èr shí èr	六 二 十 二	6 x 2 = 12
qī èr shí sì	七 二 十 四	7 x 2 = 14
bā èr shí liù	八 二 十 六	8 x 2 = 16
jiǔ èr shí bā	九 二 十 八	9 x 2 = 18
shí èr èr shí	十 二 二 十	10 x 2 = 20

Now, it's your turn to try multiplication of 3 in Chinese. The word 得 (dé) means "equals."

yī sān dé sān	一 三 得 三	1 x 3 = 3
èr sān dé liù	二 三 得 六	2 x 3 = 6
sān sān dé jiǔ	三 三 得 九	3 x 3 = 9
sì sān shí èr	四 三 十 二	4 x 3 = 12
wǔ sān shí wǔ	五 三 十 五	5 x 3 = 15
liù sān shí bā	六 三 十 八	6 x 3 = 18
qī sān èr shí yī	七 三 二 十 一	7 x 3 = 21
bā sān èr shí sì	八 三 二 十 四	8 x 3 = 24
jiǔ sān èr shí qī	九 三 二 十 七	9 x 3 = 27
shí sān sān shí	十 三 三 十	10 x 3 = 30

你知道吗？   **Did you know?**

China has a population of over 1.3 billion. This has presented many challenges for China's resources and development. In order to lower the population growth rate, the Chinese government has been promoting the "one child" policy – that means each couple is encouraged to have only one child. The "one-child" policy was introduced in 1979. There are some exceptions to the policy. If the first child has serious health problems, the couple is allowed to have a second child. If both the husband and wife are only children, they can have two children. The "one-child" policy also doesn't apply to ethnic minorities, such as Muslims, Mongolians, Tibetans, etc.

Since it was first instituted, many Chinese families have had only one child. Consequently, many young Chinese do not have brothers and sisters. You may ask: Do the Chinese still use 哥哥，姐姐，弟弟，妹妹? The answer is "Yes." When the Chinese meet each other, they often address each other according to their age relative to one another. It is common for

Three cousins.

children to address an older peer by 哥哥 or 姐姐 and to address a younger peer by 弟弟 or 妹妹. Similarly, adults often address children 小弟弟 or 小妹妹.

 课堂用语

| 今天的作业是… | Jīntiān de zuòyè shì … | Today's homework is… |
| 第五页练习三。 | Dì wǔ yè liànxí sān. | Page 5, Exercise 3.. |

2.4 家庭地址
Home Address

 对话一 Dialogue 1

Mǎlìyà: Nǐ jiā zhù zài Shànghǎi shì ma?
玛丽娅: 你 家 住 在 上海 市 吗?

Tāngmǔ: Duì.
汤姆: 对。

Mǎlìyà: Shànghǎi shénme dìfāng?
玛丽娅: 上海 什么 地方?

Tāngmǔ: Huángpǔ qū Běijīng Lù 1005 hào 201 shì.
汤姆: 黄浦 区 北京 路 1005 号 201 室。

Nǐ jiā ne?
你 家 呢?

Mǎlìyà: Wǒ jiā yě zhù zài Shànghǎi,
玛丽娅: 我 家 也 住 在 上海,

Lǎo Běi Jiē 887 hào.
老 北 街 887 号。

 对话二 Dialogue 2

Tāngmǔ: Dàwèi, nǐ yǎng chǒngwù ma?
汤姆: 大卫, 你 养 宠物 吗?

Dàwèi: Yǎng. Wǒ yǎng yī zhī gǒu, jiào "Bā Dì."
大卫: 养。 我 养 一 只 狗, 叫 "八弟"。

大卫的狗—
八弟

Tā hěn cōngmíng. Tā zhīdào wǒ jiā de dìzhǐ:
它 很 聪明。 它 知道 我 家 的 地址：

Xiānggǎng Shíyī Jiē 556 hào.
香港 十一 街 556 号。

生词 New Words

	Simplified	Traditional	Pinyin	Part of Speech	English
1.	家庭		jiātíng	*n.*	family
2.	地址		dìzhǐ	*n.*	address
3.	市		shì	*n.*	city
4.	地方		dìfāng	*n.*	place
5.	区	區	qū	*n.*	district
6.	路		lù	*n.*	road
7.	室		shì	*n.*	room, apartment
8.	街		jiē	*n.*	street
9.	宠物	寵物	chǒngwù	*n.*	pets
10.	它		tā	*pron.*	it

Proper Nouns

11.	黄浦		Huángpǔ	*p.n.*	a district in Shanghai
12.	八弟		Bādì	*p.n.*	Buddy

语言注释 Language Notes

1. 什么地方 and 哪儿

什么地方, which literally means "which place," is another way of saying 哪儿.

你住在哪儿？   (Where do you live?)

你住在什么地方？   (Where do you live?)

2. Stating your address

Unlike English, Chinese addresses are spoken and written in order of larger locality (such as a country, state, city…) to smaller locality (such as street, building number, apartment number…).

Country	Province/ state	City	District	Street	House number	Apartment number
中国	浙江省	杭州市		北京 路	335号	302室

China, Zhejiang Province, Hangzhou, 335 Beijing Rd., # 302

中国		北京市	东城区	东单大街	228号	

China, Beijing, Dongcheng District, 228 Dongdan St.

中国		上海	浦东区	花园小区	四号楼	631室

China, Shanghai, Pudong District, Huayuan Complex, Building 4, Room #631

学无止境 EXTEND YOUR KNOWLEDGE

The residential areas in Chinese cities are most often made up of high-rise apartments, townhouses and single-family houses. In recent years, for public safety and management, clusters of high-rise apartment buildings, townhouses or single-family houses are often enclosed by fences and are called 小区 (neighborhood communities). Below is a list of commonly used words that describe where people live:

dānyuán 单元 *the apartment itself* apartment	lóu 楼 story, building, building no.	mén 门 gate/door
dúlìfáng 独立房 single family house	huāyuánfáng 花园房 house with a garden	liántǐ biéshù 连体别墅 townhouse
xiǎoqū 小区 enclosed residential area, neighborhood community	gōngyù 公寓 *whole apartment building* apartment *a rent apartment*	fángjiān 房间 room

A residential community in Shanghai.

发音练习 **PRONUNCIATION PRACTICE**

1. Read aloud the following words containing the finals i and e.

When the final **i** is combined with initials **b, t, p, n, m, d, l, j, q, x**, it is pronounced [i:], as in the American English pronunciation of "sheep" or "meet."

bǐ   tí   pī   nǐ   mì   dī   lí   jī   qí   xì

When the final **i** is combined with initials **z, c, s, zh, ch, sh** and **r**, the i is not pronounced. Instead, the sound of the initial is prolonged.

zì   cí   sī   zhī   chī   shì   rì

The final **e** is pronounced as [ə], as in the American English pronunciation of "cup" or "up."

tè   hé   lè   rè   shě   zhé   chē   sè   cè   zé

2. Read the following sentences, concentrating on the correct pronunciation of i and e.

A. Tā shì Sīmǐn de jiějie, nǐ zhīdào ma?

Zhīdào. Tā jiào Zémǐn. Tā zhù zài Rìběn.

B. Míngtiān wǒmen yǒu cèyàn.

Wǒ zhīdào.

C. Lǎoshī, wǒ kěyǐ shàng cèsuǒ ma?

Bù kěyǐ. Wǒmen zhèngzài kǎoshì.

3. Read aloud the following children's rhyme.

Qīng Wā
青 蛙

Yī   zhī   qīng   wā   yī   zhāng   zuǐ,
一　　只　　青　　蛙　　一　　张　　嘴，

Liǎng   zhī   yǎn   jīng   sì   tiáo   tuǐ.
两　　只　　眼　　睛　　四　　条　　腿。

Liǎng   zhī   qīng   wā   liǎng   zhāng   zuǐ,
两　　只　　青　　蛙　　两　　张　　嘴，

Sì	zhī	yǎn	jīng	bā	tiáo	tuǐ.
四	只	眼	睛	八	条	腿。

Sān	zhī	qīng	wā	sān	zhāng	zuǐ,
三	只	青	蛙	三	张	嘴,

Liù	zhī	yǎn	jīng	shí	èr	tiáo	tuǐ.
六	只	眼	睛	十	二	条	腿。

Frogs

One frog, one mouth,

Two eyes, four legs.

Two frogs, two mouths,

Four eyes, eight legs.

Three frogs, three mouths,

Six eyes, twelve legs.

(You can continue counting...)

4. Can you say the multiplication table in Chinese?

Let's try the multiplication of 4. The word 得 (dé) means "equals."

yī sì dé sì	一 四 得 四	1 x 4 = 4
èr sì dé bā	二 四 得 八	2 x 4 = 8
sān sì shí èr	三 四 十 二	3 x 4 = 12
sì sì shí liù	四 四 十 六	4 x 4 = 16
wǔ sì èr shí	五 四 二 十	5 x 4 = 20
liù sì èr shí sì	六 四 二 十 四	6 x 4 = 24
qī sì èr shí bā	七 四 二 十 八	7 x 4 = 28
bā sì sān shí èr	八 四 三 十 二	8 x 4 = 32
jiǔ sì sān shí liù	九 四 三 十 六	9 x 4 = 36
shí sì sì shí	十 四 四 十	10 x 4 = 40

It's your turn to try the multiplication of 5 and 6. Using the multiplication table, pick some numbers to multiply by 5 and 6.

X	1	2	3	4	5	6	7	8	9	10
1	1	2	3	4	5	6	7	8	9	10
2	2	4	6	8	10	12	14	16	18	20
3	3	6	9	12	15	18	21	24	27	30
4	4	8	12	16	20	24	28	32	36	40
5	5	10	15	20	25	30	35	40	45	50
6	6	12	18	24	30	36	42	48	54	60
7	7	14	21	28	35	42	49	56	63	70
8	8	16	24	32	40	48	56	64	72	80
9	9	18	27	36	45	54	63	72	81	90

你知道吗?   **Did you know?**

Beijing (北京), situated in northern China, is the capital of the People's Republic of China (PRC). It was formerly known in English as Peking. Beijing is China's second largest city after Shanghai in terms of population. Beijing is the political, educational, and cultural center of the People's Republic of China. In recent years, its fast growing economy has turned Beijing into an economic powerhouse as well.

Beijing was the capital city during several dynasties. Its long history can be seen in many historical sites. The most famous ones are: the Tian'anmen Square, the Great Wall, the Forbidden City, the Summer Palace, the Ming Tombs, and the Temple of Heaven. Beijing attracts a lot of visitors all year around. It is easy to travel to Beijing, as it is a major transportation hub, with dozens of railways, roads and expressways entering and leaving it in all directions, as well as many domestic and international flights.

The Marble Boat at the Summer Palace, Beijing.

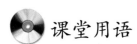 课堂用语

明天有测验。	Míngtiān yǒu cèyàn.	Tomorrow there is a quiz.
明天考试。	Míngtiān kǎoshì.	Tomorrow there is a test.

2.5 你是哪国人?
What Is Your Nationality?

 对话一 **Dialogue 1**

(Tom shows a picture of his grandparents to Maria).

Mǎlìyà: Tāmen shì shéi?
玛丽娅: 他们 是 谁?

Tāngmǔ: Tāmen shì wǒ yéye nǎinai.
汤姆: 他们 是 我 爷爷 奶奶。

Mǎlìyà: Tāmen shì Zhōngguórén ma?
玛丽娅: 他们 是 中国人 吗?

Tāngmǔ: Shì de. Tāmen zhù zài Běijīng.
汤姆: 是 的。 他们 住 在 北京。

Mǎlìyà: Nǐ yéye hái gōngzuò ma?
玛丽娅: 你 爷爷 还 工作 吗?

Tāngmǔ: Bù. Wǒ yéye nǎinai dōu tuìxiū le.
汤姆: 不。 我 爷爷 奶奶 都 退休 了。

   Kěshì yéye yǒushíhou zài jiànshēnfáng zuò yìgōng.
   可是 爷爷 有时候 在 健身房 做 义工。

对话二 **Dialogue 2**

(At the International Club, Tom makes a new friend.)

Tāngmǔ: Nǐ hǎo! Wǒ jiào Tāngmǔ. Nǐ ne?
汤姆： 你 好！ 我 叫 汤姆。 你 呢？

Shùn'ài: Nǐ hǎo! Wǒ shì Jīn Shùn'ài.
顺爱： 你 好！ 我 是 金顺爱。

Tāngmǔ: Nǐ shì nǎguórén?
汤姆： 你 是 哪国人？

Shùn'ài Wǒ shì Hánguórén. Nǐ ne?
顺爱： 我 是 韩国人。 你 呢？

Tāngmǔ: Wǒ shì Měiguórén.
汤姆： 我 是 美国人。

Shùn'ài Nǐ jiā zhù zài Měiguó ma?
顺爱： 你 家 住 在 美国 吗？

Tāngmǔ: Bù. Wǒ gēn bàba, māma hé dìdi zhù zài Shànghǎi,
汤姆： 不。 我 跟 爸爸、 妈妈 和 弟弟 住 在 上海，

yīnwèi wǒ bàba zài Shànghǎi gōngzuò. Nǐ ne?
因为 我 爸爸 在 上海 工作。 你 呢？

Nǐ jiā zhù zài Shànghǎi ma?
你 家 住 在 上海 吗？

Shùn'ài Duì. Wǒ jiā zhù zài Shànghǎi de Huángpǔ qū.
顺爱： 对。 我 家 住 在 上海 的 黄浦 区。

生词 New Words

	Simplified	Traditional	Pinyin	Part of Speech	English
1.	谁	誰	shéi, shuí	*pron.*	who, whom
2.	爷爷	爺爺	yéye	*n.*	(paternal) grandfather
3.	奶奶		nǎinai	*n.*	(paternal) grandmother
4.	还	還	hái	*adv.*	still, also
5.	退休		tuìxiū	*v.*	retire
6.	了		le	*par.*	*a particle to indicate change of a situation/ state*
7.	可是		kěshì	*conj.*	but, however
8.	有时候	有時候	yǒushíhou	*s.p.*	sometimes
9.	健身房		jiànshēnfáng	*n.*	gym
10.	义工	義工	yìgōng	*n.*	volunteer
11.	国	國	guó	*n.*	country
12.	因为	因為	yīnwèi	*conj.*	because

Proper Nouns

	Simplified	Traditional	Pinyin	Part of Speech	English
13.	中国人	中國人	Zhōngguórén	*p.n.*	Chinese
14.	金顺爱	金順愛	Jīn Shùn'ài	*p.n.*	a person's name
15.	韩国人	韓國人	Hánguórén	*p.n.*	Korean
16.	美国人	美國人	Měiguórén	*p.n.*	American
17.	美国	美國	Měiguó	*p.n.*	the United States

语言注释 Language Notes

1. Country, nationality and language

In Chinese, nationality is indicated by adding the suffix - 人 after the country's name. For example:

Country name	Nationality
中国	中国人
美国	美国人
德国	德国人
法国	法国人

It is more complicated to indicate the language that a country uses. In general, one of the two suffixes – 文 and – 语 can be placed after the country's name or the first character of the country's name. 文 refers more to the written language whereas 语 refers to language as a whole or the spoken language.

Major languages of the world (besides 汉语 and 中文):

Language	Written language	Pinyin	English
日语	日文	Rìyǔ/Rìwén	Japanese
英语	英文	Yīngyǔ/Yīngwén	English
法语	法文	Fǎyǔ/Fǎwén	French
德语	德文	Déyǔ/Déwén	German
俄语	俄文	Éyǔ/ Éwén	Russian
拉丁语	拉丁文	Lādīngyǔ/Lādīngwén	Latin
西班牙语	西班牙文	Xībānyáyǔ/Xībānyáwén	Spanish
意大利语	意大利文	Yìdàlìyǔ/Yìdàlìwén	Italian

2. 在 used as a verb

Subject	(Adverb)	在	(Place)	English meaning
他		在	中国。	He is in China.
我弟弟	不	在	家。	My brother is not home.
丁老师	不	在。		Teacher Ding is not in.

学无止境 EXTEND YOUR KNOWLEDGE

Below is a list of countries. If your country of origin is not included here, please look it up in an English-Chinese dictionary or ask your teacher.

Zhōngguó 中国 *China*	Rìběn 日本 *Japan*	Hánguó 韩国 *Korea*	Yìndù 印度 *India*
Yìndùníxīyà 印度尼西亚 *Indonesia*	Mǎláixīyà 马来西亚 *Malaysia*	Xīnjiāpō 新加坡 *Singapore*	Fēilǜbīn 菲律宾 *The Philippines*
Yuènán 越南 *Vietnam*	Měiguó 美国 *The United States*	Jiānádà 加拿大 *Canada*	Mòxīgē 墨西哥 *Mexico*
Bāxī 巴西 *Brazil*	Éguó 俄国 *Russia*	Yīngguó 英国 *The United Kingdom*	Déguó 德国 *Germany*
Fǎguó 法国 *France*	Yìdàlì 意大利 *Italy*	Xībānyá 西班牙 *Spain*	Āijí 埃及 *Egypt*

发音练习 **PRONUNCIATION PRACTICE**

The final e is pronounced [ə], as in "cup" or "up." The final ei is pronounced [ei], as in "eight" or "say." The final ie, on the other hand, is pronounced [iə], as in "here" or "near."

1. Read aloud the following words containing the initials e and ei.

tè	hé	lè	rè	shě	zhé	chē	sè	cè	zé
bēi	něi	lēi	shéi	zhèi	fèi	zéi	mèi	pēi	féi
yè	niè	miè	jié	xiē	liè	bié	piě	dié	tiē

2.   Read aloud the following sentences, concentrating on the correct pronunciation of e and ei.

A. Zhè shì shéi de cèyàn?

Zhè shì wǒ de cèyàn.

B. Zhù nǐ shēngrì kuàilè! Zhè shì wǒmen gěi nǐ de shēngrì lǐwù.

Xièxie.

C. Nǐ de yéye zhù zhèr ma?

Bù, tā zhù zài Nèiménggǔ de Rèhéshì.

D. Wǒ jiějie jīntiān méiyǒu zuòyè, kěshì wǒ yǒu zuòyè.

3. See who can read the following tongue twister fastest without any mistakes.

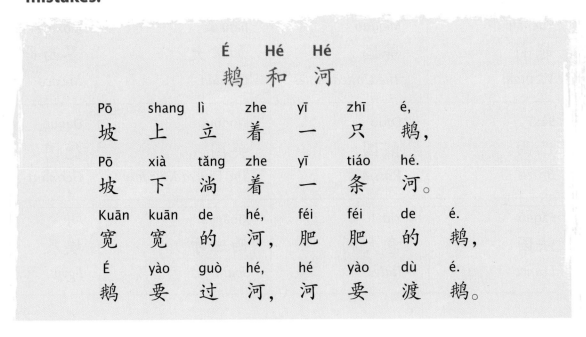

	É	Hé	Hé		
	鹅	和	河		

Pō	shang	lì	zhe	yī	zhī	é,
坡	上	立	着	一	只	鹅,
Pō	xià	tǎng	zhe	yī	tiáo	hé.
坡	下	淌	着	一	条	河。
Kuān	kuān	de	hé,	féi	féi	de	é.
宽	宽	的	河,	肥	肥	的	鹅,
É	yào	guò	hé,	hé	yào	dù	é.
鹅	要	过	河,	河	要	渡	鹅。

Bù	zhī	shì	é	guò	hé,
不	知	是	鹅	过	河，
Hái	shì	hé	dù	é.	
还	是	河	渡	鹅。	

A Goose and a River

A goose is standing on the slope,

A river is flowing under the slope.

Wide river, fat goose.

The goose wants to swim across the river; the river wants to carry the goose.

Is the goose swimming across the river,

or is the river carrying the goose?

4. Can you say the multiplication table in Chinese?

Let's try the multiplication of 7. The word 得 (dé) means "equals."

yī qī dé qī	一 七 得 七	1 x 7 = 7
èr qī shí sì	二 七 十 四	2 x 7 = 14
sān qī èr shí yī	三 七 二 十 一	3 x 7 = 21
sì qī èr shí bā	四 七 二 十 八	4 x 7 = 28
wǔ qī sān shí wǔ	五 七 三 十 五	5 x 7 = 35
liù qī sì shí èr	六 七 四 十 二	6 x 7 = 42
qī qī sì shí jiǔ	七 七 四 十 九	7 x 7 = 49
bā qī wǔ shí liù	八 七 五 十 六	8 x 7 = 56
jiǔ qī liù shí sān	九 七 六 十 三	9 x 7 = 63
shí qī qī shí	十 七 七 十	10 x 7 = 70

It's your turn to try the multiplication of 8 and 9. Using the multiplication table, pick some numbers to multiply by 8 and 9.

X	1	2	3	4	5	6	7	8	9	10
1	1	2	3	4	5	6	7	8	9	10
2	2	4	6	8	10	12	14	16	18	20
3	3	6	9	12	15	18	21	24	27	30
4	4	8	12	16	20	24	28	32	36	40
5	5	10	15	20	25	30	35	40	45	50
6	6	12	18	24	30	36	42	48	54	60
7	7	14	21	28	35	42	49	56	63	70
8	8	16	24	32	40	48	56	64	72	80
9	9	18	27	36	45	54	63	72	81	90

你知道吗？ **Did you know?**

Shanghai (上海), situated on the banks of the Yangtze River (长江 Chángjiāng) in East China, is the largest city of the People's Republic of China. Widely regarded as the stronghold of China's modern economy, the city also serves as one of the most important cultural, commercial, financial, industrial and communication centers of China.

In the late nineteenth and early twentieth century, Shanghai was the third largest financial center in the world, ranking after New York City and London, and the largest commercial city in the Far East. Adversely affected by a series of wars and revolutions from the Nationalist Revolution (1911) and the Sino-Japanese War (1937–1945) to the Civil Wars (1927–1937 and 1945–1949), Shanghai lost its glamour for several decades. Following the Chinese government's market-economic redevelopment policy and the establishment of Shanghai as a Special Economic Zone in the 1980s, Shanghai has since led China's economic growth. Shanghai's skyscrapers and rapid commercial growth provide a window to modern China.

Shanghai's Pudong District.

课堂用语

现在听写。	Xiànzài tīngxiě.	Now let's do dictation.
现在休息。	Xiànzài xiūxi.	Now let's take a break.

2.6 第二单元复习
Unit 2 Review

课文一

你们好！我是丁明。我是汉语老师。我家有五个人，爸爸、妈妈、弟弟、妹妹和我。我在上海工作。我的家人都住在北京。

我爸爸是一个公司的经理。他五十五岁。我妈妈是幼儿园老师，她五十四岁。我弟弟在美国。他在一个电脑公司工作。我妹妹是大学生。她在大学学习音乐。

我们家没有狗，也没有猫。我很喜欢狗，可是我妈妈不喜欢。

生词 New Words

Simplified	Traditional	Pinyin	Part of Speech	English
1. 家人		jiārén	*n.*	family members
2. 大学生	大學生	dàxuésheng	*n.*	university, college student

Proper Noun

3. 丁明		Dīng Míng	*p.n.*	a person's name

课文二

我叫大卫。我今年十四岁。我家有六个人，爸爸、妈妈、两个姐姐、一个弟弟和我。我们家住在香港。我妈妈是大学老师。我爸爸在电话公司工作。他是客户服务的经理。我们一家都是法国人。

我的两个姐姐都在纽约。一个在那儿上大学，一个在那儿工作。我姐姐是小学老师。我弟弟十三岁。他上中学。

我弟弟和我都喜欢"八弟"。八弟很聪明，可是许多人不喜欢它，因为它喜欢叫。

生词 New Words

	Simplified	Traditional	Pinyin	Part of Speech	English
1.	今年		jīnnián	*n.*	this year
2.	客户		kèhù	*n.*	client, customer
3.	服务		fúwù	*n.*	service
4.	那儿	那兒	nàr	*n.*	there
5.	叫		jiào	*v.*	bark, yelp

Proper Noun

6.	纽约	紐約	Niǔyuē	*p.n.*	New York

发音练习 **PRONUNCIATION PRACTICE**

1. **Read the following rhyme, paying attention to the initials j, q, x and zh, ch, sh.**

Zhè   Shì   Shén   Me?

这   是   什   么？

Shén   me   shì   jī   bù   zhǎng máo?

什   么   是   鸡   不   长   毛？

Tián   jī   shì   jī   bù   zhǎng máo.

田   鸡   是   鸡   不   长   毛。

Shén   me   shì   é   bó   bù   cháng?

什   么   是   鹅   脖   不   长？

Qǐ   é   shì   é   bó   bù   cháng.

企   鹅   是   鹅   脖   不   长。

Shén   me   shì   niú   bù   gēng   tián?

什   么   是   牛   不   耕   田？

Wō   niú   shì   niú   bù   gēng   tián.

蜗   牛   是   牛   不   耕   田。

Shén   me   shì   mǎ   bù   lā   chē?

什   么   是   马   不   拉   车

Hé   mǎ   shì   mǎ   bù   lā   chē.

河   马   是   马   不   拉   车。

Shén   me   shì   māo   bù   zhuō   shǔ?

什   么   是   猫   不   捉   鼠？

Xióng māo   shì   māo   bù   zhuō   shǔ.

熊   猫   是   猫   不   捉   鼠。

Shén   me   shì   hǔ   bù   shàng shān?

什   么   是   虎   不   上   山？

Bì   hǔ   shì   hǔ   bù   shàng shān.

壁   虎   是   虎   不   上   山。

What Is This?

What type of chicken (jī) does not have hair?

A frog (tián jī) does not have hair.

What type of goose (é) does not have a long neck?

A penguin (qǐ'é) does not have a long neck.

What type of ox (niú) does not plough the field?

A snail (wōniú) does not plough the field.

What type of horse (mǎ) does not haul a cart?

A hippopotamus (hémǎ) does not haul a cart.

What type of cat (māo) does not catch a mouse?

A panda (xióngmāo) does not catch a mouse.

What type of tiger (hǔ) does not go to the mountains?

A house lizard (bìhǔ) does not go to the mountains.

2. Read aloud the following rhyme. Chinese children sing this rhyme when they jump rope. Pay attention to using the correct numbers.

Tiào Shéng Gē
跳　　绳　　歌

Xiǎo pí qiú, xiāng jiāo lí,
小　皮　球，　香　蕉　梨，

Mǎn dì kāi huā èr shí yī.
满　地　开　花　二　十　一。

Èr wǔ liù, èr wǔ qī,
二　五　六，　二　五　七，

Èr bā èr jiǔ sān shí yī.
二　八　二　九　三　十　一。

Sān wǔ liù, sān wǔ qī,
三　五　六，　三　五　七，

Sān bā sān jiǔ sì shí yī.
三　八　三　九　四　十　一。

Sì   wǔ   liù,   sì   wǔ   qī,

四　五　六，四　五　七，

Sì   bā   sì   jiǔ   wǔ   shí   yī...

四　八　四　九　五　十　一……

(See if you can continue counting up to 101 – yī bǎi yī.)

Rope Skipping Song

Small balls, bananas, pears,

On the ground there are 21.

25-6, 25-7,

28, 29, 31,

35-6, 35-7,

38, 39, 41,

45-6, 45-7,

48, 49, 51...

(See if you can continue counting up to 101.)

学无止境 EXTEND YOUR KNOWLEDGE

How do you read a Chinese ID card?

A Chinese ID card usually includes the following information: the name or type of card, the card issuer's information, the card holder's personal information, as well as the the expiration date. Study the membership card below. Can you guess who the card issuer is? What kind of information can you learn about the card holder? If you get stuck, take a peek at the vocabulary list below the card.

上海运动俱乐部

会员姓名： 丁小朋

年龄： 16 岁

俱乐部地址：
中国上海老北街11号

会员卡有效期至
2009年12月31日

电话： 21-8888-8888

电子邮件： julebu@163.com

生词 New Words

jūlèbù	huìyuán	xìngmíng	niánlíng
俱乐部	会员	姓名	年龄
club	member	name (of a person)	age
huìyuánkǎ	yǒuxiàoqī	zhì	nián
会员卡	有效期	至	年
membership card	valid period	until	year
yuè	rì		
月	日		
month	day		

Now suppose you are a member of this sports club. Can you fill out a member card for yourself?

上海运动俱乐部

会员姓名：

年龄：

俱乐部地址：

会员卡有效期至
年 月 日

电话：

电子邮件：

Go beyond Your Classroom: Visit some local Chinese establishments and collect some Chinese business cards. Note down anything on the card that caught your eye and share what you have found with your classmates.

SELF-ASSESSMENT

In Unit 2, you have learned to talk about your family and to count in Chinese. Have you reached the learning goals of Unit 2? After completing the exercises for Unit 2 in your Workbook, fill out the following self-assessment sheet.

Yes/No	*Can you say and write these things in Chinese?*
	The number of people in your family
	Your age
	Your home address
	Your nationality

	The school you attend
	Something about your pets (dogs and cats)
	Count from 1 to 99
	Tell people your parents' professions
	Indicate your likes and dislikes
	Give a simple description of people or objects
	Give a brief introduction of your family to others, indicating each family member's name, age, relationship to you, nationality, profession and where you live.

Yes/No	*Do you know how to do these things?*
	Inquire about another person's family using interrogative questions
	Inquire about another person's age in a culturally appropriate way
	Name the major countries, nationalities and languages
	Correctly use adjectives to describe people and objects
	Correctly use adverbials of place to indicate where an event takes place
	Correctly use the measure words introduced in this unit
	Understand the written texts regarding people's personal information

16–18	yes	excellent
13–15	yes	good
10–12	yes	fair
1–9	yes	need some work

第三单元：时间、日期

UNIT 3 Time & Dates

LEARNING GOALS OF UNIT 3

By the end of this unit, you will learn:

- How to read and write 85 Chinese characters
- Words needed for telling the time, date, and day of the week
- The order of times and dates
- Adverbial of time
- Adverbial of place
- How to use 要 to describe future events
- Names of high school courses
- Chinese letter and email formats

Your knowledge will enable you to:

- Tell the time, date, and day of the week
- Talk about birthdays
- Talk about daily activities
- Talk about weekend plans
- Talk about the classes you take at school
- Make a phone call
- Make an appointment
- Write a letter or email in Chinese

3.1 我的生日
My Birthday

对话一 Dialogue 1

Kǎilì:
Nǐ   de   shēngrì   shì   jǐ   yuè   jǐ   hào?
凯丽：你 的 生日 是 几 月 几 号？

Mǎlìyà:
Sì   yuè   èrshíwǔ   hào.
玛丽娅：四 月 二十五 号。

Kǎilì:
Jīntiān   shì   sì   yuè   èrshí   hào,   xīngqīyī.
凯丽：今天 是 四 月 二十 号，星期一。

Wǒ   kàn   kan   sì   yuè   èrshíwǔ   hào   shì   xīngqī
我 看 看 四 月 二十五 号 是 星期

jǐ...   Tài   hǎo   le,   shì   xīngqīliù!
几…… 太 好 了，是 星期六！

Mǎlìyà:
Duì.
玛丽娅：对。

Kǎilì:　　　Xīngqīliù　wǒmen　méiyǒu　kè.
凯丽：　　星期六　我们　没有　课。

Wǒ　qǐng　nǐ　qù　kàn　diànyǐng,　hǎo　ma?
我　请　你　去　看　电影，　好　吗？

Mǎlìyà:　　Tài　hǎo　le.
玛丽娅：　太　好　了。

对话二 Dialogue 2

(*Tom is helping his mother to mark a birthday calendar.*)

Māma:　　Èr　yuè　shíyī　hào　shì　Jiémǐ　de　shēngrì.
妈妈：　　二　月　十一　号　是　杰米　的　生日。

Sānyuè　sānshí　hào　shì　nǐ　bàba　de　shēngrì.
三月　三十　号　是　你　爸爸　的　生日。

Liù　yuè　wǔ　hào　shì　nǐ　de　shēngrì.
六　月　五　号　是　你　的　生日。

Tāngmǔ:　Nín　de　shēngrì　shì　bù　shì　shíyī　yuè　jiǔ　hào?
汤姆：　您　的　生日　是　不　是　十一　月　九　号？

Māma:　　Shì　de.　Nǐ　zhīdào　bù　zhīdào　yéye
妈妈：　是　的。　你　知道　不　知道　爷爷

nǎinai　de　shēngrì?
奶奶　的　生日？

Tāngmǔ:　Yéye　de　shēngrì　wǒ　bù　zhīdào,　kěshì　wǒ　zhīdào
汤姆：　爷爷　的　生日　我　不　知道，可是　我　知道

nǎinai　de　shēngrì　shì　bā　yuè　yī　hào.
奶奶　的　生日　是　八　月　一　号。

Māma: Nà nǐ zhīdào bù zhīdào yéye de shēngrì shì
妈妈：那 你 知道 不 知道 爷爷 的 生日 是

nǎ nián ne?
哪 年 呢？

Tāngmǔ: Bù zhīdào.
汤姆：不 知道。

Māma: Wǒ zhǐ zhīdào yéye de shēngrì shì yī jiǔ sān sān
妈妈：我 只 知道 爷爷 的 生日 是 一 九 三 三

nián, dànshì bù zhīdào shì jǐ yuè jǐ hào. Wǒmen
年， 但是 不 知道 是 几 月 几 号。 我们

qù wèn wen bàba.
去 问 问 爸爸。

				十 月		
星期一	星期二	星期三	星期四	星期五	星期六	星期日
						1 老师的B-day
2	3 吉米生日会	4	5	6	7	8
9	10	11	12	13	14	15
16	17	18	19 小明的生日	20	21	22
23 30	24 31	25	26	27	28	29

 生词 **New Words**

	Simplified	Traditional	Pinyin	Part of Speech	English
1.	生日		shēngrì	*n.*	birthday
2.	几	幾	jǐ	*pron.*	which (month, week, day, etc.)
3.	月		yuè	*n.*	month
4.	号	號	hào	*n.*	date (in spoken Chinese)
5.	今天		jīntiān	*n.*	today
6.	星期一		xīngqīyī	*n.*	Monday
7.	看		kàn	*v.*	watch, look, see
8.	星期六		xīngqīliù	*n.*	Saturday
9.	课	課	kè	*n.*	class
10.	去		qù	*v.*	go
11.	电影	電影	diànyǐng	*n.*	movie
12.	太好了		tài hǎo le	*s.p.*	great
13.	日		rì	*n.*	date (in written Chinese); day
14.	只		zhǐ	*adv.*	only
15.	年		nián	*n.*	year
16.	问	問	wèn	*v.*	ask

语言注释 Language Notes

1. How to say a date

There are two ways of telling dates in Chinese, one is informal and the other more formal. The informal way uses 号 and the formal way uses 日. For example, March 25 can be expressed in Chinese as 三月二十五号 in speaking and informal writing, but as 三月二十五日 in more formal speaking and writing. In everyday speech, 号 is commonly used.

	Month	*Date*	*English meaning*
Informal	四月	五号	April 5
	十二月	二十五号	December 25
Formal	四月	五日	April 5
	十二月	二十五日	December 25

To ask questions regarding dates, days of the week and years, use the following expressions:

年	月	日	星期
哪年 which year	几月 which month	几日 or 几号 which date	星期几 which day of the week

2. Adverbial of time

When a time word is used to specify a point in time when an action takes place, it functions as an adverb and is called an "adverbial of time." An "adverbial of time" must precede the verb phrase in a sentence. It can be placed either before or after the subject.

Subject	*Adverbial of time*	*Verb phrase*	*English meaning*
我	星期一	有汉语课。	I have a Chinese class on Monday.

Or

Adverbial of time	*Subject*	*Verb phrase*	*English meaning*
星期一	我	有汉语课。	I have a Chinese class on Monday.

3. One verb after another

Unlike English, the Chinese language doesn't need a "connector" (such as "to") when one verb immediately follows another.

In English	In Chinese
We went to see a movie.	我们去看电影。
She comes to take a class.	她来上课。

4. 那…… "In that case"

那…… is usually used in a discussion when multiple options are given and the speaker decides to choose one of them. It can also be used in a conversation when the speaker wants to draw a conclusion from the discussion. In terms of meaning, "那……" is similar to "in that case …" in English. The following are some examples:

After discussing several new movies and deciding on a Chinese movie, the speaker may say:

那我们看中国电影吧。

After a conversation about getting together over the weekend, the speaker may say:

那我星期五晚上给你打电话吧。

5. 好吗? as a tag question

好吗? is often used after a suggestion. The speaker expects a "yes" or "no" answer from the listener.

Sentence,	好吗?	Is it OK if…? How about…?
我们去旧金山，	好吗?	Let's go to San Francisco, OK?
星期六我们看电影，	好吗?	How about going to a movie on Saturday?

The most appropriate responses to questions that end with 好吗? are "好的"、"太好了" and "对不起,……".

6. To form a yes/no question with "verb+不/没 +verb"

To form a yes/no question, you simply place the positive and the negative forms of a verb side by side, as in 你是不是学生? You do not need to use 吗 in this question format.

Subject	Adjective/Verb (positive)	Adjective/Verb (negative)	(Object)	English meaning
你	忙	不忙?		Are you busy?
你	认识	不认识	她?	Do you know her?
他	有	没有	兄弟姐妹?	Does he have siblings?

7. Duplication of a verb

A Chinese verb can be duplicated to indicate that an action is done in a casual manner or lasts for a short time. There are three ways to duplicate a Chinese verb, depending on the form of the verb:

- For single-syllable verbs, the form of duplication is AA: 看看，问问.
- For two-syllable verbs like 学习 and 工作, the form of duplication is ABAB: 学习学习，工作工作.
- For verb-object compounds like 看电影 and 玩电脑游戏, the form of duplication is AAO: 看看电影，玩玩电脑游戏.

Examples:

A: — 你认识凯丽吗？
(Do you know Kelly?)

— 不认识。你去问问玛丽娅吧。
(No. Why don't you ask Maria?)

B: 我们学习学习汉语，好吗？
(Let's study Chinese.)

C: — 星期六你做什么？
(What do you do on Saturdays?)

— 我在家里玩玩电脑游戏。
(I play computer games at home.)

学无止境 EXTEND YOUR KNOWLEDGE

1. How to say the twelve months of the year

一月	January	七月	July
二月	February	八月	August
三月	March	九月	September
四月	April	十月	October
五月	May	十一月	November
六月	June	十二月	December

2. How to say the seven days of a week

Monday	星期一	Tuesday	星期二
Wednesday	星期三	Thursday	星期四
Friday	星期五	Saturday	星期六
Sunday	星期日 or 星期天		

3. Other ways of saying the days of the week

There are two other commonly used expressions for the seven days of the week. The first is to use 礼拜 (lǐbài), which literally means the Catholic Mass, instead of 星期. The second expression is to use 周 (zhōu), meaning a cycle, instead of 星期. This form is often used in writing. Therefore you will have:

礼拜一	周一	Monday
礼拜二	周二	Tuesday
礼拜三	周三	Wednesday
礼拜四	周四	Thursday
礼拜五	周五	Friday
礼拜六	周六	Saturday
礼拜天 or 礼拜日	周日 (no 周天)	Sunday

发音练习 **PRONUNCIATION PRACTICE**

The diphthong ao is pronounced [au], as in "out" or "now"; uo is pronounced [uə], similar but not exactly the same as the "qu" sound in "quarter"; ou is pronounced [ou], as in "home" or "go."

1. Pronounce the following words containing the finals ao, uo and ou.

dào	zǎo	cǎo	máo	nào	táo	bào	zhǎo	shāo
duō	zuǒ	suǒ	cuò	mō	tuó	fó	bó	zhuō
tóu	dōu	lǒu	zǒu	sōu	gōu	kǒu	hòu	còu

2. Read aloud the following sentences, concentrating on the correct pronunciation of ao, uo and ou.

A. Lǎoshī, nín zǎo.

B. Dīng Lǎoshī yǒu duōshao gè xuésheng?

C. Wǒ jiā yǒu yī zhī gǒu. Tā jiào Jiǔ Bǎo.

D. Tāmen dōu jiào Jīn Bǎo, kěshì Dà Jīn Bǎo de tóufà duō, Xiǎo Jīn Bǎo de tóufà shǎo.

3. See who can say the following tongue twisters fastest without any mistakes.

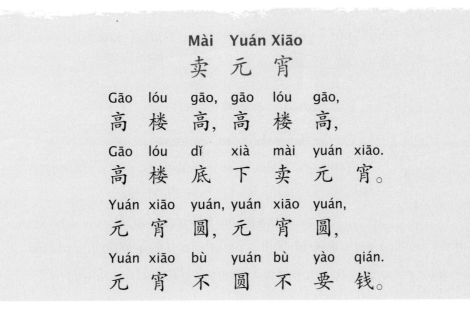

Mài   Yuán Xiāo
卖   元   宵
Gāo lóu gāo, gāo lóu gāo,
高   楼   高,   高   楼   高,
Gāo lóu dǐ   xià   mài yuán xiāo.
高   楼   底   下   卖   元   宵。
Yuán xiāo yuán, yuán xiāo yuán,
元   宵   圆,   元   宵   圆,
Yuán xiāo bù yuán bù yào qián.
元   宵   不   圆   不   要   钱。

Selling Dumplings

The building is high, the building is high,

(I am) selling dumplings by the building.

Dumplings are round, dumplings are round,

If the dumplings are not round, (I) won't charge you.

	Bō	Luó	Hé	Luò	Tuo
	菠	萝	和	骆	驼

Pō	shàng	zhǎng	bō	luó,	
坡	上	长	菠	萝，	
Pō	xià	zǒu	luò	tuo.	
坡	下	走	骆	驼。	
Pō	shàng	diào	bō	luó,	
坡	上	掉	菠	萝，	
Pō	xià	zá	luò	tuo.	
坡	下	砸	骆	驼。	
Zá	dǎo	luò	tuo	fú	luò	tuo,
砸	倒	骆	驼	扶	骆	驼，
Dǐng	pò	bō	luó	bō	bō	luó.
顶	破	菠	萝	剥	菠	萝。

Pineapples and Camels

On the slopes there grow pineapples,

Down the slopes there walk camels.

(When) the pineapples fall from the slopes,

The camels are struck by the falling pineapples.

If the camels are struck by the falling pineapples (I'll) help them stand up,

If the pineapples are crushed by the camels (I'll) peel the pineapples.

你知道吗？ **Did you know?**

In China, only special birthdays are celebrated with parties, banquets, or elaborate rituals. These "special" birthdays usually include the one-year birthday for children, and the 60, 70, 80, 90, and 100 year birthdays for the elderly. In keeping with the rapid Westernization in China, modern city residents celebrate birthdays more than rural residents, and children and elderly more than ordinary adults. The typical birthday food includes long noodles, which are called "longevity noodles" (寿面 shòumiàn) – a symbol of long life inspired by the noodle's long shape. Nowadays city dwellers will also include Western-style birthday cakes in their birthday menu. Generally speaking, birthday gifts can be pastries, wine or Chinese liquor for the elderly, and money wrapped in a red envelope for children. In many families, traditional gift-giving etiquettes are still followed. For example, gifts packaged in boxes or bottles should be given in pairs, as the Chinese believe that all good things come in pairs (好事成双, hǎo shì chéng shuāng). It is very important to remember that one should never give a clock as a birthday gift, for "giving a clock as a gift" in Chinese is 送钟 (sòng zhōng), which has the same pronunciation as 送终 (sòng zhōng, to participate in a funeral procession).

3.2 现在几点
What Time Is It?

 对话一 **Dialogue 1**

(Before class.)

Tāngmǔ:	Xiànzài	jǐ	diǎn?		
汤姆：	现在	几	点？		

Mǎlìyà:	Chà	wǔ	fēn	bā	diǎn.
玛丽娅：	差	五	分	八	点。

Tāngmǔ:	Jīntiān	wǒmen	jǐ	diǎn
汤姆：	今天	我们	几	点
	shàng	Hànyǔ	kè?	
	上	汉语	课？	

Mǎlìyà:	Bā	diǎn	shíwǔ.
玛丽娅：	八	点	十五。

Tāngmǔ:	Ò.	Míngtiān	yě	shì	bā	diǎn	shíwǔ fēn
汤姆：	哦。	明天	也	是	八	点	十五 分
	shàng	Hànyǔ	kè	ma?			
	上	汉语	课	吗？			

Mǎlìyà:	Bù	shì.	Míngtiān	shì	shí	diǎn èrshí
玛丽娅：	不	是。	明天	是	十	点 二十。

对话二 **Dialogue 2**

(Maria and David come out of a class).

Dàwèi: Xiànzài jǐ diǎn?

大卫：   现在 几 点？

Mǎliyà: Liǎng diǎn wǔshí fēn. Nǐ xiànzài huí sùshè ma?

玛丽娅：   两 点 五十 分。你 现在 回 宿舍 吗？

Dàwèi: Bù. Sān diǎn yī kè wǒ hé Tāngmǔ qù dǎ wǎngqiú.

大卫：   不。三 点 一 刻 我 和 汤姆 去 打 网球。

Mǎliyà: Shì ma? Qù nǎr dǎ?

玛丽娅：   是 吗？ 去 哪儿 打？

Dàwèi: Jiànshēnfáng. Nǐ xiànzài huí jiā ma?

大卫：   健身房。 你 现在 回 家 吗？

Mǎliyà: Bù huí. Sān diǎn bàn wǒ hé Kǎilì qù

玛丽娅：   不 回。三 点 半 我 和 凯丽 去

          diànnǎofáng zuò zuòyè.

          电脑房 做 作业。

Dàwèi: Zàijiàn.

大卫：   再见。

Mǎliyà: Zàijiàn.

玛丽娅：   再见。

木

 生词 **New Words**

	Simplified	Traditional	Pinyin	Part of Speech	English
1.	现在	現在	xiànzài	*adv.*	now, right now
2.	点	點	diǎn	*n.*	o'clock
3.	差		chà	*v.*	lack, short of
4.	分		fēn	*n.*	minute
5.	哦		ò	*int.*	oh (see Language Note 3)
6.	上课	上課	shàng kè	*v.o.*	have class
7.	明天		míngtiān	*n.*	tomorrow
8.	回		huí	*v.*	go back to
9.	宿舍		sùshè	*n.*	dormitory
10.	刻		kè	*n.*	quarter (of an hour)
11.	打		dǎ	*v*	play
12.	网球	網球	wǎngqiú	*n*	tennis
13.	半		bàn	*n*	half
14.	电脑房	電腦房	diànnǎofáng	*n*	computer lab
15.	作业	作業	zuòyè	*n*	homework

16. 过过   guo   to pass

语言注释 **Language Notes**

1. Asking time

To ask what time it is, you may say （现在）几点? or （现在）几点了?

2. Telling time

To tell the time, follow the patterns in this chart. Note in informal speech the measure word 分 to indicate minutes can be dropped when there are two or more syllables before 分.

2:00	两点★
3:00	三点
3:05	三点五分 or 三点零五分 or 三点零五
3:15	三点一刻 or 三点十五分 or 三点十五
3:30	三点半 or 三点三十分
3:45	三点三刻 or 三点四十五分 or 四点差一刻 or 差一刻四点
3:55	三点五十五分 or 四点差五分 or 差五分四点
4:00	四点

★ Use 两 instead of 二 when you say 2:00 (两点), 2:15 (两点一刻), etc.

3. Interjections in speech

Like in English, Chinese also use interjections in natural speech. The functions of these interjections are similar to those in English, as they register a certain reaction to something and express hesitation, enthusiasm, exsasperation, etc. In this unit, you have learned two commonly used interjections: 哦 and 是吗. Similar to "oh" in English, 哦 is used when you want to express some degree of understanding of the situation. 是吗 is similar to "Really?" or "Is that right?" in English. It can express surprise, understanding, or enthusiasm. Below is a list of other commonly used Chinese interjections, some of them may sound familiar to you as you probably have heard them in Chinese movies:

hēng

哼 Um, a grunting sound used to represent a hesitation in speech.

āiyōu

哎呦！ Depending on how this word is uttered, it can mean "whoops" (if said softly) or "darn" (if said forcefully) or "ouch" (if said when someone is in pain). It can express surprise, concern, enthusiasm, pain or embarrassment.

āiyā

哎呀！ "Oh no." It registers a complaint or an unfavorable reaction to something that others have done.

zhēn de

真的？ "Really?" Used to express surprise, doubt or exasperation.

zhèyàng a

这样啊？ "Is that so?" Used to express understanding, surprise or doubt.

nà hǎo

那好。 "All right, okay." Used to end a conversation.

jiù zhèyàng ba

就这样吧。 "Okay." "That's all for now." Used to end a conversation.

学无止境 EXTEND YOUR KNOWLEDGE

Here are some additional time words you can use when talking about your schedule:

shànggè yuè 上个月 *last month*	zhègè yuè 这个月 *this month*	xiàgè yuè 下个月 *next month*		
shànggè xīngqī 上个星期 *last week*	zhègè xīngqī 这个星期 *this week*	xiàgè xīngqī 下个星期 *next week*		
qiántiān 前天 *the day before yesterday*	zuótiān 昨天 *yesterday*	jīntiān 今天 *today*	míngtiān 明天 *tomorrow*	hòutiān 后天 *the day after tomorrow*

前年　　去年　　今年　　明年　　后年

last Year　　*this year*　　*ming year*　　*next next year*

发音练习 **PRONUNCIATION PRACTICE**

The final **iu** is pronounced like [**iou**], similar but not exactly the same as "yo-yo" in English. The final **ue** has no equivalent sound in English. Listen carefully as your teacher pronounces it for you.

1. Pronounce the following words containing the finals iu and ue.

jiù	yuè	qiú	qué	xiū	xuē
niū	nuè	diū	xué	liú	xuě

2. Read aloud the following sentences, concentrating on the correct pronunciation of iu and ue.

A. Xiànzài shì jiǔ diǎn shí fēn. Wǒ yào qù shàngxué le.

B. Liù yuè jiějie jiù yào qù Zhōngguó liúxué le.

C. Jiǔ yuè Běijīng de tiānqì zuì hǎo.

3. See who can say the following tongue twisters fastest without any mistakes.

Xiù Xié

绣 鞋

Xiù Xiu xiù xiù xié,

秀 秀 绣 绣 鞋，

Xiù xié Xiù Xiu xiù.

绣 鞋 秀 秀 绣。

Xiù xié Xiù Xiu xiù xié xiù,

绣 鞋 秀 秀 绣 鞋 绣，

Xiù Xiu xiù xié xiù xiù xié.

秀 秀 绣 鞋 绣 绣 鞋。

Embroidered Shoes

Xiuxiu embroiders a pair of shoes,

A pair of shoes Xiuxiu embroiders.

The embroidered shoes are embroidered by Xiuxiu,

Xiuxiu is the embroiderer of the embroidered shoes.

Wàng Jiāng Lóu

望 江 楼

Wàng Jiāng Lóu, Wàng Jiāng Lóu,

望 江 楼, 望 江 楼,

Wàng Jiāng Lóu shàng wàng jiāng liú.

望 江 楼 上 望 江 流。

Jiāng lóu qiān gǔ, jiāng liú qiān gǔ.

江 楼 千 古, 江 流 千 古。

Yìn Yuè Jǐng, Yìn Yuè Jǐng,

印 月 井, 印 月 井,

Yìn Yuè Jǐng zhōng yìn yuè yǐng.

印 月 井 中 印 月 影。

Yuè jǐng wàn nián, yuè yǐng wàn nián.

月 井 万 年, 月 影 万 年。

The River View Pagoda

River View Pagoda, River View Pagoda,

The spectacle of the river from the River View Pagoda.

The pagoda stands forever, the river flows forever.

The Moonlight Well, the Moonlight Well,

The reflection of the moon in the Moonlight Well.

The well is everlasting, the moon is everlasting.

你知道吗?   **Did you know?**

Despite China's vast geographical size, the whole of China operates under a single Standard Time — Beijing Time, which is eight hours ahead of Greenwich Mean Time (GMT+8). Beijing Time operates all year round without any Daylight Savings Time.

Public information (such as schedules for trains, flights, buses, and TV programs, and business hours for offices and shops) is usually based on a 24-hour clock, beginning at midnight, which is 零点 (0:00). 1:00 a.m. is 一点, 2:00 a.m. is 两点, 1:00 p.m. is 十三点, and so on, up until 11:00 p.m., which is 二十三点.

3.3 我的一天
My Daily Routine

🔘 课文 **Text**

(Maria is writing a letter to her pen pal 小明, who lives in Taiyuan, China).

Xiǎomíng: Nǐ hǎo!
小明：你 好！

Wǒ jiào Mǎlìyà. Wǒ shì Měiguó rén. Xiànzài zài
我 叫 玛丽娅。我 是 美国 人。现在 在

Shànghǎi Guójì Xuéxiào xuéxí. Wǒmen xuéxiào de xuésheng
上海 国际 学校 学习。我们 学校 的 学生

měitiān yǒu hěn duō kè. Wǒ měitiān zǎoshàng liù diǎn
每天 有 很 多 课。我 每天 早上 六 点

bàn qǐchuáng. Qī diǎn bàn qù xuéxiào. Wǒmen shàngwǔ bā
半 起床。七 点 半 去 学校。我们 上午 八

diǎn yī kè kāishǐ shàngkè. Zhōngwǔ shí'èr diǎn zài xuéxiào
点 一 刻 开始 上课。中午 十二 点 在 学校

chī wǔfàn. Xiàwǔ liǎng diǎn sìshíwǔ xiàkè. Xiàkè
吃 午饭。下午 两 点 四十五 下课。下课

yǐhòu, wǒ yǒushíhòu zuò zuòyè, yǒushíhòu hé péngyou
以后，我 有时候 做 作业，有时候 和 朋友

qù yùndòng. Wǒ hěn xǐhuān yùndòng. Wǎnshàng wǒ xuéxí,
去 运动。我 很 喜欢 运动。晚上 我 学习，

kàn diànshì, wán diànnǎo. Wǒ shí diǎn shuìjiào. Nǐ de
看 电视，玩 电脑。我 十 点 睡觉。你 的

yī tiān ne?   Yě hěn máng ma?
一 天 呢? 也 很 忙 吗?

zhù
祝

hǎo
好!

Nǐ de péngyǒu: Mǎlìyà
你 的 朋友: 玛丽娅

2007   nián shí yuè shíwǔ rì
2007 年 10 月 15 日

对话 Dialogue

(Maria and Tom are planning to see a movie with Kelly).

Mǎlìyà: Jīntiān wǎnshàng wǒmen qù kàn diànyǐng, hǎo ma?
玛丽娅: 今天 晚上 我们 去 看 电影, 好 吗?

Tāngmǔ: Shénme diànyǐng?
汤姆: 什么 电影?

Mǎlìyà: Chāo Rén.
玛丽娅: 《超 人》。

Tāngmǔ: Diànyǐng jǐ diǎn kāishǐ?
汤姆: 电影 几 点 开始?

Mǎlìyà: Liù diǎn.
玛丽娅: 六 点。

Tāngmǔ: Zài nǎr?
汤姆: 在 哪儿?

Mǎlìyà: Shènglì   Diànyǐngyuàn.

玛丽娅：   胜利   电影院。

Tāngmǔ: Hǎo,   wǒmen   chà   shí   fēn   liù   diǎn   zài   diànyǐngyuàn   jiàn.

汤姆：   好，我们 差 十 分 六 点   在 电影院   见。

meet

生词 New Words

	Simplified	Traditional	Pinyin	Part of Speech	English
1.	天		tiān	*n.*	day
2.	国际	國際	guójì	*adj.*	international
3.	学校	學校	xuéxiào	*n.*	school
4.	每天		měitiān	*adv.*	every day

5.	早上		zǎo shàng	*n.*	morning (before 8 a.m.)
6.	起床		qǐchuáng	*v.o.*	get up
7.	上午		shàngwǔ	*n.*	morning (8-11 a.m.)
8.	开始	開始	kāishǐ	*v.*	start, begin
9.	中午		zhōngwǔ	*n.*	noon
10.	吃		chī	*v.*	eat
11.	午饭	午飯	wǔfàn	*n.*	lunch
12.	下午		xiàwǔ	*n.*	afternoon (1-5 p.m.)
13.	下课	下課	xiàkè	*v.o.*	get out of class
14.	以后	以後	yǐhòu	*prep./conj.*	after (see Language Note 1)
15.	晚上		wǎnshàng	*n.*	evening, night
16.	电视	電視	diànshì	*n.*	TV
17.	睡觉	睡覺	shuìjiào	*v.o.*	sleep, go to bed
18.	祝		zhù	*v.*	wish
19.	电影院	電影院	diànyǐngyuàn	*n.*	cinema
20.	见	見	jiàn	*v.*	meet

Proper Nouns

21.	超人		Chāo Rén	*p.n.*	Superman
22.	胜利 电影院	勝利 電影院	Shènglì Diànyǐngyuàn	*p.n.*	Victory Movie Theater

语言注释 Language Notes

1. The use of 以后

A word, a phrase, or a sentence + 以后 forms a time phrase or a time clause. Please pay attention to the differences of word order in Chinese and English. In English, it is "after class..." In Chinese, it is "下课以后......".

Another difference is in English the time phrase/clause can go before or after the main clause. In English you can say "I went home after the class was over." In Chinese, the "after" clause always goes before the main clause – you need to say "After the class was over, I went home."

In Chinese	In English
三点以后，他在家。 下课以后，我回家。 下课以后，他去工作。	After three o'clock, he is at home. After class, I go home. After school, he goes to work.

2. Where to put adverbials of time and place

If a sentence requires both an adverbial of time and an adverbial of place, the adverbial of time comes before the adverbial of place. Here is the correct sentence order:

Subject	Adverbial of time	Adverbial of place	Verb phrase	English meaning
我们	中午	在学校	吃午饭。	At noon, we eat lunch at school.
我	下午	在电脑房	做作业。	In the afternoon, I do my homework in the computer lab.

Or

Adverbial of time	Subject	Adverbial of place	Verb phrase	English meaning
中午	我们	在学校	吃午饭。	At noon, we eat lunch at school.
下午	我	在电脑房	做作业。	In the afternoon, I do my homework in the computer lab.

3. How to say times and dates in the correct order

When telling time or saying a date in Chinese, state the larger entity before the smaller entity. The order would be: year-month-date-day of the week-time of the day-hour-minute-second. This is the same principle of larger before smaller mentioned in Unit 2.4 for stating your address.

Year	*Month*	*Date*	*Day of the week*	*a.m./p.m.*	*Hour*	*Minute*
2008年	十月	三日	星期二	晚上	六点	二十分

4. Chinese letter format

Writing a letter in Chinese requires that one strictly follow the letter format. The sample below illustrates this format:

小明：你好！

　　我叫玛丽娅。我是美国人。现在我在上海国际学校学习。…………

　　我们学校的学生每天有很多课。我每天早上六点半起床。七点半去学校。我们上午八点一刻开始上课。……

　　祝

好！

你的朋友：玛丽娅

10月15日

5. How to make an appointment in Chinese

Making an appointment in Chinese usually follows a "what-when-where" sequence. That is to say, the speakers need to be clear about what this appointment is for, then agree upon a time and place to meet. Note in the lesson dialogue, when Maria invites Tom to a movie, Tom first asks "什么电影？", then "电影几点开始？", and finally "在哪儿？". Once the appointment is made, it is customary to reconfirm the details by saying something like what Tom says in the dialogue: "好，我们六点差十分在电影院见。"

sub time place verb

学无止境 EXTEND YOUR KNOWLEDGE

The modern Chinese language divides a day into the following sections:

zǎoshàng/zǎochén 早上/早晨 early morning (5–8 a.m.)	shàngwǔ 上午 morning (8–11 a.m.)	zhōngwǔ 中午 noon (11 a.m.–1 p.m.)	xiàwǔ 下午 afternoon (1–5 p.m.)
wǎnshàng 晚上 evening (5–11 p.m.)	bànyè 半夜 midnight	língchén 凌晨 after midnight (1–4 a.m.)	

If "午饭" (wǔfàn) means lunch, how would one say "breakfast" and "dinner"?

zǎofàn 早饭 breakfast	wǎnfàn 晚饭 dinner

Sometimes people also have late night snacks, called 夜宵 (yèxiāo).

发音练习 **PRONUNCIATION PRACTICE**

The final **iao** is pronounced [**iau**], as in a cat's "meow" or the common salutation "Ciao!" The final **iu**, as we have practiced in 3.2, is pronounced like [**iou**], similar but not exactly the same as "yo-yo" in English. The final **ie** has no exact equivalent in English; listen carefully as your teacher pronounces it.

1. Pronounce the following words containing the finals iao, iu and ie.

diào	xiǎo	qiǎo	miáo	niào	tiáo	biǎo	jiāo
diū	jiǔ	xiù	qiú	yǒu	liū	miù	niú
dié	jié	xiē	miè	niè	tiě	bié	qiè

2. Read aloud the following sentences, concentrating on the correct pronunciation of iao and iu.

A. Shù shang yǒu jiǔ zhī xiǎo niǎo.

B. Xiǎo Niú hé Xiǎo Miáo yìqǐ qù fàng niú hé yáng.

C. Jiějie dié le yí gè zhǐchuán.

3. Read aloud the following rhymes.

Hái　Zi　Hé　Xié　Zi
孩　子　和　鞋　子

Hái　zi　shì　hái　zi,
孩　子　是　孩　子，

Xié　zi　shì　xié　zi.
鞋　子　是　鞋　子。

Hái　zi　bú　shì　xié　zi,
孩　子　不　是　鞋　子，

Xié　zi　bú　shì　hái　zi.
鞋　子　不　是　孩　子。

Shì　hái　zi　chuān　xié　zi,
是　孩　子　穿　鞋　子，

Bú　shì　xié　zi　chuān　hái　zi.
不　是　鞋　子　穿　孩　子。

Children and Shoes

Children (háizi) are children,

Shoes (xiézi) are shoes.*

Children are not shoes,

Shoes are not children.

It is children who wear shoes,

Not the shoes that wear children.

*This rhyme is usually used to train people who speak Hunan dialect, in which shoes are called "háizi."

		Kàn 看	**Lǎo** 姥	**Lao** 姥		
Yǒu 有	gè 个	xiǎo 小	hái 孩	jiào 叫	Qiǎo 巧	Qiǎo, 巧,
Qiǎo 巧	Qiǎo 巧	gē 哥	gē 哥	jiào 叫	Yáo 摇	Yáo. 摇。
Yáo 摇	yao 摇	huá 划	chuán 船	dài 带	Qiǎo 巧	Qiǎo, 巧,
Qiǎo 巧	Qiǎo 巧	yào 要	qù 去	kàn 看	Lǎo 姥	lao. 姥。
Lǎo 姥	lao 姥	zhàn 站	zài 在	qiáo 桥	tóu 头	xiào, 笑,
Huān 欢	yíng 迎	Qiǎo 巧	Qiǎo 巧	hé 和	Yáo 摇	Yáo. 摇。

Visiting Grandma

There is a kid named Qiao Qiao

Who has a brother named Yao Yao.

Yao Yao takes Qiao Qiao on a boat,

As Qiao Qiao wants to visit her grandma.

Grandma is smiling at the head of a bridge,

Welcoming Qiao Qiao and Yao Yao.

4. Read aloud the following classical poem.

Chūn Xiǎo

春　晓

[Táng]　Mèng Hào Rán

[唐]　孟　浩　然

Chūn mián bù jué xiǎo,　chù chù wén tí niǎo.

春　眠　不　觉　晓，　处　处　闻　啼　鸟。

Yè lái fēng yǔ shēng,　huā luò zhī duō shǎo.

夜　来　风　雨　声，　花　落　知　多　少。

A Spring Morning

By Meng Haoran [Tang Dynasty]

I awake light-hearted this morning of spring,

Everywhere round me the singing of birds —

But now I remember the night, the storm,

And I wonder how many blossoms were broken.

你知道吗? **Did you know?**

China has a vast and varied educational system, which can be divided into three tiers: primary education, secondary education and higher education.

Primary education in China includes kindergartens (幼儿园) and primary schools (小学). Secondary education comprises both regular secondary schools and vocational schools. A regular secondary school in China is called 中学. It usually consists of a middle school division (初中 chū zhōng) and a high school division (高中). Vocational schools — 中专 (zhōngzhuān) or 技校 (jìxiào) — offer specialized skill training to those who have graduated from middle school but would not go to college. Higher education in China consists of specialized professional institutes (专业学院, zhuānyè xuéyuàn), regular four-year colleges and universities (大学), as well as graduate schools (研究生院, yánjiū shēng yuàn). These higher educational institutions also offer distance learning courses and short-term adult education programs.

Chinese school-age children must finish nine years of compulsory education (six years of primary school and three years of middle school), which is required by law. In order to advance beyond the compulsory education, one must pass entrance exams. While precise data is hard to obtain, according to a report by the Xinhua News Agency, in 2005 only about 60-70 percent middle school students nationwide advanced into high schools; similarly, around 68 percent of high school graduates nationwide entered two to four year colleges.

A preschool in Shanghai.

3.4 我的课
My Classes

 对话 Dialogue

(Anthony and Maria are talking about their classes.)

Āndōngní:
Jīntiān dì yī jié nǐ shàng shénme kè?
安东尼： 今天 第一节 你 上 什么 课？

Mǎlìyà:
Jīntiān shì xīngqīsān ma?
玛丽娅： 今天 是 星期三 吗？

Āndōngní:
Duì.
安东尼： 对。

Mǎlìyà:
Wǒ kàn kan... Jīntiān dì yī jié
玛丽娅： 我 看 看…… 今天 第一节

wǒ shàng Hànyǔ, ránhòu shàng shùxué,
我 上 汉语， 然后 上 数学、

lìshǐ, Yīngyǔ, huàxué hé tǐyù.
历史、 英语、 化学 和 体育。

Nǐ ne?
你 呢？

Āndōngní:
Jīntiān wǒ hěn máng. Yǒu shùxué,
安东尼： 今天 我 很 忙。 有 数学、

Yīngyǔ, tǐyù, Fǎyǔ, Zhōngguó
英语、 体育、 法语、 中国

lìshǐ, jīngjìxué hé diànnǎo.
历史、 经济学 和 电脑。

 课文 Text

(Maria is emailing her Chinese pen pal about her course schedule.)

Xiǎomíng:　　Nǐ　　hǎo!
小明：　　你　好!

　　　　　Zhège　xuéqī　wǒ　shàng　liù　mén　kè:　　Hànyǔ,　　Yīngyǔ,
　　　　这个　学期　我　上　六　门　课：汉语、英语、

shùxué,　　wùlǐ,　　huàxué,　　tǐyù.　　Měi　mén　kè　dōu　yǒu
数学、　物理、　化学、　体育。　每　门　课　都　有

zuòyè,　　suǒyǐ　　wǒ　hěn　máng.　Wǒ　xǐhuān　Yīngyǔ　kè　hé
作业，　所以　我　很　忙。　我　喜欢　英语　课　和

Hànyǔ　kè,　bù　tài　xǐhuān　wùlǐ　kè,　yīnwèi　wùlǐ　kè　de
汉语　课，不　太　喜欢　物理　课，因为　物理　课　的

zuòyè　tài　duō　le.
作业　太　多　了。

　　　　Nǐ　zhège　xuéqī　shàng　jǐ　mén　kè?　Máng　bù　máng?
　　　你　这个　学期　上　几　门　课?　忙　不　忙?

Nǐ　xǐhuān　nǎ　mén　kè?
你　喜欢　哪　门　课?

Mǎlìyà
玛丽娅

Mǎlìyà de Kèchéngbiǎo
玛丽娅 的 课程表

	Xīngqīyī 星期一	Xīngqī'èr 星期二	Xīngqīsān 星期三	Xīngqīsì 星期四	Xīngqīwǔ 星期五
dì-yī jié 第一节	Shùxué 数学	Yīngyǔ 英语	Hànyǔ 汉语	Wùlǐ 物理	Huàxué 化学
dì-èr jié 第二节	Yīngyǔ 英语	Hànyǔ 汉语	Tǐyù 体育	Shùxué 数学	Hànyǔ 汉语
dì-sān jié 第三节	Hànyǔ 汉语	Huàxué 化学	Wùlǐ 物理	Hànyǔ 汉语	Shùxué 数学
dì-sì jié 第四节	Wùlǐ 物理	Tǐyù 体育	Huàxué 化学	Yīngyǔ 英语	Yīngyǔ 英语
dì-wǔ jié 第五节	Huàxué 化学	Wùlǐ 物理	Shùxué 数学	Huàxué 化学	
dì-liù jié 第六节	Tǐyù 体育	Shùxué 数学	Yīngyǔ 英语	Tǐyù 体育	

生词 New Words

	Simplified	Traditional	Pinyin	Part of Speech	English
1.	第……节	第……節	dì...jié	n.	number of a class period
2.	然后	然後	ránhòu	adv.	afterwards
3.	数学	數學	shùxué	n.	mathematics
4.	历史	歷史	lìshǐ	n.	history
5.	英语	英語	Yīngyǔ	n.	English
6.	化学	化學	huàxué	n.	chemistry

7.	体育	體育	tǐyù	n.	physical education
8.	物理		wùlǐ	n.	physics
9.	法语	法語	Fǎyǔ	n.	French
10.	经济学	經濟學	jīngjìxué	n.	economics
11.	课程表	課程表	kèchéngbiǎo	n.	course schedule
12.	学期	學期	xuéqī	n.	semester
13.	门	門	mén	m.w.	for an academic course
14.	所以		suǒyǐ	conj.	therefore

美术   mei shu   fine arts

语言注释 Language Notes   宗教 zōng jiào religion

1. Measure word 门

The measure word 门 is used with school courses. If you are taking five courses, you will say
我上五门课。

2. Interrogative pronoun 哪

哪 means "which." In Chinese, if you want to ask "which (noun)", you need to add a measure word between 哪 and the noun. For example:

你喜欢哪门课？　　　　Which course do you like?

我们去哪个电影院？　　Which movie therater shall we go?

There are some nouns that do not use a measure word, such as 天 and 年. In these cases, no measure word is needed. For example:

我们哪天去？　　　　　On which day shall we go?

学无止境　EXTEND YOUR KNOWLEDGE

By now you have learned many school-related words. Can you put them together and develop a general picture of the Chinese educational system?

Levels of education:

幼儿园 → 小学 → 初中 (chūzhōng) → 高中 → 大学 → 研究生院 (yánjiùshēng yuàn)

Students in each level of education:

幼儿园的小朋友 → 小学生 → 初中生 → 高中生 → 大学生 → 研究生

To attend each level of education:

上幼儿园 → 上小学 → 上初中 → 上高中 → 上大学 → 上研究生院

The general term for students: 学生

The general term students of the same class or grade use to refer to each other: 同学 (tóngxué, classmates).

发音练习 **PRONUNCIATION PRACTICE**

Please note that **in** is pronounced [**in**], as in pin, bin; **ün** is pronounced [**iun**], as in "sanguine"; **ian** is pronounced [**ian**], as in the name "Fabian."

1. **Pronounce the following words containing the finals in, ün and ian.**

jīn	xìn	qín	mín	nín	lìn	bīn	yìn
jūn (jǔn)	qún (qǔn)	xùn (xǔn)	yūn (yǔn)[1]				
diàn	jiān	xiǎn	mián	nián	tiān	biàn	qián

2. **Read aloud the following phrases or sentences, concentrating on the correct pronunciation of in, ün and ian.**

A.   Xìnxīn shízú

B.   Xīnnián dào, xīnnián dào, dàjiē xiǎoxiàng fàng biānpào.

C.   Jūn ài mín, mín yōng jūn, jūn mín tuánjié rú yì rén.

3. **Read aloud the following rhymes.**

		Huàn	**Qún**	**Zi**		
		换	裙	子		
Jūn	chē	yùn	lái	yī	duī	qún,
军	车	运	来	一	堆	裙，
Yī	sè	jūn	yòng	lǜ	sè	qún.
一	色	军	用	绿	色	裙。
Jūn	xùn	nǚ	shēng	yī	dà	qún,
军	训	女	生	一	大	群，
Huàn	xià	huā	qún	huàn	lǜ	qún.
换	下	花	裙	换	绿	裙。

[1] When **j**, **q**, and **x** are followed by **ü**, **üe**, **üan**, and **ün**, the **ü** is written as a regular **u** so that there will not be ambiguities in pronunciation. See Pinyin Spelling Rules in Appendix 1.

Changing Skirts

The army truck sent over a pile of skirts,

All of which are in olive green.

The group of girls receiving military training

All changed out of flowery skirts and into olive green skirts.

4. Read aloud the following classical poem.

Yè   Sī
夜 思

[Táng Dynasty]   Lǐ   Bái
[唐]   李 白

Chuáng	qián	míng	yuè	guāng,	yí	shì	dì	shàng	shuāng.
床	前	明	月	光,	疑	是	地	上	霜。
Jǔ	tóu	wàng	míng	yuè,	dī	tóu	sī	gù	xiāng.
举	头	望	明	月,	低	头	思	故	乡。

In the Quiet Night

By Li Bai [Tang Dynasty]

So bright a gleam on the foot of my bed —

Could there have been a frost already?

Lifting myself to look, I found that it was moonlight.

Sinking back again, I thought suddenly of home.

你知道吗？   **Did you know?**

Chinese children usually enter the first grade of primary school at 6.5–7.5 years of age. Beijing, Shanghai, and other large cities in China have six-year primary schools, which accept children at six years old. Most primary schools in China, however, have a five-year course and accept children at seven years old.

The two-semester school year consists of 9.5 months and classes meet for five days a week. The semesters begin around September 1 and March 1, with a summer vacation in July and August and a winter vacation in January and February. Urban primary schools typically divide the school week into 25–30 classes of 45 minutes each, but in the rural areas, the norm is half-day schooling during cultivating and harvesting seasons.

The primary school curriculum consists of Chinese, mathematics, physical education, music, art, and elementary instruction in science, morals and society, foreign languages and computer science, combined with practical work experiences around the school compound such as cleaning the classroom and school campus.

3.5 我的周末
My Weekend

  对话一 Dialogue 1

(Maria and Tom are chatting as they leave Friday's class.)

Tāngmǔ:　Míngtiān　nǐ　yào　zuò　shénme?
汤姆：　明天　你要　做　什么？

Mǎlìyà:　Míngtiān　shàngwǔ　wǒ　xué　gāngqín.　Xiàwǔ
玛丽娅：　明天　上午　我　学　钢琴。下午

　　　　qù　kàn　Zhāng Yéye　hé　Zhāng Nǎinai.
　　　　去　看　张　爷爷　和　张　奶奶。

Tāngmǔ:　Zhāng Yéye　Zhāng Nǎinai　shì　shéi?
汤姆：　张　爷爷　张　奶奶　是　谁？

Mǎlìyà:　Tāmen　shì　wǒmen　jiā　de　hǎo　péngyǒu.
玛丽娅：　他们　是　我们　家　的　好　朋友。

Tāngmǔ:　Tāmen　zhù　zài　nǎr?
汤姆：　他们　住　在　哪儿？

Mǎlìyà:　Tāmen　yě　zhù　zài　Shànghǎi.　Míngtiān　nǐ
玛丽娅：　他们　也　住　在　上海。明天　你

　　　　zuò　shénme?
　　　　做　什么？

Tāngmǔ:　Wǒ　shàngwǔ　hé　bàba　qù　dǎ　wǎngqiú,
汤姆：　我　上午　和　爸爸　去　打　网球，

　　　　xiàwǔ　qù　xué　wǔshù.
　　　　下午　去　学　武术。

Mǎlìyà: Zhōumò   kuàilè.
玛丽娅：   周末   快乐。

Tāngmǔ: Zhōumò   kuàilè.
汤姆：   周末   快乐。

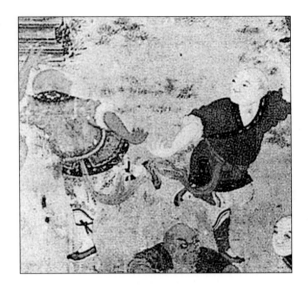

Shaolin Wushu.

 对话二 **Dialogue 2**

(Maria makes a phone call to Kelly on Saturday evening).

Mǎlìyà: Wèi, qǐng   wèn Kǎilì   zài   ma?
玛丽娅：   喂，请   问 凯丽 在 吗？

Kǎilì: Wǒ jiù shì.
凯丽：   我   就 是。

Mǎlìyà: Nǐ   hǎo, Kǎilì.   Wǒ shì Mǎlìyà.   Jīntiān
玛丽娅：   你   好，凯丽。我 是 玛丽娅。 今天

           nǐ   yǒu shì ma?
           你   有 事 吗？

Kǎilì: Jīntiān   wǒ hé bàba   māma   qù chīfàn.
凯丽：   今天   我 和 爸爸 妈妈 去 吃饭。

Mǎlìyà: Nǐ   bàba   māma zài Shànghǎi ma?
玛丽娅：   你   爸爸 妈妈 在 上海   吗？

Kǎilì:　　Duì,　tāmen　míngtiān　xiàwǔ　huí　Hángzhōu.

凯丽：　对，　他们　明天　下午　回　杭州。

Mǎlìyà:　Nà　nǐ　míngtiān　ne?

玛丽娅：　那　你　明天　呢？

*In that case/His case

Kǎilì:　　Míngtiān　shàngwǔ　wǒmen　qù　jiàotáng.　Xiàwǔ　méiyǒu　shì.

凯丽：　明天　上午　我们　去 教堂。下午 没有　事。

Mǎlìyà:　Míngtiān　xiàwǔ　wǒmen　qù　gōngyuán,　hǎo　ma?

玛丽娅：　明天　下午　我们　去　公园，　好　吗？

Kǎilì:　　Hǎo.　Jǐ　diǎn　qù?

凯丽：　好。　几　点　去？

Mǎlìyà:　Míngtiān　xiàwǔ　yī　diǎn　bàn.

玛丽娅：　明天　下午　一　点　半。

Kǎilì:　　Wǒmen　zài　nǎr　jiàn?

凯丽：　我们　在　哪儿　见？

Mǎlìyà:　Zài　Rénmín　gōngyuán　ménkǒu,　hǎo　ma?

玛丽娅：　在　人民　公园　门口，　好　吗？

Kǎilì:　　Hǎo,　míngtiān　xiàwǔ　jiàn.

凯丽：　好，　明天　下午　见。

A Catholic church in China.

生词 New Words

	Simplified	Traditional	Pinyin	Part of Speech	English
1.	要		yào	v./aux.v.	want, plan (see Language Note 1)
2.	上午		shàngwǔ	n.	morning
3.	钢琴	鋼琴	gāngqín	n.	piano
4.	下午		xiàwǔ	n.	afternoon
5.	武术	武術	wǔshù	n.	martial arts
6.	周末	週末	zhōumò	n.	weekend
7.	快乐	快樂	kuàilè	adj.	happy
8.	喂		wèi or wéi	aux.w.	hello (in a phone call)
9.	教堂		jiàotáng	n.	church
10.	事		shì	n.	matters, business
11.	有事		yǒu shì	v.	occupied, have something to do
	没有事		mei you shi	not occupied/ free.	
12.	门口	門口	ménkǒu	n.	gate, entrance
13.	打网球		da wang qiú		play tennis

Proper Nouns

	Simplified	Traditional	Pinyin	Part of Speech	English
13.	人民 公园	人民 公園	Rénmín Gōngyuán	p.n.	People's Park

语言注释 Language Notes

1. The use of 要

要 can be used either as a verb or as an optative verb. When used as a verb, 要 means "want" or "(would) like." For example:

你要什么？   What do you want?

我要一杯水。   I'd like a glass of water.

When used as an optative verb, 要 means "will," "want to," or "plan to." It is placed before another verb. For example:

我要做作业。 I will do my homework.

我要去人民公园。 I plan to go to the People's Park.

2. The use of 快乐

快乐 is often used to offer good wishes. For example:

周末快乐。 Have a good (happy) weekend.

生日快乐。 Happy birthday!

工作快乐。 Enjoy your work.

3. How to give, accept or decline an invitation

The Chinese usually give out an invitation in a rather casual way, and sometimes even at short notice. It could simply take the form of a mere suggestion: "晚上来我家吃饭吧。" A more formal invitation would be "星期六我请你吃午饭。" However, before extending a casual invitation, one needs to find out whether the invitee will be available. In Dialogue 2, for example, you hear Maria asking Kelly over the phone "今天你有事吗？" This is more than a question: it is also a hint of a forthcoming invitation or request.

To accept a causal invitation, simply say "好" and then arrange a time and location to meet, as Kelly does in Dialogue 2. If you are invited to someone's home, a small gift to the host is usually expected.

Declining an invitation in China can be tricky. One usually does not say "对不起，我有事" or "不要," which comes across as brusque. A more polite way to turn down an invitation would be to express your enthusiasm first by saying "我很想去", followed by an explanation why you can't make it to the event. However, if you are to decline an invitation for the second time, keep in mind that it may well be your last time.

发音练习 **PRONUNCIATION PRACTICE**

Please note that **an** is pronounced [ʌn]. There is no exact equivalent sound in English, but it is similar to the "Khan" in "Ghenghis Khan." The vowel sound is also like the sound you make when the doctor tells you to open your throat and say "ah." The sound **en** is pronounced [ən], as in the "**un**" sound in "under."

1. **Pronounce the following words containing the finals an and en.**

nàn	nèn	bàn	bèn
kǎn	kěn	gān	gēn
zhàn	zhèn	chán	chén
shān	shēn	fàn	fèn
màn	mèn	pán	pén

2. **Read aloud the following sentences, concentrating on the correct pronunciation of an and en.**

    A. Qǐngwèn, nǐmen xīngqītiān kàn diànyǐng ma?

    B. Xiǎo Fēn hé Xiǎo Fàn xīngqīsān xué yǔwén.

    C. Shānshàng qīngsōng gēn lián gēn.

3. **Read aloud the following rhyme.**

	Pén	**Hé**	**Píng**	
	盆	和	瓶	
Zhuō	shàng	yǒu	gè	pén,
桌	上	有	个	盆,
Pén	lǐ	yǒu	gè	píng.
盆	里	有	个	瓶。
Pēng	pēng	pēng,		
砰	砰	砰,		
Shì	píng	pèng	pén,	
是	瓶	碰	盆,	
Hái	shì	pén	pèng	píng?
还	是	盆	碰	瓶?

A Pan and a Bottle

A pan is on the table,

A bottle is in the pan.

Bang, bang, bang,

Is the bottle hitting the pan,

Or the pan hitting the bottle?

4. Read aloud the following classical poem.

Lù   Chái

鹿 柴

[Tang Dynasty]   Wáng   Wéi

[唐]   王 维

Kōng	shān	bù	jiàn	rén,	dàn	wén	rén	yǔ	xiǎng.
空	山	不	见	人，	但	闻	人	语	响。
Fǎn	jǐng	rù	shēn	lín,	fù	zhào	qīng	tái	shàng.
返	景	入	深	林，	复	照	青	苔	上。

Deer-Park Hermitage

By Wang Wei [Tang Dynasty]

There seems to be no one on the empty mountain....

And yet I think I hear a voice,

Where sunlight, entering a grove,

Shines back to me from the green moss.

你知道吗? **Did you know?**

Chinese secondary schools are called middle schools (中学) and are divided into junior 初中 (chūzhōng) and senior (高中 gāozhōng) levels. Students spend three years at junior middle school (also known as lower middle school), and those who pass the entrance examination spend three years at senior middle school (also known as upper middle school). Most students begin junior middle school at twelve years of age and senior middle school at fifteen years of age.

The regular secondary-school year usually has two semesters totaling nine months. In some rural areas, schools operate on a shift schedule to accommodate agricultural cycles. The academic curriculum consists of the Chinese language, mathematics, physics, chemistry, geology, foreign language, history, geography, politics, physiology, music, fine arts, and physical education. Some middle schools also offer vocational subjects. There are 30–35 class hours a week in addition to self-study and extracurricular activity.

A middle school classroom in China.

Although middle schools are viewed as a training ground for colleges and universities, in mainland China, a senior-middle-school graduate is considered an educated person. Entrance to universities and colleges is highly competitive and is based on excellent performance on a standardized college entrance examination. Middle schools are evaluated in terms of their success in sending graduates on for higher education.

3.6 第三单元复习
Review of Unit 3

课文 Text

我 的 妹妹 妮娜 每天 上午 八点 去 幼儿园，下午 三 点半 回家。妮娜 在 幼儿园 上 英语课、数学课、音乐 课、美术课 和 体育课。她 最 喜欢 体育课。

妮娜 在 幼儿园 有 很多 朋友。这个 星期六 妮娜 要 参 加 她 朋友 的 生日 晚会。晚会 下午 一点半 开始。 妮娜 的 朋友 住在 杭州，所以 妮娜 和 我 妈妈 上 午 要 离开 上海 去 杭州★。

星期六下午一点半妮娜去参加朋友的生日晚会。

*杭州 Hangzhou is a medium sized city to the south of Shanghai. It is best known for its beautiful scenery. It takes a little over an hour, by express train, to go from Shanghai to Hangzhou.

生词 New Words

	Simplified	Traditional	Pinyin	Part of Speech	English
1.	美术	美術	měishù	n.	fine arts
2.	参加	參加	cānjiā	v.	attend, participate
3.	晚会	晚會	wǎnhuì	n.	party
4.	离开	離開	líkāi	v.	leave

对话 Dialogue

大卫： 汤姆，这个周末你要做什么？

汤姆： 星期六上午我和爸爸打网球，下午去学武术。星期天我要做数学作业和历史作业。你呢？

大卫： 我星期六和朋友去公园。星期天上午去教堂，下午在家看球，晚上做作业。

汤姆： 看什么球？

大卫： 棒球。

汤姆： 你喜欢打棒球吗？

大卫： 非常喜欢。你呢？

汤姆： 马马虎虎。

生词 New Words

	Simplified	Traditional	Pinyin	Part of Speech	English
1.	棒球		bàngqiú	*n.*	baseball
2.	非常		fēicháng	*adv.*	very, extremely
3.	马马虎虎	馬馬虎虎	mǎma hūhu	*s.p.*	so-so

发音练习 PRONUNCIATION PRACTICE

1. Read aloud the following rhyme, paying attention to the finals.

Lí Hé Ní

梨 和 泥

Shù shàng yǒu lí, dì shàng yǒu ní.

树 上 有 梨， 地 上 有 泥。

Fēng guā lí, lí luò dì.

风 刮 梨， 梨 落 地。

Lí gǔn ní, ní zhān lí.

梨 滚 泥， 泥 沾 梨。

Pears and Mud

Pears are on the trees, mud is on the ground.

The wind blows pears, pears fall onto the ground.

Pears roll in the mud, mud sticks to pears.

Téng Hé Líng

藤 和 铃

Qīng qīng shān shàng yī kē téng,

青 青 山 上 一 棵 藤，

Qīng téng dǐ xià guà tóng líng.

青 藤 底 下 挂 铜 铃。

Fēng chuī téng dòng tóng líng dòng,

风 吹 藤 动 铜 铃 动，

Fēng tíng téng tíng tóng líng tíng.

风 停 藤 停 铜 铃 停。

A Vine and a Bell

On a green mountain grows a vine,

Under the vine there hangs a copper bell.

When the wind blows, the vine moves, and so does the bell,

When the wind stops, the vine stops, and so does the bell.

2. Read aloud the following rhyme and then recite the rhyme with a partner while playing the hand-clapping game.

Nǐ	pāi	yī,	wǒ	pāi	yī,	yī	gè	xiǎo	hái	chuān	xīn	yī.
你	拍	一,	我	拍	一,	一	个	小	孩	穿	新	衣。

Nǐ	pāi	èr,	wǒ	pāi	èr,	èr	gè	xiǎo	hái	shū	xiǎo	biànr.
你	拍	二,	我	拍	二,	二	个	小	孩	梳	小	辫儿。

Nǐ	pāi	sān,	wǒ	pāi	sān,	sān	gè	xiǎo	hái	chī	bǐng	gān.
你	拍	三,	我	拍	三,	三	个	小	孩	吃	饼	干。

Nǐ	pāi	sì,	wǒ	pāi	sì,	sì	gè	xiǎo	hái	xiě	dà	zì.
你	拍	四,	我	拍	四,	四	个	小	孩	写	大	字。

Nǐ	pāi	wǔ,	wǒ	pāi	wǔ,	wǔ	gè	xiǎo	hái	qiāo	dà	gǔ.
你	拍	五,	我	拍	五,	五	个	小	孩	敲	大	鼓。

Nǐ	pāi	liù,	wǒ	pāi	liù,	liù	gè	xiǎo	hái	jiǎn	dòu	dou.
你	拍	六,	我	拍	六,	六	个	小	孩	拣	豆	豆。

Nǐ	pāi	qī,	wǒ	pāi	qī,	qī	gè	xiǎo	hái	zuò	fēi	jī.
你	拍	七,	我	拍	七,	七	个	小	孩	坐	飞	机。

Nǐ	pāi	bā,	wǒ	pāi	bā,	bā	gè	xiǎo	hái	chuī	lǎ	bā.
你	拍	八,	我	拍	八,	八	个	小	孩	吹	喇	叭。

Nǐ	pāi	jiǔ,	wǒ	pāi	jiǔ,	jiǔ	gè	xiǎo	hái	jiāo	péng	yǒu.
你	拍	九,	我	拍	九,	九	个	小	孩	交	朋	友。

Nǐ	pāi	shí,	wǒ	pāi	shí,	shí	gè	xiǎo	hái	zhàn	de	zhí.
你	拍	十,	我	拍	十,	十	个	小	孩	站	得	直。

I clap one, you clap one, one child wears new clothes.

I clap two, you clap two, two children have pigtails.

I clap three, you clap three, three children eat cookies.

I clap four, you clap four, four children write big characters.

I clap five, you clap five, five children beat a big drum.

I clap six, you clap six, six children pick up beans.

I clap seven, you clap seven, seven children take the plane.

I clap eight, you clap eight, eight children blow horns.

I clap nine, you clap nine, nine children become friends.

I clap ten, you clap ten, ten children stand up straight.

3. Read aloud the following classical poem.

Xiāng Sī

相　思

[Táng]　Wáng Wéi

[唐]　王　维

Hóng　dòu　shēng　nán　guó,　chūn　lái　fā　jǐ　zhī.

红　豆　生　南　国，　春　来　发　几　枝。

Yuàn　jūn　duō　cǎi　jié,　cǐ　wù　zuì　xiāng　sī.

愿　君　多　采　撷，　此　物　最　相　思。

One-Hearted

By Wang Wei [Tang Dynasty]

When those red berries come in springtime,

Flushing on your southland branches,

Take home an armful for my sake,

As a symbol of our love.

SELF-ASSESSMENT

In this unit, you have learned to tell time, say the date, talk about your daily activities and weekend plans, and name some school courses. Have you reached the learning goals of Unit 3? After completing the exercises for Unit 3 in your Workbook, fill out the following self-assessment sheet.

Yes/No	*Can you say and write these things in Chinese?*
	Tell time
	Say the date
	Say the seven days of a week
	Talk about daily activities
	Make plans with friends
	Name some course offerings in a middle school or a high school
	Talk about your weekend plan
	Talk about birthdays
	Invite your friend to an event

Yes/No	*Do you know how to do these things?*
	Indicate time and date in correct order
	Correctly form an adverbial of time
	Correctly follow the sequence of adverbials of place and time
	Correctly duplicate a verb
	Write a letter in Chinese in correct letter format
	Write an email in Chinese in correct email format

13–15	yes	excellent
10–12	yes	good
7–9	yes	fair
1–6	yes	need some work

第四单元: 日常用品

UNIT 4　Things We Use Every Day

LEARNING GOALS OF UNIT 4

By the end of this unit, you will learn:

- How to read and write 80 Chinese characters
- Colors
- School supplies
- Some commonly used measure words
- Some commonly used Chinese sentence structures to indicate a sequence of actions
- Alternative questions with 还是
- Tag questions with 怎么样

Your knowledge will enable you to talk about:

- Colors
- Basic school supplies
- Sports and basic sporting goods
- Basic computer supplies
- Basic eating utensils
- A sequence of events

4.1 这是谁的书包?
Whose Backpack Is This?

🖸 对话一 Dialogue 1

(At the school library.)

Mǎlìyà: Tāngmǔ, nà gè lán shūbāo shì nǐ
玛丽娅: 汤姆, 那个 蓝 书包 是 你

de ma?
的 吗?

Tāngmǔ: Bù shì. Wǒ de shūbāo shì lǜsè
汤姆: 不 是。我 的 书包 是 绿色

de, bù shì lánsè de.
的, 不 是 蓝色 的。

Mǎlìyà: Zhè gè shūbāo bù shì nǐ de, yě
玛丽娅: 这个 书包 不 是 你 的, 也

bù shì wǒ de, shì shéi de ne?
不 是 我 的, 是 谁 的 呢?

Tāngmǔ: Shì bù shì Dàwèi de? Dàwèi yǒu
汤姆: 是 不 是 大卫 的? 大卫 有

yī gè lán shūbāo.
一 个 蓝 书包。

Mǎlìyà: Dàwèi de lán shūbāo shì jiù de,
玛丽娅: 大卫 的 蓝 书包 是 旧 的,

kěshì zhè gè shì xīn de.
可是 这个 是 新 的。

Tāngmǔ: Shūbāo shàng yǒu méiyǒu míngzì?

汤姆：书 包 上 有 没 有 名 字？

Mǎlìyà: Ràng wǒ kàn kan. Yǒu míngzì. Bādì.

玛丽娅：让 我 看 看。有 名 字。八 弟。

Tāngmǔ: Bādì? Nà shì Dàwèi de gǒu. Gǒu méiyǒu

汤姆：八 弟？那 是 大 卫 的 狗。狗 没 有

shūbāo ba?

书 包 吧？

 对话二 **Dialogue 2**

(David runs into the library.)

Dàwèi: À, wǒ de shūbāo zài zhèr.

大卫：啊，我 的 书 包 在 这 儿。

Tāngmǔ: Zhè shì nǐ de háishì Bādì de shūbāo?

汤姆：这 是 你 的 还 是 八 弟 的 书 包？

Dàwèi: Yuánlái shì Bādì de, Xiànzài shì wǒ de.

大卫：原 来 是 八 弟 的， 现 在 是 我 的。

Wǒ de shūbāo tài jiù le, suǒyǐ

我 的 书 包 太 旧 了， 所 以

wǒ yòng Bādì de shūbāo.

我 用 八 弟 的 书 包。

Mǎlìyà: Gǒu yě yòng shūbāo ma?

玛丽娅：狗 也 用 书 包 吗？

Dàwèi: Duì. Fàng gǒu de wánjù.

大卫：对。放 狗 的 玩 具。

生词 New Words

	Simplified	Traditional	Pinyin	Part of Speech	English
1.	蓝（色）	藍	lán(sè)	*adj.*	blue (color)
2.	书包	書包	shūbāo	*n.*	school bag
3.	绿（色）	綠	lǜ(sè)	*adj.*	green (color)
4.	新		xīn	*adj.*	new
5.	旧	舊	jiù	*adj.*	old
6.	上		shàng	*n.*	on (see Language Note 2)
7.	让	讓	ràng	*v.*	let, allow (see Language Note 3)
8.	这儿	這兒	zhèr	*n.*	here
9.	原来	原來	yuánlái	*adv.*	originally
10.	太…了		tài…le	*s.p.*	too
11.	用		yòng	*v.*	use
12.	放		fàng	*v.*	put, place
13.	玩具		wánjù	*n.*	toy

Handwritten annotations: 老 lao (with more love) [next to row 5]; to give / ask [next to row 7]; 这里 = zhe li [next to row 8]; It turns out that [next to row 9]; adj [next to row 10]

语言注释 Language Notes

1. Talking about colors

You may use a color word in two ways.

Color word	Noun	English meaning
蓝(色的)	书包	blue school bag
绿(色的)	书包	green school bag

Or,

Subject	是	Color word 的	Word omitted	English meaning
书包	是	蓝(色)的。	(书包)	The school bag is blue.

2. 上 to indicate location

书包上   on the bag
钢琴上   on the piano

3. The use of 让

Subject	让	Someone	Do something	Let/allow/ask someone (to) do something.
	让	我	看看	Let me take a look.
老师	让	他们	学习。	The teacher is asking them to study.

4. 吧 in a question

When you expect an affirmative answer to your question, you can use 吧 instead of 吗.

你是大卫吧？

(You are quite sure that the person you speak to is David. You expect the answer is "yes".)

你是大卫吗？

(You are not sure whether the person you speak to is David. You do not know whether you will get a "yes" or "no" answer.)

5. Alternative questions with 还是 _hi shi_ => _or_ <= _"或者" but only used in statement / huò zhe_

还是 is used to connect two choices in an alternative question. The choices can be nouns or verbs.

这个书包是你的还是她的？

Is the schoolbag yours or hers?

她学习还是工作？

Is she studying or working?

你喜欢蓝色的还是绿色的？

Do you like the blue one or the green one?

6. 太 + **adj.** + 了 **(too...)**

太 旧 了   too old

太 小 了   too small

学无止境 EXTEND YOUR KNOWLEDGE

Do you remember how to say the primary colors in Chinese?

银灰色 yin(sè) silver ←hui

金色 jin(sè) gold

红(色)	hóng(sè)	red
橙(色)	chéng(sè)	orange
黄(色)	huáng(sè)	yellow
绿(色)	lǜ(sè)	green
蓝(色)	lán(sè)	blue
紫(色)	zǐ(sè)	purple

Here are some other colors that you may want to learn:

白(色)	bái(sè)	white
黑(色)	hēi(sè)	black
粉(色) or 粉(红)色	fěn(sè)	pink (cosmetic powder color)
米(色)	mǐ(sè)	beige (rice color)
棕(色)	zōng(sè)	brown
灰(色)	huī(sè)	grey
浅蓝(色)	qiǎn lán(sè)	light blue
深绿(色)	shēn lǜ(sè)	dark green

发音练习 **PRONUNCIATION PRACTICE**

1. Read aloud the syllables, paying special attention to the tones.

yī	yí	yǐ	yì	shī	shí	shǐ	shì
一	姨	以	意	师	十	史	是

bāo	báo	bǎo	bào	mā	má	mǎ	mà
包	薄	宝	抱	妈	麻	玛	骂

2. Read aloud the tongue twister, paying special attention to the tones.

Rén	Míng	Hé	Rèn	Mìng
人	名	和	任	命

Rén	míng	shì	rén	míng,
人	名	是	人	名，

Rèn	mìng	shì	rèn	mìng.
任	命	是	任	命。

Rèn	mìng	bù	shì	rén	mìng,
任	命	不	是	人	命，

Rén	míng	bù	shì	rèn	míng.
人	名	不	是	认	名。

Names and Appointments

A name is a name,

An appointment (to an official position) is an appointment.

Appointing someone to a position is not (asking for) one's life,

A name is not the same as recognizing a name.

中国文化一瞥 A Glimpse into Chinese Culture

For more information and activities related to Chinese culture, please go to http://my.cheng-tsui.com/huanying.

1. Read aloud the poem, paying special attention to your tones.

Poetry has been an important part of Chinese culture—and education—for thousands of years. In ancient China, reciting poems was an important part of a scholar's education, and essential for passing the imperial exam which would lead to an official government post. Nowadays, Chinese children still memorize and recite classical poems in grade school. Can you memorize them?

Jué   Jù

绝 句

Táng   Dù   Fǔ

[唐] 杜 甫

Liǎng	gè	huáng	lí	míng	cuì	liǔ,
两	个	黄	鹂	鸣	翠	柳，
Yī	**háng**	**bái**	**lù**	**shàng**	**qīng**	**tiān.**
一	行	白	鹭	上	青	天。
Chuāng	**qián**	**xī**	**lǐng**	**qiān**	**qiū**	**xuě,**
窗	前	西	岭	千	秋	雪，
Mén	**bó**	**dōng**	**Wú**	**wàn**	**lǐ**	**chuán.**
门	泊	东	吴	万	里	船。

Two Golden Orioles Sing in the Green Willows

Du Fu [Tang Dynasty]

Two golden orioles sing in the green willows,

A row of white egrets against the blue sky.

The window frames the western hills' snow of a thousand autumns,

At the door is moored, from eastern Wu, a boat of ten thousand li.

2. Chinese Proverbs and Idioms

Proverbs 成语 (chéngyǔ) and idioms 惯用语 (guànyòngyǔ) are an essential part of the Chinese language. Similar to English, Chinese proverbs and idioms are phrases that are established and accepted through use. A Chinese proverb is often made of a fixed number of Chinese characters, and most are four characters long.

Chinese idioms and proverbs are a unique and fun part of the Chinese language and culture. Some idioms and proverbs are derived from stories and have meanings that are not readily apparent. Chinese speakers usually include proverbs and idioms in their speech and writing to make the language more vivid and interesting. Understanding them and learning to use them appropriately are important for building up your language proficiency.

Below are two simple examples of Chinese proverbs:

wǔ yán liù sè
五 颜 六 色
colorful

wǔ guāng shí sè
五 光 十 色
a great variety of colors

你知道吗？ **Did you know?**

Colors represent different things in different cultures. The traditional Chinese system regarded five colors—black, red, greenish blue, white and yellow—as standard colors. In ancient China, the color black was believed to be the color of heaven. Therefore, it was the king of all colors. In the eyes of ancient Chinese, the color white symbolized brightness, purity and fullness. The color red symbolized good fortune and joy. This tradition has been kept for thousands of years, and red is still used as a holiday and wedding color. In some areas, red eggs are given to family and friends when a baby is born. The color yellow represented the center of all things and was regarded as the most beautiful color of all. The color green-blue (青) symbolized the spring when everything is full of vigor and life.

Chinese emperors traditionally wore colorful robes of yellow.

4.2 我带书去学校
I Take Books to School

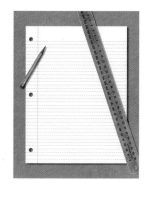

 对话一 **Dialogue 1**

(Nina watches Maria putting things into her school bag.)

Nínà:	Míngtiān nǐ dài jǐ běn kèběn qù
妮娜:	明天 你 带 几 本 课本 去
	xuéxiào?
	学校?
Mǎlìyà:	Wǔ běn. Nǐ kàn, yǒu shùxué,
玛丽娅:	五 本。 你 看, 有 数学、
	Hànyǔ, Yīngyǔ, lìshǐ, hé huàxué.
	汉语、 英语、 历史、 和 化学。
Nínà:	Nǐ dài běnzi ma?
妮娜:	你 带 本子 吗?
Mǎlìyà:	Dài. Wǒ dài liǎng běn liànxíběn.
玛丽娅:	带。 我 带 两 本 练习本。
Nínà:	Nǐ měitiān dài nàme duō shū hé
妮娜:	你 每天 带 那么 多 书 和
	běnzi qù xuéxiào ma?
	本子 去 学校 吗?
Mǎlìyà:	Duì. Nǐ ne?
玛丽娅:	对。 你 呢?

Nínà: Wǒ dài yī běn Yīngyǔ shū, yī
妮娜: 我 带 一 本 英语 书， 一

běn liànxíběn hé yī hé làbǐ.
本 练习本 和 一 盒 蜡笔。

对话二 **Dialogue 2**

(After class.)

Tāngmǔ: Kǎilì, jiè wǒ yī zhī bǐ yòng yong,
汤姆: 凯丽， 借 我 一 支 笔 用 用，

hǎo ma?
好 吗？

Kǎilì: Hǎo, nǐ yào shénme yánsè de?
凯丽: 好， 你 要 什么 颜色 的？

Tāngmǔ: Hóng de. Nǐ yǒu ma?
汤姆: 红 的。 你 有 吗？

Kǎilì: Duìbùqǐ, wǒ zhǐ yǒu lán de hé hēi de.
凯丽: 对不起， 我 只 有 蓝 的 和 黑 的。

Tāngmǔ: Shéi yǒu hóng de?
汤姆: 谁 有 红 的？

Mǎlìyà: Dīng Lǎoshī yǒu.
玛丽娅: 丁 老师 有。

生词 New Words

	Simplified	Traditional	Pinyin	Part of Speech	English
1.	带		dài	v.	take, take along
2.	本		běn	m.w.	for books, notebooks
3.	课本	課本	kèběn	n.	textbook
4.	本子		běnzi	n.	notebook
5.	练习本	練習本	liànxíběn	n.	notebook
6.	那么	那麼	nàme	adv.	so
7.	多		duō	adj.	many
8.	书	書	shū	n.	book
9.	盒		hé	n/m.w.	box
10.	蜡笔	蠟筆	làbǐ	n.	crayon
11.	借(给)		jiè	v.	borrow, lend
12.	支		zhī	m.w.	for pens
13.	笔	筆	bǐ	n.	pen
14.	颜色	顏色	yánsè	n.	color
15.	红(色)	紅(色)	hóng(sè)	adj.	red (color)
16.	黑(色)		hēi(sè)	adj.	black (color)

(handwritten annotations: 丝练习册 work book CC; 少 shǎo small; measure word; 给 give; 笔记本 bǐjì běn notebook (also notebook computer))

语言注释 Language Notes

1. 几 (how many?)

几 is used in a question when the number is <u>fewer</u> than ten.

你有几本本子？

How many notebooks do you have?

你有几个兄弟姐妹？

How many brothers and sisters do you have?

2. 那么 + adjective (so, such)

那么多课本   so many textbooks

那么好的学生   such a good student

3. The meaning of 对不起

You can use 对不起 to apologize for your mistake. For instance, when you bump into someone, you can say 对不起. You can also use 对不起 to express your regret. For example, if you can't go to a party because you have other engagements, you can say 对不起.

 发音练习 **PRONUNCIATION PRACTICE**

1. Read aloud the syllables, paying special attention to the tones.

shì	shí	shì	shí	huà	huá	huà	huá
是	十	是	十	化	滑	化	滑

xī	xǐ	xī	xǐ	tāng	tǎng	tāng	tǎng
西	喜	西	喜	汤	淌	汤	淌

2. Read aloud the tongue twister, paying special attention to the tones.

	Dà	Māo	Hé	Xiǎo	Māo	
	大	猫	和	小	猫	
Dà	māo	máo	duǎn,			
大	猫	毛	短,			
Xiǎo	māo	máo	cháng.			
小	猫	毛	长。			
Dà	māo	máo	bǐ	xiao	māo	duǎn,
大	猫	毛	比	小	猫	短,
Xiǎo	māo	māo	bǐ	dà	māo	cháng.
小	猫	毛	比	大	猫	长。

The Big Cat and the Kitten

The big cat has short hair,

The kitten has long hair.

The big cat's hair is shorter than the kitten's,

the kitten's hair is longer than the big cat's.

 中国文化一瞥 **A Glimpse into Chinese Culture**

For more information and activities related to Chinese culture, please go to http://my.cheng-tsui.com/huanying.

1. Read aloud the following poem, paying special attention to your tones.

Dēng Guàn Què Lóu
登　鹳　雀　楼

Táng　Wáng　Zhīhuàn
[唐]　王　之涣

Bái　rì　yī　shān　jìn,　Huáng　hé　rù　hǎi　liú.
白　日　依　山　尽，　黄　河　入　海　流。

Yù　qióng　qiān　lǐ　mù,　gèng　shàng　yī　céng　lóu.
欲　穷　千　里　目，　更　上　一　层　楼。

At Heron Lodge

Wang Zhihuan [Tang Dynasty]

Mountains cover the white sun,

And oceans drain the golden river.

But you widen your view three hundred miles,

By going up one flight of stairs.

2. Chinese Proverbs and Idioms

yú   gōng   yí   shān

愚　公　移　山

the Foolish Old Man who moved mountains

This proverb is used to praise someone who is not afraid of difficulties and has the determination to win. The story behind the proverb:

A long, long time ago, there lived an old man by the name of "the Foolish Old Man" in northern China. He was about ninety years old and lived in a house that faced two great mountains. It was rather inconvenient each time he and his family went out and returned home. The Foolish Old Man decided to remove them.

One day, he told his children and grandchildren about his plan, and they all agreed with him. The next morning and every morning thereafter the Foolish Old Man and his family would dig into the mountains. They worked at the mountains with diligence and great determination.

His neighbor, the Wise Old Man, saw what was going on. He went to talk to the Foolish Old Man, "How foolish of you to do this. It is impossible for the few of you to remove these two huge mountains. Besides, you are an old man. Why bother?"

The Foolish Old Man replied, "When I die, my sons will carry on; when they die, there will be my grandsons, and then their sons and grandsons… Even though the mountains are high, they cannot grow any higher. With every bit we dig, they will become much lower. Why can't we remove the mountains?"

The Foolish Old Man and his family went on digging every day, unshaken in their conviction. Their determination moved the gods. Heaven sent two angels down to the earth and they carried away the mountains on their backs.

wáng   yáng   bǔ   láo

亡　羊　补　牢

to fix the fence after a sheep is lost

This proverb's original meaning is that taking action after a problem has already occurred is too late. However, it can also be used to advise people that it is never too late to take action to prevent future problems.

你知道吗？ **Did you know?**

To write Chinese characters, what supplies do you need? You need a brush, ink, paper and ink stone, commonly referred to as the "four treasures of study" (文房四宝 wén fáng sì bǎo).

Writing brushes are varied, and white goat's hair, black rabbit's hair and yellow weasel's hair are three major types. The shaft is usually made from bamboo, but some fancy ones are made from ivory, jade, crystal, gold, silver, porcelain, ox horn, etc. There are both soft and hard brush for writing in different styles. There is a special way to hold the brush because writing characters with a brush needs a good coordination of the fingers and the wrist. Schoolchildren in China spend many hours practicing how to write with a brush.

To make ink, you add a few drops of water on to the ink stone and grind the ink stick on it. In the old days, when students took Chinese calligraphy class they needed to bring the heavy ink stone to school. Nowadays, they only need to bring a bottle of ready-made ink (usually in a light tiny plastic bottle).

4.3 买文具
Buying School Supplies

 对话一 Dialogue 1

(Maria and Kelly are at a stationery store).

Mǎlìyà: Nǐ   yào   mǎi   shénme?
玛丽娅：   你   要   买   什么？

Kǎilì: Wǒ   yào   mǎi   liànxíběn.
凯丽：   我   要   买   练习本。

Mǎlìyà: Liànxíběn   zài   nàr.
玛丽娅：   练习本   在   那儿。

     Wǒmen   qù   nàr.
     我们   去   那儿。

Kǎilì: Zhè   zhǒng   liànxíběn   hěn   hǎo,   kěshì
凯丽：   这   种   练习本   很   好，   可是

     wǒ   bù   xǐhuān   huáng   de.
     我   不   喜欢   黄   的。

Mǎlìyà: Nǐ   xǐhuān   lǜ   de   ma?   Zhèr   yǒu
玛丽娅：   你   喜欢   绿   的   吗？ 这儿   有

     lǜ   de,   bái   de,   zǐ   de   hé
     绿   的、 白   的、 紫   的   和

     lán   de.
     蓝   的。

凯丽： Zǐsè hěn hǎokàn, wǒ mǎi yī běn zǐ de.
凯丽： 紫色 很 好看， 我 买 一 本 紫 的。

玛丽娅： Wǒmen qù kàn kan bǐ. Wǒ yào mǎi qiānbǐ.
玛丽娅： 我们 去 看 看 笔。 我 要 买 铅笔。

凯丽： Nǐ kàn, zhè zhī yuánzhūbǐ shì zǐ de.
凯丽： 你 看， 这 支 圆珠笔 是 紫 的。

Wǒ mǎi yī zhī.
我 买 一 支。

玛丽娅： Nǐ shì bù shì hěn xǐhuān zǐ sè?
玛丽娅： 你 是 不 是 很 喜欢 紫色？

凯丽： Shì de.
凯丽： 是 的。

玛丽娅： Zhèr yǒu zǐsè de xiàngpí hé zǐsè de
玛丽娅： 这儿 有 紫色 的 橡皮 和 紫色 的

chǐzi. Nǐ yào ma?
尺子。 你 要 吗？

凯丽： Hǎo, wǒ zài mǎi yī kuài zǐsè de xiàngpí
凯丽： 好， 我 再 买 一 块 紫色 的 橡皮

hé yī bǎ zǐsè de chǐzi.
和 一 把 紫色 的 尺子。

对话二 Dialogue 2

玛丽娅： Wǒmen qù nàr kàn kan, wǒ yào mǎi yī
玛丽娅： 我们 去 那儿 看 看， 我 要 买 一

gè wénjiànjiā.
个 文件夹。

Kǎilì: Zhè gè wénjiànjiā hěn hǎokàn.

凯丽： 这 个 文件夹 很 好看。

Mǎlìyà: Kěshì tài dà le, wǒ yào yī gè xiǎo de.

玛丽娅： 可是 太 大 了， 我 要 一 个 小 的。

Kǎilì: Zhèr yǒu xiǎo de.

凯丽： 这儿 有 小 的。

Mǎlìyà: Hǎo, wǒ mǎi yī gè. Nǐ kàn, zhèr yǒu

玛丽娅： 好， 我 买 一 个。 你 看， 这儿 有

MPsān bōfàngqì. Nǐ yǒu MP sān bōfàngqì ma?

MP3 播放器。 你 有 MP3 播放器 吗？

Kǎilì: Wǒ yǒu yī gè. Nǐ ne?

凯丽： 我 有 一 个。 你 呢？

Mǎlìyà: Wǒ méiyǒu.

玛丽娅： 我 没有。

🔘 生词 **New Words**

sell 卖 mài

	Simplified	Traditional	Pinyin	Part of Speech	English
1.	买	買	mǎi	v.	buy
2.	文具		wénjù	n.	stationery
3.	种	種	zhǒng	n./m.w.	type, kind
4.	黄（色）		huáng(sè)	adj.	yellow (color)
5.	白（色）		bái(sè)	adj.	white (color)
6.	紫（色）		zǐ(sè)	adj.	purple (color)
7.	铅笔	鉛筆	qiānbǐ	n.	pencil
8.	圆珠笔	圓珠筆	yuánzhūbǐ	n.	ballpoint pen
9.	橡皮		xiàngpí	n.	eraser
10.	尺（子）		chǐ(zi)	n.	ruler
11.	块	塊	kuài	m.w.	for pieces
12.	把		bǎ	m.w.	for a handful
13.	文件夹	文件夾	wénjiànjiā	n.	file folder
14.	大		dà	adj.	big
15.	MP3播放器		MP sān bōfàngqì	n.	MP3 player

东西 dōng xi

语言注释 **Language Notes**

1. Using 是不是 to form a question and A 不 A Pattern (Yes No Question)

Has nothing to do with "to be" or 是 actually.

Subject	是不是	Rest of the sentence	English meaning
你	是不是	认识 他?	You know him, right?
她	是不是	喜欢 红色?	She likes the color red, right?
你	是不是	没有 弟弟?	You don't have a brother, do you?

2. Measure words

Here is a summary of the measure words that we have learned so far:

Measure word	Example	English meaning
个	一个学生	one student
个	一个文件夹	one file folder
本	两本课本	two textbooks
盒	三盒蜡笔	three boxes of crayons
种	四种练习本	four types of notebooks
支	五枝笔	five pens *also for music / melody*
块	六块橡皮	six erasers
把	七把尺子	seven rulers

3. Using 吧 to make a suggestion

When making a suggestion or giving an order, 吧 can be added to the end of a sentence to soften the tone.

星期日下午，我们去打网球吧。

Let's play tennis on Sunday afternoon.

你去看看吧。

(You) go and take a look.

发音练习 **PRONUNCIATION PRACTICE**

1. **Read aloud the syllables, paying special attention to the tones.**

hóng	hǒng	hóng	hǒng	lán	lǎn	lán	lǎn
红	哄	红	哄	蓝	懒	蓝	懒

hú	hǔ	hú	hǔ	máng	mǎng	máng	mǎng
湖	虎	湖	虎	忙	蟒	忙	蟒

2. **Read aloud the tongue twister, paying special attention to the tones.**

		Sōng	Shǔ	Hé	Sōng	Shù		
		松	鼠	和	松	树		
Sōng	shù	zhù	sōng	shǔ,				
松	树	住	松	鼠,				
Sōng	shǔ	pá	sōng	shù.				
松	鼠	爬	松	树。				
Shǔ	pá	sōng	shù	shù	zhù	shǔ,		
鼠	爬	松	树	树	住	鼠,		
Shǔ	zhù	sōng	shù	shǔ	pá	shù.		
鼠	住	松	树	鼠	爬	树。		

A Squirrel and a Pine Tree

A squirrel lives in the pine tree,

A squirrel climbs on the pine tree.

The squirrel climbs on the pine tree to live on the pine tree,

The squirrel lives on the pine tree so he has to climb on the pine tree.

中国文化一瞥 **A Glimpse into Chinese Culture**

For more information and activities related to Chinese culture, please go to http://my. cheng-tsui.com/huanying.

1. Read aloud the poem, paying special attentions to your tones.

Yǒng É

咏　鹅

[Táng]　Luò　Bīn　Wáng

[唐] 骆　宾　王

É　　é　　é,

鹅　　鹅　　鹅，

Qū　jǐng　xiàng　tiān　gē.

曲　颈　向　天　歌。

Bái　máo　fú　lǜ　shuǐ,

白　毛　浮　绿　水，

Hóng　zhǎng　bō　qīng　bō.

红　掌　拨　清　波。

Ode to the Goose

Luo Binwang [Tang Dynasty]

Goose, goose, goose,

You bend your neck towards the sky and sing.

Your white feathers float on the emerald water,

Your red feet push the clear waves.

2. Chinese Proverbs and Idioms

qí   hǔ   nán   xià

骑 虎 难 下

difficult to get off the tiger that you are riding

This is a metaphor for describing someone who is in a difficult situation.

zǒu   mǎ   guān   huā

走 马 观 花

appreciate flowers while riding a horse

This metaphor is used to describe someone who is not very careful in examining all aspects of things.

你知道吗? **Did you know?**

Where do Chinese students buy their school supplies? Most stationery shops in China are small and scattered around neighborhoods. It is easy to find one or two near a school. Street peddlers also display many school supplies on street carts and wait at the school's entrance during the hours when students get in and out of school. It is common for students to shop around to find the best design, color, and price. In the past few years, more and more supermarkets and department stores have opened up in China. They usually have a school supplies section.

网上词典
Online Dictionaries

4.4

🔘 对话一 **Dialogue 1**

(At the computer lab).

Dàwèi: Nǐ   yǒu   Hàn-Yīng   cídiǎn   ma?
大卫：   你 有 汉英 词典 吗?

Tāngmǔ: Méiyǒu.   Kěshì   wǎngshàng   yǒu.
汤姆：   没有。 可是 网上 有。

            Nǐ   wéishénme   bù   yòng   wǎngshàng   de
            你 为什么 不 用 网上 的

            cídiǎn?
            词典?

Dàwèi: Zài   nǎ   gè   wǎngzhàn?
大卫：   在 哪个 网站?

Tāngmǔ: Zài   http://www.tigernt.com.   Wǎngshàng   cídiǎn
汤姆：   在 http://www.tigernt.com。 网上 词典

            hěn   róngyì   yòng.
            很 容易 用。

Dàwèi: Xièxie.   Tīng   shuō   xiànzài   wǎngshàng *online*
大卫：   谢谢。 听 说 现在 网上

            hái   yǒu   xǔduō   shū,   fēicháng   fāngbiàn. *convenient*
            还 有 许多 书, 非常 方便。

Tāngmǔ: Duì, wǒ cháng cháng yòng wǎngshàng cídiǎn, yīnwèi
汤姆： 对， 我 常 常 用 网上 词典， 因为

wǒ xǐhuān shàng wǎng kàn shū.
我 喜欢 上 网 看 书。

Dàwèi: Nǐ xǐhuān kàn shénme shū?
大卫： 你 喜欢 看 什么 书？

Tāngmǔ: Wǒ zuì xǐhuān kàn lìshǐ shū.
汤姆： 我 最 喜欢 看 历史 书。

Dàwèi: Wǒ yǒu yī zhāng guāngpán. Zhè zhāng guāngpán
大卫： 我 有 一 张 光盘。 这 张 光盘

shàng yǒu hěn duō běn lìshǐ shū.
上 有 很 多 本 历史 书。

Wǒ míngtiān gěi nǐ.
我 明天 给 你。

Tāngmǔ: Tài hǎo le! Nǐ de guāngpán shàng yǒu shìjiè
汤姆： 太 好 了！ 你 的 光盘 上 有 世界

lìshǐ shū ma?
历史 书 吗？

Dàwèi: Yǒu shìjiè lìshǐ, yě yǒu Zhōngguó lìshǐ, Měiguó
大卫： 有 世界 历史， 也 有 中国 历史、 美国

lìshǐ, Yīngguó lìshǐ, hái yǒu diànnǎo lìshǐ,
历史、 英国 历史， 还 有 电脑 历史、

diànyǐng lìshǐ, diànshì lìshǐ. Wǒ zuì
电影 历史、 电视 历史。 我 最

xǐhuān kàn diànnǎo lìshǐ.
喜欢 看 电脑 历史。

对话二 Dialogue 2

Kǎilì: Zhè shì nǐ de MP sān ma? Zhème
凯丽：   这 是 你 的 MP3 吗？ 这么

xiǎo.
小。

Mǎlìyà: Bù shì. Zhè shì yōupán. Wǒ yòng
玛丽娅：   不 是。 这 是 优盘。 我 用

yōupán cún wénjiàn.
           save *file*
优盘 存 文件。

Kǎilì: Wǒ yuánlái yòng cípán cún wénjiàn,
凯丽：   我 原来 用 磁盘 存 文件，

xiànzài yòng MP sān.
现在 用 MP3。

Mǎlìyà: Nǐ xǐhuān nǐ de MP sān ma?
玛丽娅：   你 喜欢 你 的 MP3 吗？

Kǎilì: Hěn xǐhuān. Wǒ yòng MP sān tīng yīnyuè,
凯丽：   很 喜欢。 我 用 MP3 听 音乐，

yě yòng MP sān cún diànnǎo wénjiàn.
也 用 MP3 存 电脑 文件。

生词 **New Words**

zì diǎn

字典 =

	Simplified	Traditional	Pinyin	Part of Speech	English
1.	词典	詞典	cídiǎn	*n.*	dictionary
2.	网上	網上	wǎngshàng	*n.*	online
3.	为什么	為甚麼	wèishénme	*adv.*	why
4.	网站	網站	wǎngzhàn	*n.*	website, web address
5.	容易		róngyì	*adj.*	easy
6.	方便		fāngbiàn	*adj.*	convenient
7.	听说	聽說	tīngshuō	*s.p.*	it is said
8.	常常		chángcháng	*adv.*	often
9.	上网	上網	shàng wǎng	*v.o.* verb/obj	go online
10.	世界		shìjiè	*n.*	world
11.	最		zuì	*adv.*	most
12.	光盘	光盤	guāngpán	*n.*	CD, DVD
13.	给	給	gěi	*v./prep.*	give, to
14.	张	張	zhāng	*m.w.*	*for flat objects*
15.	优盘	優盤	yōupán	*n.*	USB flash drive
16.	存		cún	*v.*	store, save
17.	文件		wénjiàn	*n.*	file
18.	磁盘	磁盤	cípán	*n.*	floppy diskette

语言注释 Language Notes

1. 听说 (It is said…, I heard [from somewhere]…)

听说丁老师是北京人。

(I) heard Teacher Ding is from Beijing.

听说优盘上有许多电脑文件。

It is said there are many computer files on a USB drive.

2. 有…也有…还有 (there are A, B, and C)

You can use this structure to list things/people.

我们学校有美国人，也有日本人，还有很多韩国人。

There are Americans, Japanese, as well as Koreans in my school.

这种文件夹有很多颜色：有黄的，也有蓝的，
还有红的。

yanse

This kind of file folder comes in many colors: there are yellow, blue, and red (ones).

3. 最 (most)

最 is an adverb that goes before a verb or an adjective to make a superlative adjective in Chinese.

最好 best	最大 largest	最新 newest
最多 most	最喜欢 like most	最要 want most

4. 这么 / 那么 + adjective (so/such…)

这么小 or 那么小   so small

这么美丽 or 那么美丽   so beautiful

5. 是…的 ([It] is for…)

If you want to tell what something is used for, you can use the following structure:

Subject	是	*Verb phrase*	的	*English meaning*
优盘	是	存文件	的。	A USB drive is for storing computer files.
笔	是	写字	的。	A pen is for writing.
书包	是	放书	的。	A book bag is for putting books in.

学无止境 EXTEND YOUR KNOWLEDGE

How do the Chinese read a web address? Taking "www.zhongwen.com" as an example, this is how a web address is read in China: "sān dábùliu diǎr zhōngwén diǎr kàngmu".

Now, try it yourself. How would you read these web addresses? See page 199 for answers.

www.china.com   www.yahoo.com   www.baidu.com   www.alibaba.com

Below is a list of Internet-related Chinese words that have been created in recent years:

Characters	Pinyin	English
因特网	yīntèwǎng	Internet
互联网	hùliánwǎng	World Wide Web
网址	wǎngzhǐ	web address
网页	wǎngyè	web page
网站	wǎngzhàn	website
网吧	wǎngbā	Internet café
上网	shàng wǎng	go online
网上	wǎngshàng	online
网上聊天	wǎngshàng liáotiān	online chat
网上聊天室	wǎngshàng liáotiān shì	Internet chat room
版主	bǎnzhǔ	webmaster
免费下载	miǎnfèi xiàzài	free download

Answers to 学无止境 Extend Your Knowledge:

www.china.com: sān dábùliu diǎr china diǎr kàngmu

www.yahoo.com: sān dábùliu diǎr yǎhǔ diǎr kàngmu

www.baidu.com: sān dábùliu diǎr bǎidù diǎr kàngmu

www.alibaba.com: sān dábùliu diǎr ālǐbābā diǎr kàngmu

 发音练习 **PRONUNCIATION PRACTICE**

1. Read aloud the syllables, paying special attention to the tones.

yǐ	yī	yǐ	yī	shǐ	shí	shǐ	shí
以	一	以	一	史	实	史	实

bǎo	bao	bǎo	bao	mǎ	mā	mǎ	mā
宝	宝	宝	宝	玛	妈	玛	妈

2. Read aloud the tongue twister, paying special attention to the tones.

		Shǐ	Lǎo	Shī		
		史	老	师		

Lǎo	shī	jiào	Lǎo	Shǐ,		
老	师	叫	老	史，		

Lǎo	Shǐ	shì	lǎo	shī.		
老	史	是	老	师。		

Lǎo	shī	wèi	hé	jiào	Lǎo	Shǐ?
老	师	为	何	叫	老	史？

Lǎo	Shǐ	wèi	hé	shì	lǎo	shī?
老	史	为	何	是	老	师？

Teacher Shi

The teacher (laoshi)'s name is Lao Shi,

Lao Shi is a teacher (laoshi).

Why would the teacher (laoshi) have the name Lao Shi?

Why would Lao Shi work as a teacher (laoshi)?

中国文化一瞥 **A Glimpse into Chinese Culture**

For more information and activities related to Chinese culture, please go to http://my. cheng-tsui.com/huanying.

1. Read aloud the poem, paying attention to your tones.

Yóu   Zǐ   Yín
游   子   吟

[Táng]   Mèng   Jiāo
[唐]   孟   郊

Cí   mǔ   shǒu   zhōng   xiàn,   yóu   zǐ   shēn   shàng   yī.
慈   母   手   中   线，   游   子   身   上   衣。

Lín   xíng   mì   mì   féng,   yì   kǒng   chí   chí   guī.
临   行   密   密   缝，   意   恐   迟   迟   归。

Shéi   yán   cùn   cǎo   xīn,   bào   de   sān   chūn   huī?
谁   言   寸   草   心，   报   得   三   春   辉?

A Traveler's Song

Meng Jiao [Tang Dynasty]

The thread in the hands of a fond-hearted mother

makes clothes for the body of her wayward boy.

Carefully she sews and thoroughly she mends,

dreading the delays that will keep him late from home.

But how much love has the inch-long grass

for three spring months of the light of the sun?

2. Chinese Proverbs and Idioms

yī   sī   bù   gǒu
一   丝   不   苟

not overlook a single imperfection

This proverb is used to describe someone who is very meticulous and thorough.

yī   shì   wú   chéng
一   事   无   成

haven't accomplished a single task

This proverb is often used to describe someone who has no aspiration in life, or has accomplished nothing in life.

你知道吗? **Did you know?**

As computers and Internet technology have become increasingly available in the world, the number of Internet users in China has climbed. In 2007, there were an estimated 137 million Internet users in China, a number which grew by about 20 percent per year between 2004 and 2007.[1]

According to a survey conducted by China Internet Network Information Center (CNNIC) in 2007[2], 77.3 percent of online use in China is dedicated to reading news, 74.8 percent searching the Internet, and 55.4 percent e-mailing. Although some Chinese have Internet access at work or at home, most people, particularly those in rural areas, depend on Internet cafés. Internet cafés are easy to find in China, whether you are in a big city or in a small rural village.

[1] Fallows, Deborah. China's Online Population Explosion: What It May Mean for the Internet Globally...and for the U.S. Pew Internet and American Life Project. http://www.pewinternet.org/pdfs/China_Internet_July_2007.pdf.

[2] China Internet Network Information Center. Statistical Survey Report on the Internet Development in China. Published online July 15, 2007. Accessed on January 22, 2008. http://www.cnnic.cn/download/2007/20thCNNICreport-en.pdf.

4.5 我带滑板
I Will Take a Skateboard

Skateboarding in front of the Eastern Catholic Church in Beijing.

对话一 Dialogue 1

Dàwèi:	Xīngqīliù	wǒmen	qù	Rénmín	Gōngyuán,	hǎo	ma?
大卫:	星期六	我们	去	人民	公园，	好	吗？

LD TAG Q = suggestion

Mǎlìyà:	Hǎo,	wǒmen	qù	dǎ	qiú,	hǎo	ma?
玛丽娅:	好，	我们	去	打	球，	好	吗？

Tāngmǔ:	Hǎo	a.	Nǐmen	yǒu	zúqiú	ma?
汤姆:	好	啊。	你们	有	足球	吗？

Kǎilì:	Wǒmen	qù	dǎ	lánqiú	ba.	Wǒ	yǒu	lánqiú.
凯丽:	我们	去	打	篮球	吧。	我	有	篮球。

Mǎlìyà:	Hǎo.	Dǎ	qiú	yǐhòu,	wǒmen	qù	liū	hànbīng,
玛丽娅:	好。	打	球	以后，	我们	去	溜	旱冰，

zěnmeyàng?	Nǐmen	xǐhuān	liū	hànbīng	ma?
怎么样？	你们	喜欢	溜	旱冰	吗？

Kǎilì: Hěn xǐhuān. Míngtiān wǒ dài hànbīngxié.
凯丽: 很 喜欢。 明天 我 带 旱冰鞋。

Tāngmǔ: Wǒ yě dài yī shuāng.
汤姆: 我 也 带 一 双。

Dàwèi: Wǒ xǐhuān wán huábǎn. Wǒ dài wǒ de
大卫: 我 喜欢 玩 滑板。 我 带 我 的

huábǎn.
滑板。

Tāngmǔ: Tài hǎo le, dǎ lánqiú yǐhòu, Dàwèi wán
汤姆: 太 好 了， 打 篮球 以后， 大卫 玩

huábǎn, wǒmen sān gè liū hànbīng.
滑板， 我们 三 个 溜 旱冰。

对话二 Dialogue 2

Māma: Míngtiān wǒmen qù gōngyuán yěcān, hǎo ma?
妈妈: 明天 我们 去 公园 野餐， 好 吗?

Jiémǐ: Tài hǎo le. Wǒmen yào dài shénme?
杰米: 太 好 了。 我们 要 带 什么?

Bàba: Wǔfàn.
爸爸: 午饭。

Māma: Hái yào dài sì gè bēizi, sì gè pánzi,
妈妈: 还 要 带 四 个 杯子、 四 个 盘子、

sì bǎ dāo, chā hé yīxiē zhǐjīn.
四 把 刀、 叉 和 一些 纸巾。

→ future tense

Bàba:　Wǒmen shì bù shì zài dài yī gè zúqiú?

爸爸：　我们 是 不 是 再 带 一 个 足球？

→ one more

　　　　Yěcān yǐqián, wǒmen tī zúqiú.

　　　　野餐 以前， 我们 踢 足球。

Tāngmǔ:　Hǎo. Wǒ hé Jiémǐ yī duì, bàba māma

汤姆：　好。 我 和 杰米 一 队， 爸爸 妈妈

　　　　yī duì.

　　　　一 队。

we are in one team
mom, dad on one team

Jiémǐ:　Wǒmen dài "lǎohǔ" qù ma?

杰米：　我们 带 "老虎" 去 吗？

⇒ no need to say "去"

Tāngmǔ:　Dài

汤姆：　带。

↳ to bring him the park

Jiémǐ:　"Lǎohǔ" yě hé wǒmen yī duì.

杰米：　"老虎" 也 和 我们 一 队。

Exercise equipment in a school playground.

Dancing in a residential park.

生词 New Words

	Simplified	Traditional	Pinyin	Part of Speech	English
1.	打球		dǎqiú	v.o.	play ball
2.	啊		a	par.	*a mood particle*
3.	足球		zúqiú	n.	soccer (in the U.S.), football
4.	篮球	籃球	lánqiú	n.	basketball
5.	溜旱冰		liū hànbīng	v.o.	roller skate
6.	鞋		xié	n.	shoe
7.	双	雙	shuāng	m.w.	*a pair*
8.	滑板		huábǎn	n.	skateboard
9.	野餐		yěcān	n.	picnic
10.	还	還	hái	adv.	also, additionally
11.	杯子		bēizi	n.	cup
12.	盘子	盤子	pánzi	n.	plate
13.	刀(子)		dāo	n.	knife
14.	叉(子)		chā	n.	fork
15.	纸巾	紙巾	zhǐjīn	n.	paper napkin
16.	再		zài	adv.	also, again
17.	以前		yǐqián	prep./conj.	before
18.	踢		tī	v.	kick
19.	队员	隊	duì	n.	team

[handwritten] 20. 勺 sháo (子) spoon

语言注释 Language Notes

1. Time phrase/clause with 以前 or 以后

A word, a phrase, or a sentence +以前 or 以后 forms a time phrase or a time clause. Please note: the time phrase/clause comes before the predicate in a sentence.

三点以前，我们在学校。

We are at school before three o'clock.

看电影以前，我们去吃饭。

Before the movie, we will go eat.

下课以后，他做作业。

He does his homework after class.

他去公园以后玩滑板。

After going to the park, he skated on his skateboard.

(See Unit 3.3 Language Note 1 for more examples of time phrases with 以后.)

2. Tag questions with 怎么样

In this type of tag question, 怎么样 is tagged after a proposition or a suggestion to ask for others' opinions.

我们去公园溜旱冰，怎么样？

How about we go roller skating in the park?

我们明天去，怎么样？

How about we go there tomorrow?

3. 再 and 还

Both 再 and 还 are adverbs. There is a slight difference between the two words. 再 is used to indicate an action in the future, whereas 还 can be used for an action that has taken place or will take place. 再 often means "again" or "once more" (as in 再见 "see you again") while 还 usually means "also, in addition, too, as well as."

她买了一块橡皮，再要买一块。

She has bought an eraser and wants to buy another one.

她买了一支圆珠笔和一本练习本，
还买了一块橡皮。

She bought a pen and a notebook, as well as an eraser.

发音练习 **PRONUNCIATION PRACTICE**

1. **Read aloud the following syllables, paying special attention to the tones.**

yì	yi	yì	yi	shì	shí	shì	shí
意	义	意	义	事	实	事	实
mìng	míng	mìng	míng	bào	bǎo	bào	bǎo
命	名	命	名	抱	宝	抱	宝

2. **Read aloud the tongue twister, paying special attention to the tones.**

	Tiě	Dīng	Tiě	Bǎn,
	铁	钉	铁	板
Tiě	dīng	dīng	tiě	bǎn,
铁	钉	钉	铁	板，
Tiě	bǎn	dīng	tiě	dīng.
铁	板	钉	铁	钉。
Dīng	dīng	bǎn,		
钉	钉	板，		
bǎn	dīng	dīng.		
板	钉	钉。		

Iron Nails and Iron Boards

The nails are hammered into the iron board,
Into the iron board the nails are hammered.
The nails are hammered into the board,
Into the board the nails are hammered.

中国文化一瞥 **A Glimpse into Chinese Culture**

For more information and activities related to Chinese culture, please go to http://my.cheng-tsui.com/huanying.

1. Read aloud the poem, paying special attention to your tones.

Cūn Jū

村 居

Qīng Gāo Dǐng

[清] 高 鼎

Cǎo	zhǎng	yīng	fēi	èr	yuè	tiān,
草	长	莺	飞	二	月	天,

Fú	tí	yáng	liǔ	zuì	chūn	yān.
拂	堤	杨	柳	醉	春	烟。

Ér	tóng	sǎn	xué	guī	lái	zǎo,
儿	童	散	学	归	来	早,

Máng	chèn	dōng	fēng	fàng	zhǐ	yuān.
忙	趁	东	风	放	纸	鸢。

Village Life

Gao Ding [Qing Dynasty]

Grass grows, orioles fly in the early spring,

willows stroke the river banks in the spring air.

Children come home early from school,

hurrying to fly kites in the east wind.

2. Chinese Proverbs and Idioms

xué yǒu suǒ chéng

学　有　所　成

learned and accomplished

This idiom is used to describe someone who is diligent in learning and become successful.

wēn gù zhī xīn

温　故　知　新

revisit the past to learn about the future

This saying is originally from Confucius. It is often used to remind students of the importance of reviewing what you have learned.

你知道吗？ **Did you know?**

People in China are generally quite active in their daily lives. Basketball, soccer, badminton, ping-pong (table tennis), volleyball, swimming, roller skating, and jogging are popular sports in China. Older people like Taijiquan (太极拳), know as Tai Chi in the West. It is a soft-style martial art with slow motion routines that combines exercise and meditation. Bicycling and walking, which may be considered exercise in the West, are the only means of transportation for many Chinese to get around. Therefore, most Chinese do not consider them "sports."

To help everyone keep fit, almost all schools, businesses, and offices have set aside "exercise time" during the school/working day. During the "exercise time," everyone will practice a ten-minute stretching routine in groups. The exercise is accompanied by music and instruction. It is known as 广播体操 (guǎngbō tǐcāo – broadcast exercise). Because the movements are quite simple and light, people of all ages and physical conditions can usually follow.

4.6 第四单元复习
Review of Unit 4

对话 Dialogue

玛丽娅：　你每天上网吗？

汤姆：　　对。

玛丽娅：　在学校还是在家？

汤姆：　　有时候在学校，有时候在家。

玛丽娅：　你上网做什么？

汤姆：　　看email，听音乐，用网上词典，玩电脑游戏。

玛丽娅：　你们家用电话上网吗？

汤姆：　　不。我爸爸是电脑工程师，有时候要上网。因为用电话上网不方便，所以他用宽带上网。你们家呢？

玛丽娅：　我们也用宽带。爸爸、妈妈、安东尼和我都上网，用电话上网太不方便了。

课文 Text

玛丽娅带妮娜去买蜡笔。蜡笔有大盒和小盒的。小盒的蜡笔有八色、十六色、和二十四色，大盒的蜡笔有九十六色。妮娜喜欢大盒的，可是带大盒的蜡笔去幼儿园不方便，所以玛丽娅给妮娜买了一盒大的，一盒小的。大的在家用，小的去幼儿园用。妮娜还要买一个铅笔盒，放她的铅笔、圆珠笔、橡皮和尺子。

生词 New Words

Simplified	Traditional	Pinyin	Part of Speech	English
宽带	（寬带）	kuāndài	n.	broadband
铅笔盒	（鉛筆盒）	qiānbǐhé	n.	pencil box

SELF-ASSESSMENT

In Unit 4, you have learned primary colors, some basic school supplies, sporting equipment, computer supplies and eating utensils. Have you reached the learning goals of Unit 4? After completing the exercises for Unit 4 in your Workbook, fill out the following self-assessment sheet.

Yes/No	*Can you say and write these things in Chinese?*
√	Discuss basic school supplies: indicate the name, color, size and number of the item
√	Talk about surfing the Internet
√	Arrange an outing
√	Talk about some common sports and sporting goods

Yes/No	*Do you know how to do these things?*
√	Name the primary colors
√	Name some basic school supplies, such as notebooks, pens, pencils, erasers, etc.
√	Name some basic computer supplies, such as USB flash drive, file, CD, DVD, etc.
No	Name some basic eating utensils
No	Know how to use these measure words: 把、本、盒、块、双、张、支、种

7–9	yes	excellent
3–6	yes	good
1–2	yes	need some work

第五单元: 娱乐活动

UNIT 5　Things I Do for Fun

LEARNING GOALS OF UNIT 5

By the end of this unit, you will learn:

- How to read and write 73 Chinese characters
- Words for some common recreational activities, including computer games, TV programs, musical instruments, movies, concerts, sports, and travel
- How to describe an action in progress
- Optative verbs to express intent, ability, permission and wish
- Conjunctions to describe when two or more actions take place (immediately after one another, at the same time, and sequentially)
- Using words and phrases to modify a noun
- Time spent on an activity

Your knowledge will enable you to:

- Talk about recreational activities, including computer games, TV programs, musical instruments, movies, concerts, sports, and travel
- Express intent, ability, permission and wish
- Describe an action in progress or say that you are in the middle of doing something
- Talk about two actions that take place at the same time
- Talk about a sequence of actions
- Talk about time spent on an activity

5.1 看电影
Seeing a Movie

A movie theater in China.

对话一 Dialogue 1

（大家在玛丽娅家。）

要 = already decided
想 = not decided.

| Āndōngní: | Jīntiān | wǎnshàng | wǒ | xiǎng | qù | kàn | Zhōngguó | diànyǐng, |

安东尼： 今天 晚上 我 想 去 看 中国 电影，

Time word

nǐmen xiǎng qù ma?

你们 想 去 吗?

Tāngmǔ: Shénme diànyǐng?

汤姆： 什么 电影?

Āndōngní: «Měilì Shànghǎi».

安东尼:《美丽 上海》。

Tāngmǔ: Hǎo, wǒmen xiànzài qù ma?

汤姆： 好, 我们 现在 去 吗?

Āndōngní: Bù, wǎnshàng qù.

安东尼: 不, 晚上 去。

Nínà: Wǒ yě yào qù.

妮娜: 我 也 要 去。

Āndōngní: Bù néng dài nǐ qù.
安东尼： 不 能 带 你 去。

Nínà: Wèishénme?
妮娜： 为什么？

Āndōngní: Yīnwèi nǐ shì yòu'éryuán de, bù néng kàn
安东尼： 因为 你 是 幼儿园 的， 不 能 看

zhè gè diànyǐng. Zài shuō, diànyǐng bā diǎn
这 个 电影。 再 说， 电影 八 点

kāishǐ, kěshì nǐ měitiān bā diǎn bàn shuìjiào.
开始， 可是 你 每天 八 点 半 睡觉。

Nínà: Mǎlìyà, jīntiān wǎnshàng nǐ kěyǐ dài wǒ qù
妮娜： 玛丽娅， 今天 晚上 你 可以 带 我 去

kàn diànyǐng ma?
看 电影 吗？

Mǎlìyà: Jīntiān wǎnshàng wǒ méi kōngr, yīnwèi wǒ yào
玛丽娅： 今天 晚上 我 没 空儿， 因为 我 要

zuò zuòyè, míngtiān wǒ kěyǐ
做 作业， 明天 我 可以

dài nǐ qù kàn diànyǐng.
带 你 去 看 电影。

Nínà: Wǒmen qù kàn 《Mù Lán》,
妮娜： 我们 去 看《木兰》，

hǎo ma?
好 吗？

Mǎlìyà: Hǎo.
玛丽娅： 好。

Mù Lán
木兰

对话二 **Dialogue 2**

（安东尼去看电影以前，问爸爸要钱。）

Āndōngní: Bàba, nín néng gěi wǒ yī diǎnr qián ma?
安东尼： 爸爸，您 能 给 我 一 点儿 钱 吗？

Jīntiān wǎnshàng wǒ yào qù kàn diànyǐng.
今天 晚上 我 要 去 看 电影。

Bàba: Hǎo ba.
爸爸： 好 吧。

Āndōngní: Xièxie Bàba. Bàba, zàijiàn.
安东尼： 谢谢 爸爸。 爸爸， 再见。

Bàba: Diànyǐng bā diǎn kāishǐ, xiànzài cái liù diǎn,
爸爸： 电影 八 点 开始， 现在 才 六 点，

nǐ yào qù nǎr?
你 要 去 哪儿？

Āndōngní: Wǒ hé Tāngmǔ xiān qù shūdiàn, zài qù
安东尼： 我 和 汤姆 先 去 书店， 再 去

diànyǐngyuàn.
电影院。

Bàba: Nǐ jǐ diǎn huí jiā?
爸爸： 你 几 点 回 家？

Āndōngní: Shí diǎn bàn.
安东尼： 十 点 半。

Bàba: Tài wǎn le ba?
爸爸： 太 晚 了 吧？

Āndōngní: «Měilì Shànghǎi» yào kàn liǎng gè xiǎoshí.

安东尼：《美丽上海》 要 看 两 个 小时。

Bàba: Hǎo ba, zǎo qù zǎo huí.

爸爸： 好 吧，早 去 早 回。

Āndōngní: Bàba, zàijiàn.

安东尼：爸爸，再见。

rui shio norean addition

生词 New Words

	Simplified	Traditional	Pinyin	Part of Speech	English
1.	想		xiǎng	v./o.v.	would like to, want, intend /miss/think
2.	美丽	美麗	měilì	adj.	beautiful
3.	能		néng	o.v.	have the ability to, can
4.	再说 =还有	再說	zàishuō	adv.	moreover, in addition
5.	可以		kěyǐ	o.v.	may
6.	没空儿 freetime 没時间 shi jian ⇒ no time.	沒空兒	méikòngr	v.o.	do not have free time
7.	有点儿(adj) (一)点儿 (er)	一點	yīdiǎn (n)	det.	a little, some
8.	钱	錢	qián	n.	money
9.	才		cái	adv.	only
10.	先…再…		xiān…zài…	s.p.	first…then…
11.	晚		wǎn	adj.	late
12.	小时	小時	xiǎoshí	n.	hour
13.	早		zǎo	adj.	early

⇒有空 you kong have free time.
⇒多少钱 duo shao qian how much

早去早回 xiao qui xiao hui go early come early / 快去快回 kuai qui kuai hui go quick come back Quick

娱乐活动 yu le huo dong recreational activities.

漂亮 piao liang beautiful   还有 hai you also have   多少 duo shao how much

Proper Noun

| 14. | 木兰 | 木蘭 | Mù Lán | *p.n.* | Mu Lan |

语言注释 Language Notes

1. Optative verbs

能, 可以, and 要 are optative verbs that are used before verbs to indicate ability, possibility, intent, or wish. They are made negative by using 不.

Subject	（不）	Optative verb	Verb	Object	English meaning
我		想	看	电影。	I'd like to see a movie.
你	不	能	去。		You cannot go.
你		可以	问	老师。	You may ask the teacher.

In positive form, 可以 and 能 are similar in meaning and use. They mark "internal ability" and "external permissibility". For example, 我可以去 and 我能去 are interchangeable in meaning and in use.

In asking permission, 可以 is used more often than 能. For example, 我可以去吗? 我可以看看书吗?

In negative form, 不能 and 不可以 have slightly different meanings. 不能 often implies inability to do something while 不可以 often implies being prohibited or forbidden from doing something. For example, 他不能来 (He cannot come.) 他不可以来 (He is prohibited to come.)

2. 先···再··· (first...then...)

This phrase is used to show the sequence of two actions. Both 先 and 再 are adverbs, and they need to be followed by verbs/verbal phrases.

我们先去学校，再去电影院。
We will go to school first, and then to the cinema.

爸爸说："你可以先做作业，再玩电脑游戏。"
His father says, "You can do your homework first, and play computer games later."

3. 一点 (a little, some)

一点 indicates an unspecified quantity of something.

请给我一点钱。

Please give me some money.

4. 才 (only)

才 is a versatile adverb. Its meanings vary according to different contexts. One of its uses is to indicate a small "amount" or "number" of something. 才 is placed before a numerical phrase.

For example:

现在才三点。

(It's only three o'clock.)

我们的汉语老师才二十一岁。

(Our Chinese teacher is only 21 years old.)

 中国文化一瞥 **A Glimpse into Chinese Culture**

For more information and activities related to Chinese culture, please go to http://my. cheng-tsui.com/huanying.

1. Read aloud the poem, paying special attention to your tones.

Yuè   Yè
月　夜

[Táng]　Liú　Fāng　Píng
[唐]　刘　方　平

Gēng	shēn	yuè	sè	bàn	rén	jiā,	běi	dǒu	lán	gān	nán	dǒu	xié.
更	深	月	色	半	人	家，	北	斗	阑	干	南	斗	斜。

Jīn	yè	piān	zhī	chūn	qì	nuǎn,	chóng	shēng	xīn	tòu	lǜ	chuāng	shā.
今	夜	偏	知	春	气	暖，	虫	声	新	透	绿	窗	纱。

A Moonlit Night

Liu Fangping [Tang Dynasty]

When the moon has coloured half the house,

With the North Star at its height and the South Star setting,

I can feel the first motions of the warm air of spring

In the singing of an insect at my green-silk window.

2. Chinese Proverbs and Idioms

shuǐ dī shí chuān

水 滴 石 穿

drops of water outwear the stone (constant effort brings success)

你知道吗？ **Did you know?**

Motion pictures were introduced to China in 1896. The first Chinese movie was made in 1913. In the 1930s and 1940s the Chinese movie industry flourished and Shanghai became the movie center of China. Many excellent works were made during that period, such as *Street Angel* (1937), *Crossroad* (1937), *Spring River Flows Eastward* (1947), *Light of a Million Hopes* (1948) and *The Crow and the Sparrow* (1949).

Since 1949, China's movie industry has experienced ups and downs. In the 1950s and early 1960s, many fine movies were showing on the screen. During the Cultural Revolution (1966–1976), filmmaking experienced severe setbacks. Very few movies were made and these movies were strongly influenced by revolutionary thinking, with little artistic value.

In the 1980s and 1990s, China's movie industry once again began to prosper. Chinese movies started to be internationally recognized for their high artistic quality. Many Chinese movies have won awards in international film festivals, such as *Red Sorghum* (1987), *Farewell My Concubine* (1993), and *To Live* (1994).

In the twenty-first century, the situation of Chinese movie industry is both encouraging and challenging. It is encouraging because China produces more than 100 movies a year and some movies are of high quality, such as *Beijing Bicycle* (2002) directed by Wang Xiaoshuai, *Together* (2002) directed by Chen Kaige, and *Still Life* (2006) directed by Jia Zhangke. It is challenging because the movie market has become sluggish in the last few years due to competition from other forms of entertainment, such as DVD, TV and the Internet. China's movie industry is working to regain its prosperity by providing high-quality movies and services for viewers.

5.2 音乐
Music

对话一 **Dialogue 1**

（汤姆给玛丽娅打电话。）

Tāngmǔ: Mǎlìyà, nǐ zài kàn diànshì ma? Fǎguó duì hé
汤姆： 玛丽娅，你 在 看 电视 吗？法国 队 和

Měiguó duì zhèngzài bǐsài ne.
美国 队 正在 比赛 呢。

Mǎlìyà: Méiyǒu, wǒ zài xiàzǎi diànnǎo yóuxì ne.
玛丽娅： 没有，我 在 下载 电脑 游戏 呢。

Tāngmǔ: Nǎ gè yóuxì?
汤姆： 哪个 游戏？

ball game

Mǎlìyà: Super Mario. Nǐ zài kàn qiúsài ma?
玛丽娅： Super Mario. 你 在 看 球赛 吗？

Tāngmǔ: Duì. Wǒ yě yībiān kàn qiú, yībiān xiàzǎi yīnyuè

汤姆： 对。我 也 一边 看 球，一边 下载 音乐

ne.

呢。

Mǎlìyà: Shénme yīnyuè?

玛丽娅：什么 音乐？

Tāngmǔ: U2 de.

汤姆： U2 的。

Mǎlìyà: Nǐ wéishénme bù mǎi tāmen de CD ne?

玛丽娅：你 为什么 不 买 他们 的 CD 呢？

Tāngmǔ: CD shàng de gē, wǒ yǒu de xǐhuān, yǒu de

汤姆： CD 上 的 歌，我 有 的 喜欢，有 的

bù xǐhuān. Zài wǎngshàng, wǒ kěyǐ zhǐ xiàzǎi

不 喜欢。在 网上， 我 可以 只 下载

wǒ xǐhuān de gē.

我 喜欢 的 歌。

Mǎlìyà: Nǐ qù nǎge wǎngzhàn xiàzǎi?

玛丽娅：你 去 哪个 网站 下载？

Tāngmǔ: Wǒ qù yīnyuè wǎngzhàn.

汤姆： 我 去 音乐 网站。

对话二 **Dialogue 2**

（下课以后，玛丽娅和凯丽在说话。）

are talking

Mǎlìyà: Zhège xīngqī wǔ wǎnshàng xuéxiào yǒu gāngqín bǐsài.

玛丽娅：这个 星期五 晚上 学校 有 钢琴 比赛。

Kǎilì: Shì wǒmen xuéxiào xuésheng de gāngqín bǐsài ma?

凯丽：是 我们 学校 学生 的 钢琴 比赛 吗？

Mǎlìyà: Bù shì. Shì Shànghǎi yòu'éryuán xuésheng de gāngqín

玛丽娅：不 是。是 上海 幼儿园 学生 的 钢琴

bǐsài. Wǒ mèimei Nínà yào lái cānjiā.

比赛。我 妹妹 妮娜 要 来 参加。

Kǎilì: Nínà huì tán gāngqín ma?

凯丽：妮娜 会 弹 钢琴 吗？

studying　　　　　　　　*can play a little*

Mǎlìyà: Tā zhèngzài xuéxí tán gāngqín, huì tán yīdiǎnr.

玛丽娅：她 正在 学习 弹 钢琴，会 弹 一点儿。

Tā de gāngqín lǎoshī ràng tā lái cānjiā

她 的 钢琴 老师 让 她 来 参加

asked　　*come to participate*

bǐsài.

比赛。

Kǎilì: Nǐ yě huì tán gāngqín ma?

凯丽：你 也 会 弹 钢琴 吗？

Mǎlìyà: Huì. Wǒ hái huì lā xiǎotíqín. Nǐ ne?

玛丽娅：会。我 还 会 拉 小提琴。你 呢？

↳I also can play

Kǎilì:

Wǒ huì tán shùqín. Wǒ jiā de rén dōu
凯丽： 我 会 弹 竖琴。我 家 的 人 都

hěn xǐhuān yīnyuè. Wǒ māma huì tán gāngqín,
很 喜欢 音乐。我 妈妈 会 弹 钢琴，

wǒ bàba huì lā dàtíqín, wǒ jiějie huì tán
我 爸爸 会 拉 大提琴，我 姐姐 会 弹

jítā.
吉他。

生词 New Words

	Simplified	Traditional	Pinyin	Part of Speech	English
1.	正		zhèng	adv.	indicates an action in progress (see Language Note 1)
2.	比赛	比賽	bǐsài	n./v.	(sports) match, competition
3.	下载	下載	xiàzǎi	v.	download
4.	球赛	球賽	qiúsài	n.	ball game
5.	一边···一边···	一邊···一邊···	yībiān... yībiān...	s.p.	at the same time, while (indicates doing two things simultaneously; see Language Note 3)
6.	歌		gē	n.	song
7.	有的		yǒude	s.p.	some
8.	弹	彈	tán	v.	play (piano, guitar)
9.	会	會	huì	o.v.	know how to, be likely to (see Language Note 2)
10.	拉		lā	v.	play (violin, viola, cello...)
11.	小提琴		xiǎotíqín	n.	violin
12.	竖琴	豎琴	shùqín	n.	harp
13.	大提琴		dàtíqín	n.	cello
14.	吉他		jítā	n.	guitar

Proper Noun

	Simplified	Traditional	Pinyin	Part of Speech	English
15.	法国	法國	Fǎguó	p.n.	France

Handwritten annotations:

参加 canjia join, participate
给...打电话 gěi dǎdiànhuà call someone
音乐会 yīn yue hui concert
yue qi musical instruments
吹 chui blow
下棋 xia qi play chess
画画 hua hua painting
二胡 di zi er hu flute two string violin

语言注释 Language Notes

1. An action in progress *tense*

To indicate that an action is in progress, place 正, 正在, or 在 before the verb, or place 呢 at the end of the sentence. 正，正在， or 在 can also be used together with 呢.

Subject	正/在/正在	Verb	(Object)	（呢）	English meaning
我	正	看	书。		I am (was) reading a book.
我	正	看	书	呢。	
我	在	看	书。		
我	在	看	书	呢。	
我	正在	看	书。		
我	正在	看	书	呢。	
我		看	书	呢。	

The above sentences have the same meaning. However, 我看书呢 is usually used in informal speech.

The negative form of this structure is 没有 or 没. *Only use* 在 <u>not</u> 正, 正在

A: 他正在打网球吗?

B: 他没有打网球。Or 他没打网球。Or 没有。

A: Is he playing tennis?

B: No.

2. The optative verb 会

会 is an optative verb (also called an "auxiliary verb") meaning "be likely to," "know how to," and "have the ability to." When you use 会 to indicate an ability to do something, it usually means an acquired ability, such as the ability to play a musical instrument or speak a foreign language.

我会弹钢琴。

I can play the piano. (I know how to play the piano.)

你会说法语吗？

Can you speak French? (Do you know how to speak French?)

他明天会来吗？

Will he come tomorrow? (Is he likely to come tomorrow?)

3. 一边…一边…

This structure is used to indicate that two actions take place simultaneously.

Subject	一边	Action 1	一边	Action 2	English meaning
他	一边	做作业	一边	听音乐。	He is doing homework and listening to music at the same time.
他	一边	下载音乐	一边	打电话给朋友。	He is calling his friend while downloading music.

4. 有的 (some), can be used in list

This set phrase is used to refer to a segment of a group. 有的 is usually followed by a noun, such as 有的书，有的学生…. But sometimes, the noun is omitted if the noun is understood from the context, as CD 上的歌，我有的喜欢，有的不喜欢。

有的 can be used both as the subject or the object of a sentence, but it can never appear after a verb in a sentence. If it is used as the object of a sentence, the sentence order needs to be changed from SVO (subject + verb + object) to OSV or SOV. For example:

有的书我喜欢。

我有的书喜欢，有的不喜欢。

(I like some of the books.)

5. Word/phrase/clause + 的 + noun

To modify a noun, 的 is placed between a word/phrase/clause and a noun. The format is:
word/phrase/clause + 的 + noun.

Here are some examples:

Adjective (with two or more than two characters) + 的 + noun

快乐的歌   happy song

聪明的学生   smart student

Verb + 的 + noun

来的老师   teachers who came

参加比赛的学生   students who participate in the competition

Phrase + 的 + noun

在电脑房学习的学生   students who study in the computer lab

MP3 播放器上的歌   the songs on a MP3 player

Clause (subject + verb) + 的 + noun

我喜欢的书   the book that I like

他下载的音乐   the music that he downloaded

When to omit the noun after 的?

a. Generally speaking, when the noun after 的 is understood from the context, it can be omitted.

我的狗是白色的，你的（狗）呢？

My dog is white. How about yours?

有的书我喜欢，有的（书）我不喜欢。

I like some of the books.

b. If the same noun is to be used twice in a sentence, one of them is usually omitted to avoid redundancy.

他下载的（音乐）是U2的音乐。 or 他下载的音乐是U2的（音乐）。

What he downloaded is music from U2.

中国文化一瞥 **A Glimpse into Chinese Culture**

For more information and activities related to Chinese culture, please go to http://my. cheng-tsui.com/huanying.

1. Read aloud the poem, paying special attention to your tones.

Chí   Shàng

池　　上

[Táng]　　Bái　Jū　Yì

[唐]　白　居　易

Shān　sēng　duì　qí　zuò,　jú　shàng　zhú　yīn　qīng.

山　僧　对　棋　坐，局　上　竹　阴　清。

Yìng　zhú　wú　rén　jiàn,　shí　wén　xià　zǐ　shēng.

映　竹　无　人　见，时　闻　下　子　声。

On the Lake

Bai Juyi [Tang Dynasty]

Two monks sit, facing each other over a chess board,

The shadow of bamboo on the board is clear.

No one sees the bamboo shadow,

From time to time one hears the pieces being moved.

2. Chinese Proverbs and idioms

léi　shēng dà,　yǔ　diǎn　xiǎo

雷　声　大，雨　点　小

loud thunder but small rain drops (much said but little done)

你知道吗？   **Did you know?**

There are a great variety of traditional Chinese musical instruments. They are typically made of bamboo, metal, wood, animal hides, silk, stone and other natural materials. Since there are approximately 100 different types of musical instruments, let's focus on some of the best-known ones.

Guqin (古琴 gǔqín) is a seven-stringed zither without bridges. It is the most classical Chinese instrument, with over 3,000 years of history. In Imperial China, scholars were expected to master four arts, namely *qin* (琴, *guqin* playing); *qi* (棋 qí, *qi*-playing or *weiqi*, which is known as "Go" in the West); *shu* (书, calligraphy); and *hua* (画, painting).

Some popular plucked string instruments include *pipa* (琵琶, pípá), *liuqin* (柳琴 liǔqín) and *yueqin* (月琴 yuèqín). *Pipa* is a four-stringed lute with a pear-shaped body. It has a history of over 2,000 years. *Liuqin* is a smaller version of the pipa that sounds similar to a mandolin. *Yueqin* has four strings and a moon-shaped body. Both *liuqin* and *yueqin* are often played to accompany folk songs and local operas.

二胡
(èrhú)

The better-known bowed string instruments include the *erhu* (二胡 èrhú) and the *morin khur* or horse-headed violin (马头琴 mǎtóuqín). *Erhu* is a two-stringed fiddle. It is one of the most popular Chinese instruments in the huqin family. *Morin khur* is a typical Mongolian bowed instrument with two strings. Another popular instrument is the *yangqin* (扬琴 yángqín), which is a Chinese hammered dulcimer with a trapezoidal soundboard. In addition to the string instruments, various types of flutes made of bamboo, bronze bells, and drums in different shapes are widely played as well.

A man plays the Chinese 笙 (shēng) on the Thames River.

5.3 电脑游戏
Computer Games

💿 对话一 **Dialogue 1**

（玛丽娅给汤姆打电话。）

Mǎlìyà: Wèi, Tāngmǔ zài ma?
玛丽娅：喂，汤姆 在 吗？

Tāngmǔ: Wǒ jiù shì Tāngmǔ.
汤姆： 我 就 是 汤姆。

Mǎlìyà: Nǐ hǎo, Tāngmǔ, wǒ shì Mǎlìyà.
玛丽娅：你 好， 汤姆， 我 是 玛丽娅。

Wǒ zài zuò shùxué zuòyè, jiǔshíbā yè
我 在 做 数学 作业，九十八 页

shàng yǒu yī gè wèntí wǒ bù dǒng,
上 有 一 个 问题 我 不 懂，

Xiǎng wèn wen nǐ. Nǐ yě zài zuò
想 问 问 你。你 也 在 做

shùxué zuòyè ma?
数学 作业 吗？

Tāngmǔ: Méiyǒu. Wǒ zài wán diànnǎo yóuxì ne.
汤姆： 没有。我 在 玩 电脑 游戏 呢。

Mǎlìyà: Shénme? Nǐ bù zhīdào míngtiān yǒu
玛丽娅：什么？你 不 知道 明天 有

shùxué kǎoshì ma?
数学 考试 吗？

Tāngmǔ: Zhīdào, wǒ xiān wán yīhuìr, zài zuò

汤姆: 知道，我 先 玩 一会儿，再 做

zuòyè.

作业。

Mǎlìyà: Nǐ fùmǔ ràng nǐ wánr diànnǎo yóuxì ma?

玛丽娅: 你 父母 让 你 玩儿 电脑 游戏 吗？

Tāngmǔ: Měitiān wǒ kěyǐ wán yī gè xiǎoshí.

汤姆: 每天 我 可以 玩 一 个 小时。

Mǎlìyà: Nà nǐ xiān wánr ba, wǒ děng yīhuìr

玛丽娅: 那 你 先 玩儿 吧，我 等 一会儿

zài gěi nǐ dǎ diànhuà.

再 给 你 打 电话。

对话二 Dialogue 2

（五点半，汤姆的妈妈回来了。）

Māma: Tāngmǔ, nǐ zài zuò shénme?

妈妈: 汤姆，你 在 做 什么？

饺子

Tāngmǔ: Wǒ zài wán diànnǎo yóuxì.

汤姆: 我 在 玩 电脑 游戏。

Māma: Nǐ yìnggāi shǎo wánr diànnǎo yóuxì. Měitiān

妈妈: 你 应该 少 玩儿 电脑 游戏。每天

nǐ zuì duō kěyǐ wánr yī gè xiǎoshí.

你 最 多 可以 玩儿 一 个 小时。

Jiémǐ ne? Tā zài zuò shénme?

杰米 呢？ 他 在 做 什么？

Tāngmǔ: Tā zhèngzài kàn kǎtōng ne.

汤姆: 他 正在 看 卡通 呢。

Māma: Tā zuòyè zuò le ma?
妈妈：他 作业 做 了 吗？

Tāngmǔ: Āiyōu, nín de bǎobèi Jiémǐ měitiān huí le jiā
汤姆：哎呦，您 的 宝贝 杰米 每天 回 了 家

baby (→ what you treasure)

jiù zuò zuòyè.
就 做 作业。

Māma: Nǐ yīnggāi xuéxí Jiémǐ.
妈妈：你 应该 学习 杰米。 ▷ *I should, I should! (angry?)*

Tāngmǔ: Yīnggāi, yīnggāi! Wǒ chī le wǎnfàn jiù zuò.
汤姆：应该，应该！我 吃 了 晚饭 就 做。

Māma: Jīntiān wǎnshàng nǐ xiǎng chī shénme?
妈妈：今天 晚上 你 想 吃 什么？

Tāngmǔ: Wǒmen kěyǐ chī jiǎozi ma?
汤姆：我们 可以 吃 饺子 吗？

Māma: Kěyǐ, jiā lǐ yǒu yī *some* xiē bīng jiǎozi, děng
妈妈：可以，家 里 有 一 些 冰 饺子，等

nǐ bàba huí lái le wǒmen jiù xià jiǎozi chī.
你 爸爸 回 来 了 我们 就 下 饺子 吃。

💿 生词 **New Words**   *one hour and a half*
一个半小时

	Simplified	Traditional	Pinyin	Part of Speech	English
1.	就		jiù	*adv.*	then, precisely, just
2.	考试	考試	kǎoshì	*n./v.*	test, exam
3.	一会儿	一會兒	yīhuìr	*n./time word*	a little while
4.	父母		fùmǔ	*n.*	parents
5.	卡通		kǎtōng	*n.*	cartoon
6.	应该	應該	yīnggāi	*o.v.*	should, ought to

indication of earliness (than usual)

才 cai *indication of lateness (than usual)*

+ verb

roughly / somewhere after subject 最多/少 *at most / at least*   懂/明白 *to understand*   多久 *how long*
Zui do xiao   dǒng míng bai (spoken) (formal)   duo jiu long

喂 wéi
hello on phone

页 yè page

回来
used
without ←
a place.

6 → negative
like a
blame

7.	怎么	怎麼	zěnme	*adv.*	how come.../how
8.	晚饭	晚飯	wǎnfàn	*n.*	dinner
9.	饺子	餃子	jiǎozi	*n.*	dumpling
10.	冰		bīng	*n.*	frozen, ice
11.	回来	回來	huílái	*v.c.*	return, come back
12.	下饺子		xià jiǎozi	*v.o.*	cook dumplings

→ when 回来 + a place take out 来 so 回 + a place is correct

下 = put in boiling
water to cook

问题
wen ti
question

向...学习
to learn from
xiàng xuéxi

语言注释 Language Notes

一...就...
Yì jiù
as soon as
you

又...又
both

1. Time spent

To talk about how much time you spend doing something, you need to put the "time spent" (or "time duration") phrase after the verb, as the time duration is a complement to the verb.

There are three basic patterns to describe time spent (S=subject, V=verb, O=object):

1. S V time spent →answering
2. S V O V (repeated) time spent
3. S V time spent (的) O

Compare with the "adverbial of time" explained in 3.1, where the time phrase that tells when an event happens needs to go before the verbal phrase. For example: 我们每天上午八点上课。

Subject	Optative verb	Verb	Time spent	English meaning
我	可以	玩	一个小时。	I am allowed to play for an hour.
他们	要	去	一个星期。	They will be gone for a week.

Subject	Verb/ object	Optative verb	Verb (repeated)	Time spent	English meaning
你	看电视	可以	看	半个小时。	You can watch TV for half an hour.
我们	做作业	要	做	两个小时。	We need two hours to do our homework.

Subject	Verb	Time spent	（的）	Object	English meaning
我	看	半个小时	（的）	电视。	I will watch TV for half an hour.
我们	打	一会儿		篮球。	We will play basketball for a while.

2. Summary of optative verbs

Optative verb	Pinyin	English meaning	Negative form
想	xiǎng	want, intend, would like to	不想
要	yào	want, need, should, will	不要
应该	yīnggāi	should, ought to	不应该
能	néng	1) have the ability to 2) can (subject to conditions)	不能
会	huì	1) know how to 2) be likely to	不会
必须	bìxū	must, have to, ought to	不用
得	děi	have to	不用
可以	kěyǐ	1) may, have permission to 2) can (subject to conditions)	不可以

When asking a yes/no question with an optative verb in it, you can use one of the following forms:

A. Sentence + 吗

你能去吗？
你会弹钢琴吗？

B. Subject + Optative verb + 不 + Optative verb + Rest of the sentence

你能不能去？
你会不会弹钢琴？

C. Sentence + 不 + Optative verb

你能去不能？
你会弹钢琴不会？

3. 多 or 少 + verbal phrase

This structure means "do more of…" or "do less of…" It is used when giving advice and therefore is often used with an optative verb.

你应该少玩电脑游戏，多学习。

You should play fewer computer games and study more.

她应该多运动，少吃汉堡。

She should exercise more and eat fewer hamburgers.

4. V1 了就 V2 (as soon as…)

We have learned in Lesson 2.6 that 了 can indicate a change of situation or state. 了 has another function, that is, to indicate the completion of an action. In this pattern, 了 symbolizes the completion of the first action (V1). *→ after verb always*

The structure of "Verbal phrase 1 + 了 + 就 + Verbal phrase 2" is used when two actions take place, with one immediately following the other.

A. Both activities are done by the same person

他回了家就做作业。

After he got home, he immediately did his homework.

我知道了就告诉你。

As soon as I know it, I will tell you.

B. The two activities are done by different people

妈妈回了家，爸爸就带我去打球。

As soon as mom comes back home, dad will take me to play ball.

老师来了我们就做作业。

As soon as the teacher arrives, we will do our homework.

things {
东西 *dong xi*
what you can touch = item

事情 *shi qing*
what you cannot touch
}

中国文化一瞥 **A Glimpse into Chinese Culture**

For more information and activities related to Chinese culture, please go to http://my. cheng-tsui.com/huanying.

1. Read aloud the poem, paying special attention to your tones.

Zá   Shī
杂 诗

[Táng]   Wáng Wéi
[唐]   王 维

Jūn   zì   gù   xiāng lái,   yìng   zhī   gù   xiāng   shì.
君   自   故   乡   来， 应   知   故   乡   事。

Lái   rì   qǐ   chuāngqián,   hán   méi   zhù   huā   wèi.
来   日   琦   窗   前， 寒   梅   著   花   未。

Lines

Wang Wei [Tang Dynasty]

You who have come from my old country,

Tell me what has happened there —

Was the plum, when you passed my silken window,

Opening its first blossom?

2. Chinese Proverbs and Idioms

dāo   shān   huǒ   hǎi
刀   山   火   海

a mountain of swords and a sea of flames (extremely dangerous places, most severe trials)

你知道吗？   **Did you know?**

The China Internet Network Information Center (CNNIC) reported that in June 2007, the total number of Internet users in China reached 162 million.* Because of China's large population, these 162 million users only make up 12.3 percent of the Chinese population. More than 75 perent of Internet users live in cities. That means that only 5 percent of rural residents have access to the Internet.

The majority of Chinese Internet users are educated, urban young people. More than 70 percent are below the age of 30, and 36.7 percent are students. On average, Chinese Internet users spend 18–19 hours a week online. The most popular online activities are reading news, using search engines, emailing, instant messaging, listening to music, watching video and playing online games. Fewer than 20 percent of users use the Internet for online business, such as banking, looking for jobs, shopping, and stock trading.

An Internet café in Xinjiang.

*Source: http://www.forbes.com/2006/03/31/china-internet-usage-cx_nwp_0403china.html

5.4 旅行
Travel

🔘 对话一 **Dialogue 1**

（玛丽娅一家周末要去南京旅行。）

Nínà: Mǎlìyà, wǒmen xīngqīliù qù Nánjīng,
妮娜： 玛丽娅，我们 星期六 去 南京，

nǐ dài shénme?
你 带 什么？

Mǎlìyà: Wǒ yào dài Hànyǔ shū. Wǒmen xīngqīyī
玛丽娅：我 要 带 汉语 书。我们 星期一

yǒu Hànyǔ kǎoshì, wǒ zuò chē de
有 汉语 考试， 我 坐 车 的

shíhòu, kěyǐ kàn shū.
时候， 可以 看 书。

Nínà: Wǒ yào dài Xióngmāo hé Mīmī.
妮娜： 我 要 带 熊猫 和 咪咪。

Nǐ kàn shū de shíhòu, wǒ kěyǐ
你 看 书 的 时候， 我 可以

hé tāmen wán.
和 它们 玩。

Mǎlìyà: Nǐ kěyǐ dài Xióngmāo, bù néng dài
玛丽娅：你 可以 带 熊猫， 不 能 带

Mīmī. Mīmī shàng le chē jiù bù
咪咪。 咪咪 上 了 车 就 不

gāoxìng. Tā bù xǐhuān zuò chē.
高兴。 它 不 喜欢 坐 车。

Nínà:
妮娜： Wèishénme gǒu xǐhuān zuò chē, māo bù
为什么 狗 喜欢 坐 车, 猫 不
xǐhuān ne?
喜欢 呢?

Mǎlìyà:
玛丽娅： Wǒ yě bù zhīdào, nǐ kěyǐ wèn yī
我 也 不 知道, 你 可以 问 一
wèn Mīmī, tā wèishénme bù xǐhuān
问 咪咪, 它 为什么 不 喜欢
zuò chē.
坐 车。

Nínà:
妮娜： Kěshì Mīmī bù huì shuō huà. Tā zhǐ
可是 咪咪 不 会 说 话。 它 只
huì shuō: "mī mī."
会 说: "咪咪。"

🔘 对话二 **Dialogue 2**

（在去南京的车上。玛丽娅的父母坐在前边，三个孩子坐在后边。）

Āndōngní:
安东尼： Māma, wǒmen néng bù néng tīng
妈妈, 我们 能 不 能 听
yīnyuè?
音乐?

Māma:
妈妈： Hǎo a. Nǐmen yào tīng gǔdiǎn yīnyuè
好 啊。 你们 要 听 古典 音乐
háishì liúxíng yīnyuè?
还是 流行 音乐?

Āndōngní: Wǒ xǐhuān liúxíng yīnyuè.
安东尼：我 喜欢 流行 音乐。

Mǎlìyà: Wǒ yě shì.
玛丽娅：我 也 是。

Māma: Hǎo ba, wǒmen tīng liúxíng yīnyuè.
妈妈： 好 吧，我们 听 流行 音乐。

Nínà: Māma, wǒ yào hē shuǐ.
妮娜： 妈妈，我 要 喝 水。

Mǎlìyà: Zhèr yǒu shuǐ, nǐ hē ba.
玛丽娅：这儿 有 水，你 喝 吧。

Māma: Wǒmen kěyǐ zài qiánbiān tíng yī tíng ma?
妈妈： 我们 可以 在 前边 停 一 停 吗？

Nàr de fēngjǐng hěn měi. Wǒmen kěyǐ kàn yī
那儿 的 风景 很 美。我们 可以 看 一

kàn fēngjǐng.
看 风景。

Āndōngní: Wǒ è le. Wǒmen qù nǎr chī wǔfàn?
安东尼：我 饿 了。我们 去 哪儿 吃 午饭？

Bàba: Nǐmen è ma?
爸爸： 你们 饿 吗？

Āndōngní: Wǒ hěn è. Nǐmen ne?
安东尼：我 很 饿。你们 呢？

Mǎlìyà: Wǒ yǒu yīdiǎnr è.
玛丽娅：我 有 一点儿 饿。

Bàba: Nǐmen xiǎng chī Zhōngcān háishì Xīcān?
爸爸： 你们 想 吃 中餐 还是 西餐？

Mǎlìyà: Wǒ   xiǎng   chī   Zhōngcān.

玛丽娅：我 想 吃 中餐。

Āndōngní: Wǒ   suíbiàn.

安东尼：我 随便。

Nínà: Māma,   wǒ   yào   qù   cèsuǒ.

妮娜：妈妈， 我 要 去 厕所。

Māma: Nǐ   kěyǐ   děng   yī   děng   ma?

妈妈：你 可以 等 一 等 吗？

Nínà: Wǒ   kěyǐ   děng   wǔ   fēnzhōng.

妮娜：我 可以 等 五 分钟。

Āndōngní: Bàba,   nǐ   kàn,   qiánbiān   yǒu   Hànbǎowáng,   wǒmen

安东尼：爸爸， 你 看， 前边 有 汉堡王， 我们

kěyǐ   zài   nàr   tíng   chē.   Nínà   kěyǐ   qù

可以 在 那儿 停 车。 妮娜 可以 去

cèsuǒ.

厕所。

wèishēngjiān

卫生间

(handwritten: little bit ⟨ 一点儿 +n / 有点儿 +adj)

(handwritten: 去 a place 旅行 / 想 emotional verb)

生词 New Words

	Simplified	Traditional	Pinyin	Part of Speech	English
1.	旅行 or 旅游 *(you)*		lǚxíng	v./n.	travel
2.	坐		zuò		ride, sit *(开 cai drive)*
3.	车	車	chē	n.	vehicle *(两 is m.w.)*
4.	时候	時候	shíhou	n.	time
5.	熊猫	熊貓	xióngmāo	n.	panda
6.	咪咪		mīmī	n.	meow
7.	说	說	shuō	v.	speak, say
8.	话	話	huà	n.	spoken language, words
9.	前边	前邊	qiánbiān *(side)*	n.	front
10.	古典		gǔdiǎn	adj.	classical
11.	流行		liúxíng	adj.	popular
12.	水		shuǐ	n.	water
13.	停		tíng	v.	stop
14.	风景	風景	fēngjǐng	n.	scenery
15.	美		měi	adj.	beautiful
16.	饿	餓	è	adj.	hungry
17.	中餐		Zhōngcān	n.	Chinese food
18.	西餐		Xīcān	n.	Western food
19.	随便	隨便	suíbiàn	adj./adv.	anything will do; easy-going, *whatever*
20.	厕所	廁所	cèsuǒ	n.	bathroom, washroom, *like toilet*
21.	等		děng	v.	wait
22.	分钟	分鐘	fēnzhōng	n.	minute

(handwritten notes: 24. 后边 behind hòu biān; 分 is for time; 分钟 for how long 20 minutes amount of time; 23. 孩子 child hái zǐ)

Proper Nouns

23.	南京	Nánjīng	*p.n.*	Nanjing
24.	汉堡王　漢堡王	Hànbǎowáng	*p.n.*	Burger King

语言注释 Language Notes

1. …的时候 (when…)

This time phrase or time clause can only be placed before a main clause.

他看书的时候听音乐。

When he reads, he listens to music.

做作业的时候你不应该看电视。

When doing homework, you should not watch TV.

2. Verb — verb

This structure indicates a brief action, or doing something informally.

请问一问他。　　　　　　Please ask him.

停一停车，好吗？　　　　Stop the car for a minute, OK?

⤷ Does not work with verb with two characters
ex) 听 — 听

学无止境 EXTEND YOUR KNOWLEDGE

Since the 1980s, many Western fast food and beverage companies have opened franchises or begun to distribute their products in China. The following ones are the most popular:

Kěndéjī 肯德基 *Kentucky Fried Chicken*	Màidāngláo 麦当劳 （麥當勞） *McDonald's*	Hànbǎowáng 汉堡王 （漢堡王） *Burger King*	Bìshèngkè 必胜客 （必勝客） *Pizza Hut*
Àobàikè 澳拜客 *Outback Steak House*	Xīngbākè 星巴克 *Starbucks*	Kěkǒu Kělè 可口可乐 （可口可樂） *Coca-Cola*	Bǎishì Kělè 百事可乐 （百事可樂） *Pepsi-Cola*
Qīxǐ 七喜 *Seven-Up*	Xīngqīwǔ Cāntīng 星期五餐厅 *T.G.I. Friday's*	Bàng Yuēhàn 棒约翰 *Papa John's*	Quècháo kāfēi 雀巢咖啡 *Nestlé coffee*

中国文化一瞥 **A Glimpse into Chinese Culture**

For more information and activities related to Chinese culture, please go to http://my. cheng-tsui.com/huanying.

1. Read aloud the poem, paying special attention to your tones.

Zhú   Lǐ   Guǎn

竹　里　馆

[Táng]　Wáng　Wéi

[唐]　王　维

Dú　zuò　yōu　huáng lǐ,　tán　qín　fù　cháng xiào.

独　坐　幽　篁　里，　弹　琴　复　长　啸。

Shēn　lín　rén　bù　zhī,　míng　yuè　lái　xiāng　zhào.

深　林　人　不　知，　明　月　来　相　照。

In a Retreat Among Bamboos

Wang Wei [Tang Dynasty]

Leaning alone in the close bamboos,

I am playing my lute and humming a song

Too softly for anyone to hear —

Except my comrade, the bright moon.

2. Chinese Proverbs and Idioms

luàn   tán   qín
乱   弹   琴

Recklessly play the piano — Act or talk like a fool; talk nonsense.

duì   niú   tán   qín
对   牛   弹   琴

Play music to cows — speak to someone who is clueless and uncultivated.

你知道吗？   **Did you know?**

In China, travel peak seasons are usually tied to Chinese festivals. Spring Festival (Chinese New Year, which is the first day of the first month on the Lunar Calendar and usually falls between late January and early February) is the busiest travel time for the Chinese. No matter where they live and work, most people go home to celebrate the New Year's Day with their families. Trains and buses are packed during the Spring Festival time.

Other tourism peak seasons occur during the "golden" holiday week, such as the National Day Holiday (October 1–7). October is considered the best time for travel because of the mild climate in most places in China at this time of the year. During the golden holiday week, many families visit popular tourist sites, such as scenic spots, historical sites, and recreational areas.

The travel expenses during the peak seasons are higher than usual. Despite the higher cost, it is not easy to secure a train ticket or a hotel room. Therefore, when traveling during the peak seasons, it is always a good idea to book tickets and lodging in advance.

5.5 看电视
Watching TV

去 aplace 旅行

对话一 Dialogue 1

（下课的时候，玛丽娅和汤姆在谈电视节目。）

tán

Mǎlìyà:　Nǐ　xǐhuān　kàn　nǎxiē　diànshì　jiémù?
玛丽娅：你　喜欢　看　哪些　电视　节目？

Tāngmǔ:　Wǒ　xǐhuān　kàn　qiú,　kàn　diànyǐng,　hái
汤姆：　我　喜欢　看　球，看　电影，还

xǐhuān　kàn　MTV　de　yīnyuè　jiémù.
喜欢　看　MTV　的　音乐　节目。

Nǐ　ne?
你　呢？

TV drama

Mǎlìyà:　Wǒ　xǐhuān　kàn　diànshìjù.　Yě　xǐhuān　kàn
玛丽娅：我　喜欢　看　电视剧。也　喜欢　看

xīnwén,　kěshì　wǒ　zuì　xǐhuān　kàn
新闻，可是　我　最　喜欢　看

Zhōngyāng　diànshìtái　de　wényì　jiémù.
中央　电视台　的　文艺　节目。

Tāngmǔ:　Nǐ　xǐhuān　kàn　lǚyóu　jiémù　ma?
汤姆：　你　喜欢　看　旅游　节目　吗？

Mǎlìyà:　Fēicháng　xǐhuān.　Kěshì　Āndōngní　bù
玛丽娅：非常　喜欢。可是　安东尼　不

xǐhuān.　Wǒ　yī　kàn　lǚyóu　jiémù,
喜欢。我　一　看　旅游　节目，

tā jiù hǎnzhe yào kàn tǐyù jiémù. Tā yī
他 就 喊着 要 看 体育 节目。他 一

hǎnzhe yào kàn tǐyù jiémù, Nínà jiù shuō yào
喊着 要 看 体育 节目，妮娜 就 说 要

kàn kǎtōngpiàn. Wǒ kàn, wǒmen zuì hǎo yī rén
看 卡通片。我 看，我们 最 好 一 人

yǒu yī tái diànshìjī.
有 一 台 电视机。

Tāngmǔ: Duì. Wǒ bù xǐhuān wǒ fùmǔ kàn de diànshì jiémù.
汤姆： 对。我 不 喜欢 我 父母 看 的 电视 节目。

Wǒ māma cháng cháng kàn Yīngyǔ jiémù. Wǒ bàba
我 妈妈 常常 看 英语 节目。我 爸爸

měitiān kàn jīngjì xīnwén. Zuìhǎo wǒ yǒu zìjǐ de
每天 看 经济 新闻。最好 我 有 自己 的

diànshìjī.
电视机。

对话二 Dialogue 2

（汤姆在给爷爷打电话。）

Tāngmǔ: Yéye, nín hǎo. Wǒ shì Tāngmǔ.
汤姆： 爷爷， 您 好。我 是 汤姆。

Yéye: A, Tāngmǔ, nǐmen dōu hǎo ma?
爷爷： 啊，汤姆，你们 都 好 吗？

Tāngmǔ: Wǒmen dōu hěn hǎo. Yéye, nín hé nǎinai zài
汤姆： 我们 都 很 好。爷爷，您 和 奶奶 在

zuò shénme ne?
做 什么 呢？

Yéye: Wǒ zài kàn bào, nǎinai zài kàn dì wǔ píndào
爷爷：我 在 看 报，奶奶 在 看 第 五 频道

de diànshìjù.
的 电视剧。

Tāngmǔ: Yéye, nín bù xǐhuān kàn nǎinai de diànshìjù ma?
汤姆：爷爷，您 不 喜欢 看 奶奶 的 电视剧 吗？

Yéye: Hā hā... wǒ xǐhuān kàn diànshì xīnwén. Yǒushíhou,
爷爷：哈哈... 我 喜欢 看 电视 新闻。有时候，

kàn yīxiē lǎo diànyǐng. Nǐmen nàr yě yǒu
看 一些 老 电影。你们 那儿 也 有

xǔduō diànshì jiémù ba?
许多 电视 节目 吧？

Tāngmǔ: Duì, wǒmen jiā dìng yǒuxiàn diànshì, kěyǐ shōudào
汤姆：对，我们 家 订 有线 电视，可以 收到

wǔshí duō gè píndào.
五十 多 个 频道。

Yéye: Nàme duō?
爷爷：那么 多？

Tāngmǔ: Shì a, yǒu xīnwén píndào, diànyǐng píndào,
汤姆：是 啊，有 新闻 频道、电影 频道、

tǐyù píndào, hái yǒu Yīngyǔ píndào.
体育 频道，还 有 英语 频道。

Yéye: Shì ma? Nǐ měitiān kàn diànshì ma?
爷爷：是 吗？你 每天 看 电视 吗？

Tāngmǔ: Měitiān kàn, kěshì kàn de shíjiān bù cháng. Māma
汤姆： 每天 看，可是 看 的 时间 不 长。妈妈

shuō, wǒ měitiān zuì duō néng kàn yī gè
说，我 每天 最 多 能 看 一 个

xiǎoshí. Tā rang wǒ shǎo kàn diànshì, duō kàn
小时。她 让 我 少 看 电视，多 看

shū, duō yùndòng.
书，多 运动。

Yéye: Duì. Nǐ yīnggāi duō kàn shū, zhǐ kàn diànshì, bù
爷爷： 对。你 应该 多 看 书，只 看 电视 不

kàn shū huì bèn. Nǐ yě yīnggāi duō yùndòng,
看 书 会 笨。你 也 应该 多 运动，

zhǐ kàn diànshì bù yùndòng huì pàng.
只 看 电视 不 运动 会 胖。

Tāngmǔ: Yéye, bàba yào hé nín shuō huà. Yéye, zàijiàn.
汤姆： 爷爷，爸爸 要 和 您 说话。爷爷，再见。

Yéye: Zàijiàn.
爷爷： 再见。

生词 New Words

	Simplified	Traditional	Pinyin	Part of Speech	English
1.	节目	節目	jiémù	*n.*	(entertainment) program
2.	电视剧	電視劇	diànshìjù	*n.*	TV drama
3.	新闻	新聞	xīnwén	*n.*	news
4.	中央		zhōngyāng	*adj.*	central
5.	电视台	電視臺	diànshìtái	*n.*	TV station
6.	文艺	文藝	wényì	*n.*	arts and culture (entertainment)
7.	旅游	旅遊	lǚyóu	*n./v.*	travel, tourism
8.	喊		hǎn	*v.*	yell out, shout
9.	着	著	zhe	*par.*	*indicates accompanying action (see Language Note 4)*
10.	卡通片		kǎtōngpiàn	*n.*	cartoon film
11.	电视机	電視機	diànshìjī	*n.*	TV set
12.	报	報	bào	*n.*	newspaper
13.	有线电视	有線電視	yǒuxiàn diànshì	*n.*	cable TV
14.	收到		shōudào	*v.c.*	receive
15.	第		dì	*par.*	*a prefix used to form ordinal numbers (see Language Note 5)*
16.	频道	頻道	píndào	*n.*	(TV) channel
17.	少		shǎo	*adj.*	less
18.	胖		pàng	*adj.*	fat, overweight
19.	订	訂	dìng	*v.*	subscribe

Handwritten annotations:
- (next to 4/5) central tv station
- (next to 6) or arts (entertainment)
- (next to 9) ✗ (grammar word)
- (next to 10) (movie)
- (next to 12) 时报 Times / shí bào
- (next to 15) (sequencial word)
- (next to 19) / order

谈 tán talk / discuss
台 tái m.w of machine
笨 bèn stupid

Proper Noun

20.	中央 中央 电视台 電視臺	Zhōngyāng Diànshìtái	*p.n.*	CCTV (China Central Television)

语言注释 Language Notes

1. Interrogative pronoun 哪

When using 哪 to get more specific information about a person, place or thing, add a measure word after 哪.

你要哪本书？

Which book do you want?

哪些学生会说中文？

Which students can speak Chinese?/

哪个电影好看？

Which movie is good?

2. 一···就··· (as soon as...)

The structure "一 verbal phrase 1 就 verbal phrase 2" is used when two actions/events take place, one immediately after the other.

Subject	*一 V1*	*就 V2*	*English meaning*
杰米	一回家	就做作业。	As soon as Jimmy came home, he did his homework.
我们	一下课	就回家。	As soon as class is dismissed, we will go home.

If the two actions are done by two different people, the structure is as follows:

Subject 1 — V1	Subject 2 就 V2	English meaning
爸爸 一回家	我们 就下饺子。	As soon as father returns, we will cook the dumplings.
她 一来	我们 就开始玩。	As soon as she comes, we will start playing.

3. 最好··· (it's ideal... it's best that ...) *or 2 word*

最好 can be used in front of a verbal phrase or a sentence to express your preference.

最好明天不下雨。

It will be ideal if it doesn't rain tomorrow.

你最好去问她。

It's best if you ask her.

4. Action 1 着 action 2

Verb 着 can be used to indicate that a major action (action 2) is accompanied by a secondary action (action 1).

安东尼喊着要看体育节目。

Anthony shouts that he wants to watch the sports channel.

他常常听着音乐做作业。

He often does his homework while listening to music.

妮娜要带着熊猫去旅游。

Nina wants to travel with "Panda."

5. 第

第 is a prefix. It is used before numerals to form ordinal numbers.

第一	first	第二	second
第一天	the first day	第五个人	the fifth person

中国文化一瞥 A Glimpse into Chinese Culture

For more information and activities related to Chinese culture, please go to http://my. cheng-tsui.com/huanying.

1. **Read aloud the poem, paying special attention to your tones.**

Dēng Guàn Què Lóu
登　鹳　雀　楼

[Táng]　Wáng Zhī Huàn
[唐]　王　之　涣

Bái rì yī shān jìn, huáng hé rù hǎi liú.
白　日　依　山　尽，黄　河　入　海　流。

Yù qióng qiān lǐ mù, gèng shàng yī céng lóu.
欲　穷　千　里　目，更　上　一　层　楼。

At Heron Lodge

Wang Zhihuan [Tang Dynasty]

Mountains cover the white sun,
And oceans drain the golden river;
But you widen your view hundreds of miles,
By going up one flight of stairs.

2. Chinese Proverbs and Idioms

tóng gān gòng kǔ

同 甘 共 苦

share comfort and hardship through thick and thin

tóng xīn xié lì

同 心 协 力

shoulder to shoulder, hand in hand

你知道吗? **Did you know?**

Although television didn't enter most Chinese homes until the late 1970s, watching TV has become an integral part of everyday life in China. At present, more than 95 percent of Chinese families have TV sets. Watching TV has become the most common recreational activity for ordinary Chinese, whether they live in a city or in a village.

China has more than 100 million cable TV subscribers. That means it is the largest cable TV market in the world. There are more than 1000 TV channels, although a typical cable TV subscriber only has access to 40–50 channels. As the Chinese government closely monitors the production of TV programs, the content of most TV programs has little variation. TV programs are shown twenty-four hours a day seven days a week. The most watched programs include news, soap operas, sports, and game shows.

5.6 第五单元复习
Unit 5 Review

 课文一 Text 1

凯丽一家和音乐

凯丽家的人都非常喜欢音乐。凯丽的爸爸会拉大提琴，她妈妈会弹钢琴，她姐姐会弹吉他，凯丽会弹竖琴。有时候，他们在一起练习。有的朋友说，凯丽家可以开家庭音乐会。可是凯丽说："我们不能开，因为我和爸爸妈妈想开古典音乐会，可是姐姐要开流行音乐会。"

凯丽的姐姐说："古典音乐和流行音乐都很好听。我们可以开一个有古典音乐，也有流行音乐的音乐会。你们可以表演古典音乐，我可以一边弹吉他一边唱歌。"

今年春节凯丽家要开一个家庭音乐会。很多朋友会来参加。一些中国朋友也要来。凯丽的姐姐正在学唱中国歌呢。凯丽正在练习弹中国音乐。

课文二 Text 2

大卫 给 汤姆 打 电话 的 时候，汤姆 正在 做 作业。大卫 最近 下载 了 一个 电脑 游戏，可是 那个 游戏 有一些 病毒，那些 病毒 常常 让 大卫 的 电脑 不能 运行。大卫 想，汤姆 也 常常 下载 音乐 和 游戏，可以问问 他，哪些 游戏 不 应该 下载。汤姆 告诉 大卫，他 应该 去 一个 网站 下载 去 病毒 的 软件。那个 软件 非常 有用。

汤姆 和 大卫 都 很 喜欢 玩 电脑 游戏，可是 不能 每天 玩。他们 的 父母 都 让 他们 多 学习，少 玩电脑。大卫 告诉 汤姆："以后，我 要 做 电脑 游戏工程师，这样 每天 可以 玩 电脑 游戏。"

汤姆 说："你 做 了 电脑 游戏 工程师，就 要 每天 写 游戏 软件，所以 还是 不 能 每天 玩 游戏。"

生词 New Words

	Simplified	Traditional	Pinyin	Part of Speech	English
1.	开	開	kāi	v.	hold (a meeting, party, conference, etc.)
2.	表演		biǎoyǎn	n./v.	perform, performance
3.	唱		chàng	v.	sing
4.	一些		yīxiē	det.	some, several
5.	春节	春節	chūnjié	n.	Spring Festival
6.	练习	練習	liànxí	n./v.	practice
7.	病毒		bìngdú	n.	virus

8.	运行	運行	yùnxíng	v./n.	v. run, operate n. operation
9.	去		qù	v.	eliminate
10.	软件	軟件	ruǎnjiàn	n.	software

语言注释 Language Notes

些 (indicates a plural number of things)

一些 indicates an unspecified quantity of things.

一些学生	some students
那些书	those books
这些练习本	these notebooks

SELF-ASSESSMENT

In Unit 5, you have learned how to talk about some recreational activities. You have also learned to express your intention, ability, and wish. After completing the exercises for Unit 5 in your Workbook, fill out the following self-assessment sheet.

Yes/No	*Can you say and write these things in Chinese?*
	Some TV programs
	Some musical instruments and types of music
	You are able to do something (能)
	You know how to do something (会)
	You intend to do something (要)
	You are permitted to do something (可以)

	You ought to do something (应该)
	You are doing two things at the same time (一边，一边)
	You do one thing immediately after another (V1 了就 V2，一···就···)
	You do things in a sequence (先···再···)
	The time you spent doing something

9–11   yes   excellent
6–8   yes   good
0–5   yes   need some work

第六单元：我们生活的地方

di fang (handwritten annotation above 地方)

UNIT 6 The Places Where We Live

By the end of this unit, you will learn:

- How to read and write 68 Chinese characters
- Words needed for talking about school buildings
- Words needed for talking about the rooms in a house
- Words needed for talking about locations and positions
- Words needed for talking about future plans
- Basic sentence structures for indicating distance between two things
- Basic structure for indicating the completion of an action

Your knowledge will enable you to:

- Describe locations and positions
- Describe the layout of a house
- Describe the major buildings in a school
- Describe the surroundings of your home and school
- Describe where some major Chinese cities are
- Describe your future plans

6.1 中国的城市
Chinese Cities

新疆维吾尔自治区

甘肃

内蒙古

黑龙江

吉林

辽宁

区

自治

北京市

河北

天津市

山西

山东

江苏

上海市

浙江

安徽

青海

西藏

自治区

陕西

四川

重庆市

湖北

河南

湖南

江西

福建

台湾

贵州

云南

广西壮族自治区

广东

香港特别行政区

澳门特别行政区

湖南

中华人民共和国

💿 课文 Text

(Teacher Ding is showing a map of China to her class.)

Qǐng kàn Zhōngguó dìtú. Zhè shì Běijīng. Běijīng shì
请 看 中国 地图。 这 是 北京。 北京 是

Zhōngguó de shǒudū, zài Zhōngguó de běibù.
中国 的 首都, 在 中国 的 北部。

Zhōngguó de běibù hái yǒu yī gè dà chéngshì, jiào
中国 的 北部 还 有 一 个 大 城市，叫

Tiānjīn. Nà shì Shànghǎi. Shànghǎi shì Zhōngguó zuì dà de
天津。那 是 上海。上海 是 中国 最 大 的

chéngshì, zài Zhōngguó de dōngbù. Wǒmen zài lái kàn
城市，在 中国 的 东部。我们 再 来 看

yī kàn Zhōngguó de xībù hé nánbù. Zhōngguó de xībù
一 看 中国 的 西部 和 南部。中国 的 西部

yǒu yī gè hěn gǔlǎo de dà chéngshì, jiào Xī'ān.
有 一 个 很 古老 的 大 城市，叫 西安。

Zhè shì Guǎngzhōu, zài Zhōngguó de nánbù. Nà shì
这 是 广州，在 中国 的 南部。那 是

Chóngqìng. Chóngqìng zài Zhōngguó de zhōngbù. Xǔduō rén
重庆。重庆 在 中国 的 中部。许多 人

zhù zài zhè xiē dà chéngshì lǐ.
住 在 这 些 大 城市 里。

北京的天安门广场

Beijing's Tiananmen Square

学无止境 EXTEND YOUR KNOWLEDGE

There are 23 provinces (including Taiwan), 5 autonomous regions, 4 municipalities and 2 special administrative regions in China.

省	shěng	province	(23)
自治区	zìzhìqū	autonomous region	(5)
直辖市	zhíxiáshì	municipality	(4)
特别行政区	tèbié xíngzhèngqū	special administrative region	(2)

You can find their names in the pronunciation exercises for Unit 1.3. To learn more about the administrative divisions in the People's Republic of China, please refer to the "Do You Know" section at the end of this lesson.

对话 Dialogue

(Kelly and David are talking about their weekend plans.)

Dàwèi: Kǎilì, zhè gè zhōumò nǐ yào zuò shénme?
大卫： 凯丽, 这个 周末 你 要 做 什么？

Kǎilì: Wǒ yào huí Hángzhōu kàn fùmǔ. Nǐ huí jiā
凯丽： 我 要 回 杭州 看 父母。 你 回 家

ma?
吗？

Dàwèi: Wǒ bù huí jiā. Wǒ jiā zhù zài Xiānggǎng. Tài
大卫： 我 不 回 家。 我 家 住 在 香港。 太

yuǎn le. Yǒu cháng zhōumò de shíhou, wǒ zài
远 了。 有 长 周末 的 时候, 我 再

huí jiā.
回 家。

Kǎilì: Nǐ xiǎng qù Hángzhōu ma? Hángzhōu zài Shànghǎi de
凯丽： 你 想 去 杭州 吗？ 杭州 在 上海 的

nánbiān, zuò huǒchē liǎng gè xiǎoshí, bù tài
南边, 坐 火车 两 个 小时, 不 太

yuǎn. Nǐ kěyǐ qù wǒ jiā guò zhōumò.
远。 你 可以 去 我 家 过 周末。

Dàwèi: Zhēnde ma? Bùhǎoyìsi dǎrǎo nǐ fùmǔ.
大卫： 真的 吗？ 不好意思 打扰 你 父母。

Kǎilì: Bù huì de. Wǒ fùmǔ yīdìng huì hěn huānyíng nǐ
凯丽： 不 会 的。 我 父母 一定 会 很 欢迎 你

qù wánr.
去 玩儿。

Dàwèi: Nà tài hǎo le. Tīngshuō Hángzhōu hěn měilì,

大卫：那 太 好 了！听说 杭州 很 美丽，

shì ma?

是 吗？

Kǎilì: Duì. Hángzhōu yǒu yī gè hú, jiào Xīhú. Xīhú

凯丽：对。杭州 有 一 个 湖，叫 西湖。西湖

hěn dà. Xīhú de pángbiān yǒu xǔduō xiǎo gōngyuán,

很 大。西湖 的 旁边 有 许多 小 公园，

fēngjǐng fēicháng měilì. Wǒmen kěyǐ qù Xīhú

风景 非常 美丽。我们 可以 去 西湖

zǒu zou kàn kan.

走 走 看 看。

Dàwèi: Tài hǎo le. Xièxie nǐ qǐng wǒ qù nǐ jiā

大卫：太 好 了。谢谢 你 请 我 去 你 家

guò zhōumò. Wǒmen xīngqīwǔ háishì xīngqīliù qù?

过 周末。我们 星期五 还是 星期六 去？

Kǎilì: Wǒmen zuò xīngqīwǔ xiàwǔ wǔdiǎn de huǒchē qù,

凯丽：我们 坐 星期五 下午 五点 的 火车 去，

hǎo ma?

好 吗？

Dàwèi: Hǎo.

大卫：好。

生词 **New Words**

[handwritten: 图 = picture or map]

	Simplified	Traditional	Pinyin	Part of speech	English
1.	地图	地圖	dìtú	*n.*	map
2.	首都		shǒudū	*n.*	capital
3.	北部		běibù	*n.*	north, northern part
4.	城市		chéngshì	*n.*	city
5.	东部	東部	dōngbù	*n.*	east, eastern part
6.	西部		xībù	*n.*	west, western part
7.	古老		gǔlǎo	*adj.*	ancient
8.	南部		nánbù	*n.*	south, southern part
9.	中部		zhōngbù	*n.*	middle, the central part
10.	这些	這些	zhèxiē	*det.*	these
11.	远	遠	yuǎn	*adj.*	far
12.	长	長	cháng	*adj.*	long
13.	南边	南邊	nánbiān	*n.*	south
14.	火车	火車	huǒchē	*n.*	train
15.	过	過	guò	*v.*	spend, celebrate
16.	不好意思		bùhǎoyìsī	*s.p.*	feel ill at ease, feel indebted
17.	打扰	打擾	dǎrǎo	*v.*	disturb
18.	一定		yīdìng	*adv.*	definitely
19.	欢迎	歡迎	huānyíng	*v.*	welcome
20.	湖		hú	*n.*	lake
21.	旁边	旁邊	pángbiān	*n.*	side, next to

[handwritten notes:]
城市 → syn + syn = new word
中间 zian
那些 those na xie
哪些 which na xie ones
近 jin close/near
打扰你的不好意思

短 duǎn short length (horizontal) only
低 dī short, low
矮 ǎi short, low (vertical) only

离 lí from
从 A 离 B from

Proper Nouns

22.	天津		Tiānjīn *p.n.*	Tianjin
23.	西安		Xī'ān *p.n.*	Xi'an
24.	广州	廣州	Guǎngzhōu *p.n.*	Guangzhou
25.	重庆	重慶	Chóngqìng *p.n.*	Chongqing
26.	西湖		Xīhú *p.n.*	West Lake

学无止境 EXTEND YOUR KNOWLEDGE

So far you have learned two forms of transportation: 坐火车 and 坐(汽)车 (Unit 5.4).
Below is a list of other modes of transportation:

坐飞机	zuò fēijī	travel by plane
坐船	zuò chuán	travel by boat
坐公共汽车	zuò gōnggòng qìchē	travel by bus
坐公车	zuò gōngchē	travel by bus (Taiwan) /
坐电车	zuò diànchē	travel by trolley
坐地铁	zuò dìtiě	travel by subway
坐出租汽车	zuò chūzū qìchē	travel by taxi /
坐计程车	zuò jìchéng chē	travel by taxi (Taiwan) /
打的	dǎ dī	take a cab (colloquial)
骑摩托车	qí mótuóchē	ride a motorcycle
骑自行车	qí zìxíngchē	ride a bike /
骑脚踏车	qí jiǎotàchē	ride a bike (Taiwan) /
走路	zǒu lù	travel on foot

开 lai drive

语言注释 Language Notes

1. Position words

东部、北部、南边、旁边、中部 and so on are position words. Position words are nouns. They can be used as the subject, object, or an attributive of a noun in a sentence.

In terms of their meanings, 东部、西部、南部、北部 and 中部 refer to different parts or sections within a region. 东边、西边、南边 and 北边 have two different meanings: first, they refer to the immediate area outside of the border of a region; second, they refer to different sections of an architectural structure or a region.

北京在中国的北部。	Beijing is in the northern part of China. (within China)
南京在上海的北边。	Nanjing is north of Shanghai. (outside of the Shanghai city limits)
教室在校园的北边。	Classrooms are located in the northern part of the campus. (within the campus, but at the northern edge of the campus)
上海的东边是海。	East of Shanghai is the ocean.

2. Three commonly used sentence structures for location/position/the existence of something

To indicate the location, position or existence of something, the most commonly used verbs include 是, 在 and 有.

Sentence Structure 1: Use 是

Noun phrase with Position word	是	*Noun phrase*	*English meaning*
北京的西部	是	山地。	The western part of Beijing is mountainous area.
美国的南边	是	墨西哥。	South of the United States is Mexico.

Sentence Structure 2: Use 在

Noun Phrase 1	在	Noun Phrase with Position word	English meaning
北京	在	中国的北部。	Beijing is in northern China.
杭州	在	上海的南边。	Hangzhou is south of Shanghai.

Sentence Structure 3: Use 有

Noun phrase with position word	有	Noun phrase 2	English meaning
中国的南部	有	广州。	Guangzhou is in southern China.
西湖旁边	有	一些小公园。	There are some small parks by the West Lake.

There are some subtle differences among the above structures. 有 is used to introduce new information (similar to "there is" in English). 是 places more emphasis on the identity or the name of the object. 在 is often used to indicate the specifics of a location and position.

3. The use of 再

再 can be used in the following three ways:

1) To mean "again" in the future:

再见!
See you again!

明年我们再去一次中国。
Next year we will go to China again.

2) To indicate a sequence of actions:

我们先看看中国的北部，再看看中国的南部。
We will take a look at northern China before looking at southern China.

3) To indicate that an action is postponed to a later date (in this usage, 再 comes after a time phrase):

我家太远了。我们有长周末的时候我再回家。
My house is too far away from here. I will go home when we have a long weekend (instead of now).

玩了游戏，再吃饭吧。
Let's eat after playing a game (we will first play a game, and then eat.)

4. Politeness

The Chinese way of expressing politeness may not be the same as that in the Western cultures. For example, when offered something, a Chinese person would first decline. But the host/hostess would insist. Only at the second (or sometimes, third) round of offering would a Chinese accept the invitation/offer. Read the following part of the lesson dialogue and pay attention to how David accepts Kelly's invitation:

凯丽：你想去杭州吗？杭州在上海的南边，坐火车两个小时，不太远。你可以去我家过周末。

大卫：真的吗？不好意思打扰你父母。

凯丽：不会的。我父母一定会很欢迎你去玩儿。

大卫：那太好了！听说杭州很美丽，是吗？

Chinese speakers use the colloquial expression 不好意思 to show politeness and respect. A direct English translation of this expression is "feel ill at ease," "feel embarrassed" or "feel indebted." Chinese are sensitive to social status. To show respect, the common practice is to put yourself lower than the other party. The "lower" status has little to do with reality. It is a token of politeness. You can use it to apologize for your imperfect performance and abilty, or to show your gratitude to someone's kindness. For example:

1) 不好意思，我的汉语不好。
   I am embarrassed that my Chinese is not good.

2) 不好意思，我可以问您一个问题吗？
   Excuse me (I am obliged), may I ask you a question?

中国文化一瞥 A Glimpse into Chinese Culture

For more information and activities related to Chinese culture, please go to http://my.cheng-tsui.com/huanying.

1. Read aloud the lyrics of a Chinese folk song, paying special attention to your tones.

This folk song by an anonymous writer dates back to the Ming-Qing dynasties (1368–1911).

Sāi　Hóng Qiū · Shān Xíng Jǐng

塞　鸿　秋 · 山　行　警

Dōng	biān	lù,	xī	biān	lù,	nán	biān	lù.
东	边	路、	西	边	路、	南	边	路。

Wǔ	lǐ	pù,	qī	lǐ	pù,	shí	lǐ	pù.
五	里	铺、	七	里	铺、	十	里	铺。

Xíng	yī	bù,	pàn	yī	bù,	lǎn	yī	bù.
行	一	步、	盼	一	步、	懒	一	步。

Shà	shí	jiān	tiān	yě	mù,	rì	yě	mù,	yún	yě	mù,
霎	时	间	天	也	暮、	日	也	暮、	云	也	暮，

Xié	yang	mǎn	dì	pù,	huí	shǒu	shēng	yān	wù.
斜	阳	满	地	铺，	回	首	生	烟	雾。

Wù	de	bù	shān	wú	shù,	shuǐ	wú	shù,	qíng	wú	shù.
兀	的	不	山	无	数、	水	无	数、	情	无	数。

Roads to the east, to the west, to the south,

Villages in five miles, seven miles, ten miles.

Take a step, expect another step, withhold a step,

Suddenly dusk embraces the sky, the sun, and the clouds.

The setting sunshine covers the land, the roads I traveled are immersed in fog.

Endless mountains, waters, and love I have yet to experience.

2. Chinese Proverbs and Idioms

sān   sān   liǎng   liǎng

三　三　两　两

small groups of people

sān   yán   liǎng   yǔ

三　言　两　语

in a few words → *language*

你知道吗？ Did you know?

The administrative divisions of the People's Republic of China consist of five levels: province, region, county/city, town/district, and village/neighborhood. At the province level, China has 23 provinces (省 shěng) (including Taiwan), four municipalities (直辖市 zhíxiáshì) (Beijing, Shanghai, Tianjin, and Chongqing), five autonomous regions (自治区 zìzhìqū) (Xinjiang, Ningxia, Tibet, Inner Mongolia, and Guangxi), and two special administrative regions (特别行政区 tèbié xíngzhèngqū) (Hong Kong and Macau).*

A province is made up of several regions. A region consists of counties and cities. In other words, a region usually includes rural and urban areas. As agriculture played a primary economic role in China for a long time, "county" used to refer to rural areas and "city" to urban areas. Under the county government, there are towns and villages, whereas under the city government, there are urban districts and neighborhoods. In recent years, due to rapid urbanization, the distinction between urban and rural areas has become blurred. Nowadays, it is quite common to find a county government in a newly developed industrial city. Town and district government is the lowest administrative level because administration at the village/neighborhood level becomes informal. Village and neighborhood affairs are usually managed by a group of individuals who are often selected (not elected) by villagers or residents. They tend to be elders who have lived in the village/neighborhood for a long time and know most people quite well.

*You can find their names in the pronunciation exercises for Unit 1.3.

6.2 我们的学校
Our School

 对话一 **Dialogue 1**

(Tom is talking to his grandfather over the phone.)

Tāngmǔ: Yéye, nín hǎo! Wǒ shì Tāngmǔ.
汤姆: 爷爷，您 好！我 是 汤姆。

Yéye: Tāngmǔ, nǐ hǎo ma?
爷爷: 汤姆，你 好 吗？

Tāngmǔ: Wǒ hěn hǎo.
汤姆: 我 很 好。

Yéye: Xuéxí máng bù máng?
爷爷: 学习 忙 不 忙？

Tāngmǔ: Xuéxí hěn máng. Wǒ hái cānjiā le xuéxiào de
汤姆: 学习 很 忙。我 还 参加 了 学校 的

also participate

wǎngqiú duì, xīngqīyī hé xīngqīsān xiàwǔ yào
网球 队，星期一 和 星期三 下午 要

team

xùnliàn.
训练。

Yéye: Nǐ men   de   xuéxiào   zài   nǎr?

爷爷：你们 的 学校 在 哪儿？

Tāngmǔ: Zài   Shànghǎi   de   *west* xībiān.

汤姆：在 上海 的 西边。

Yéye: Lí   nǐ men   jiā   yuǎn   ma?

爷爷：离 你们 家 远 吗？

Tāngmǔ: Bù   yuǎn.   Wǒ   měitiān   zǒu   lù   qù   xuéxiào.

汤姆：不 远。我 每天 走 路 去 学校。

Yéye: Zǒu   lù   hǎo.   Zǒu   lù   yě   shì   yī   zhǒng

爷爷：走 路 好。走 路 也 是 一 种 *one type/kind*

yùndòng.   Wǒ   měitiān   zǒu   lù   qù   gōngyuán.

运动。我 每天 走 路 去 公园。

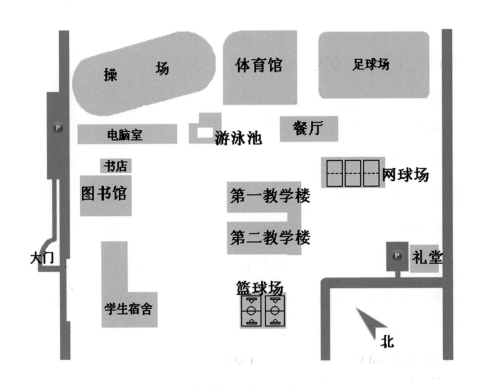

对话二 Dialogue 2

(Tom is telling his grandfather about his school.)

Yéye: Nǐmen de xuéxiào dà ma?
爷爷： 你们 的 学校 大 吗？

Tāngmǔ: Bù dà bù xiǎo. Xuéxiào yǒu liǎng gè jiàoxuélóu,
汤姆： 不 大 不 小。学校 有 两 个 教学楼，

yī gè túshūguǎn, hái yǒu cāntīng, lánqiúchǎng
一 个 图书馆、还 有 餐厅、 篮球场

shénme de.
什么 的。

Yéye: Nǐ de jiàoshì zài nǎgè jiàoxuélóu?
爷爷： 你 的 教室 在 哪个 教学楼？

Tāngmǔ: Wǒ de jiàoshì zài dì yī jiàoxuélóu.
汤姆： 我 的 教室 在 第 一 教学楼。

Yéye: Xuéxiào yǒu wǎngqiúchǎng ma?
爷爷： 学校 有 网球场 吗？

Tāngmǔ: Yǒu. Wǎngqiúchǎng zài jiàoxuélóu yòubiān.
汤姆： 有。网球场 在 教学楼 右边。

Jiàoxuélóu qiánbiān shì lánqiúchǎng, zuǒbiān shì
教学楼 前边 是 篮球场， 左边 是

túshūguǎn.
图书馆。

Yéye: Xuésheng cāntīng zài nǎr?
爷爷： 学生 餐厅 在 哪儿？

Tāngmǔ: Xuésheng cāntīng zài jiàoxuélóu hòubiān.
汤姆： 学生 餐厅 在 教学楼 后边。

Yéye: Nǐ měitiān zài xuéxiào cāntīng chī wǔfàn ma?

爷爷： 你 每天 在 学校 餐厅 吃 午饭 吗?

Tāngmǔ: Yǒushíhòu zài xuéxiào cāntīng chī, yǒu shíhòu

汤姆： 有时候 在 学校 餐厅 吃, 有时候

zài xuéxiào wàibiān chī.

在 学校 外边 吃。

生词 New Words

	Simplified	Traditional	Pinyin	Part of Speech	English
1.	训练	訓練	xùnliàn	*v./n.*	*v.* train, *n.* training
2.	西边	西邊	xībiān	*n.*	west side
3.	离	離	lí	*prep.*	from, off, away
4.	走路		zǒu lù	*v.o.*	walk
5.	教学	教學	jiàoxué	*n./v.*	teaching
6.	教室		jiàoshì	*n.*	classroom
7.	楼	樓	lóu	*n.*	building
8.	餐厅	餐廳	cāntīng	*n.*	restaurant, cafeteria
9.	篮球场	籃球場	lánqiúchǎng	*n.*	basketball court
10.	网球场	網球場	wǎngqiúchǎng	*n.*	tennis court
11.	右边	右邊	yòubiān	*n.*	right (side)
12.	左边	左邊	zuǒbiān	*n.*	left (side)
13.	后边/面	後邊	hòubiān /miàn	*n.*	back, behind
14.	外边/面	外邊	wàibiān	*n.*	outside

Handwritten annotations:

v. jiāo
n. jiào

边 biān / edge, side

面 miàn / face, side

15. 前边 qian bian front

16. 上边/面 shang bian on, above

17. 下边/面 xia bian under

18. 中间 zhong jian middle, center (smaller), in between

19. 对面 dùi mian across bian

20. 里边 li bian inside

21. 旁边 beside
pong bian

学无止境 EXTEND YOUR KNOWLEDGE

Below is a list of words related to school buildings:

dàmén ✓	lǐ táng	diànnǎoshì ✓	shíyànshì
大门	礼堂	电脑室	实验室
main entrance	*auditorium*	*computer lab*	*laboratory*
tǐ yùguǎn ✓	cāochǎng	yóuyǒngchí ✓	xuésheng sùshè ✓
体育馆	操场	游泳池	学生宿舍
gymnasium	*exercise field; playground*	*swimming pool*	*student dorm*
xuésheng huódòng zhōngxīn ✓	jiàodǎochù	xiàozhǎng bàngōngshì ✓	bàngōnglóu
学生活动中心	教导处	校长办公室	办公楼
student activity center	*dean's office*	*principal's office*	*office building*

语言注释 Language Notes

1. The use of 离

离 is a preposition to indicate a distance in time or space.

Location/Time 1	离	Location/Time 2	Comment	*How far?*
你家	离	学校	远吗？	A: 有多远？ 有多近
Is your house far away from the school?				
北京	离	上海	不近。	
Beijing is not close to Shanghai.				
现在	离	2020年	有几年？	
How many years are there until 2020?			*Past* 过去	
现在	离	上课	还有几分钟？	
How many minutes are there until the next class?				

For people / everything

2. 什么的 (and so on, and so forth, etc.) / 等等 *deng deng (etc)*

When listing things, 什么的 meaning "and so on, so forth" is often used at the end of the list. 什么的 is most often used in casual spoken language.

我爸爸喜欢看足球、篮球、网球什么的。
My father likes to watch football, basketball, tennis, and so on.

我们去买本子、笔、文件夹什么的。
We are going to buy notebooks, pens, file folders, etc.

3. 有时候···，有时候··· (sometimes…sometimes…)

他有时候看电视，有时候玩电脑。
He sometimes watches TV, sometimes plays on the computer.

我有时候在家吃饭，有时候在学校吃饭。
I sometimes eat at home, and sometimes eat at school.

4. Completion aspect particle 了

了 can be added to a verb to show the perfect aspect of an action, or that an action has been completed. It is very important to understand that 了 is NOT a particle for past tense. Rather, it is quite similar to the present perfect tense in English. The verb- 了 can be used with a future action, a present action, or a past action, depending on the context of the conversation; the emphasis is on completion of the action. For example, in 5.3 we have learned the expression "等爸爸回来了我们就下饺子。" In this sentence, obviously Dad is not back yet. The 了 in the sentence only indicates the completion of the first action, which is 等爸爸回来.

Depending on the form of the verb, the completion aspect particle 了 is placed in different places in a sentence:

1) When the verb does not take an object, 了 is added after the verb at the end of a sentence.

我们学习了。
We have studied.

他们走了。
They have left.

2) When the verb takes on a simple (or general) object, 了 is added after the simple object.

我们看电影了。
We watched a movie.

他们打网球了。
They played tennis.

3) When the verb takes on a modified/quantified (or specified) object, 了 is inserted between the verb and the modified object.

我参加了学校的网球队。
I have joined the school's tennis team.

我们参观了北京国际学校。
We visited the Beijing International School.

他们看了三个电影。
They have watched three movies.

Please also refer to Language Note 4 in Unit 5.3.

5. 边 and 面 in location words

前边、后边、左边、右边、上边、下边、里边 and 外边 have another form, which uses 面 instead of 边. Therefore you will also hear people say 前面，后面，左面，右面，上面，下面，里面 and 外面. In terms of meaning, they are basically the same.

中国文化一瞥 **A Glimpse into Chinese Culture**

For more information and activities related to Chinese culture, please go to http://my. cheng-tsui.com/huanying.

1. **Read aloud the lyrics of an old Chinese folk song, paying special attention to your tones.**

This folk song was written between 1127 and 1130 during the Song Dynasty. At that time, because of wars and corruption, most ordinary people lived difficult lives, while the rich and the powerful still lived in luxury. This song highlights the differences in people's lives.

Yuè	Ér	Wān	Wān	Zhào	Jiǔ	Zhōu
月	儿	弯	弯	照	九	洲

Yuè	ér	wān	wān	zhào	jiǔ	zhōu
月	儿	弯	弯	照	九	洲，

Jǐ	jiā	huān	lè	jǐ	jiā	chóu
几	家	欢	乐	几	家	愁，

Jǐ	jiā	fū	qī	tóng	luó	zhàng
几	家	夫	妻	同	罗	帐，

Jǐ	jiā	piāo	ling	zài	wài	tóu
几	家	飘	零	在	外	头。

The Moon Shines Everywhere

The moon shines everywhere,
Some families are in joy and some are in sorrow.
Some couples are in their comfortable beds, and
Some are wandering homeless.

2. Chinese Proverbs and Idioms

谢　天　谢　地

xiè　tiān　xiè　dì

thank heaven

冰　天　雪　地

bīng　tiān　xuě　dì

a world of ice and snow

你知道吗?　Did you know?

In China, almost all schools have a 1.5-hour lunch break. In the past, most elementary and secondary school students would go home for lunch because their families lived nearby. Moreover, the Chinese love a freshly cooked hot lunch. This tradition, however, has changed in recent years. Now most students eat lunch at the school's cafeteria. Their lunch comes in a lunch box, usually containing some steamed rice, a small bowl of soup, and two dishes of stir-fried vegetables with meat, fish or eggs. Students have stopped going home for lunch for many reasons. One major reason is the fast urban development. Many families have moved to newer and bigger apartments in the suburbs. Since many schools remain where they are in the city, parents like to send their children to the good schools in the old neighborhoods. Consequently, students need to take public transportation to school. For some, the commute can take an hour one way. It becomes impossible for some to go home at lunch break. Another reason is that most women are working and do not have the luxury of preparing a hot lunch for their children at lunchtime.

This lifestyle change has its bright side, though. As most students are the "only child" in their families, lunch hours have become social hours for many. This is the only time that they can play and talk freely with their peers, without worrying too much about schoolwork or under the close observation of their overly protective parents.

6.3 我的房间
My Room

A traditional-style Chinese house.

对话一 Dialogue 1

(Maria is in Hangzhou for the weekend. She is visiting Kelly's home.)

Mǎlìyà: Kǎilì, nǐ jiā de kètīng zhēn piàoliang. Nǐmen
玛丽娅：凯丽，你 家 的 客厅 真 漂亮！。你们

yǒu jǐ jiān wòshì?
有 几 间 卧室？

Kǎilì: Sān jiān. Lái, wǒ dài nǐ cānguān cānguān ba.
凯丽：三 间。来，我 带 你 参观 参观 吧。

Zhè shì kètīng. Zhè shì wǒmen de chúfáng
这 是 客厅。这 是 我们 的 厨房
hé fàntīng. Fàntīng pángbiān shì wǒ fùmǔ
和 饭厅。饭厅 旁边 是 我 父母
de shūfáng. Kètīng de zuǒbiān shì wǒ
的 书房。 客厅 的 左边 是 我
fùmǔ de wòshì, lǐbiān yǒu yī gè wèishēngjiān.
父母 的 卧室，里边 有 一 个 卫生间。
Wǒ hé jiějie de wòshì zài guòdào de zhèbiān.
我 和 姐姐 的 卧室 在 过道 的 这边。
Wǒmen liǎ de wòshì zhōngjiān yě yǒu yī gè
我们 俩 的 卧室 中间 也 有 一 个
wèishēngjiān.
卫生间。

Mǎlìyà:	Wāsai, Nǐ jiā de fángzi zhēn dà!
玛丽娅：	哇噻，你 家 的 房子 真 大！
Kǎilì:	Shì a. Zǒu, wǒmen qù wǒ de fángjiān ba.
凯丽：	是 啊。走，我们 去 我 的 房间 吧。
Mǎlìyà:	Āiyou, nǐ de fángjiān yě gòu dà de.
玛丽娅：	哎呦，你 的 房间 也 够 大 的。
Kǎilì:	Wǒ jiějie de fángjiān gèng dà. Tā de fángjiān
凯丽：	我 姐姐 的 房间 更 大。她 的 房间
	jiù zài duìmiàn. Nǐ xiǎng qù shūfáng kàn kan
	就 在 对面。你 想 去 书房 看 看
	ma?
	吗？

Mǎlìyà:　Hǎo　a!　Nǐmen　jiā　de　shūfáng　lǐ　yǒu　zhème
玛丽娅：好 啊！你们 家 的 书房 里 有 这么

　　　　　duō　shū!　Hái　yǒu　liǎng　tái　diànnǎo　ne.
　　　　　多 书！还 有 两 台 电脑 呢。

Kǎilì:　Zhè　tái　diànnǎo　shì　bàba　de,　nà　tái　shì
凯丽：这 台 电脑 是 爸爸 的，那 台 是

　　　　　māma,　jiějie　hé　wǒ　de.
　　　　　妈妈、姐姐 和 我 的。

Mǎlìyà:　Nǐ　bù　yòng　nǐ　bàba　de　diànnǎo　ma?
玛丽娅：你 不 用 你 爸爸 的 电脑 吗？

Kǎilì:　Bù　yòng.　Tā　de　diànnǎo　tài　màn　le.
凯丽：不 用。他 的 电脑 太 慢 了。

🖸 对话二 **Dialogue 2**

(David is visiting Tom's home.)

Dàwèi:　Zhè　shì　nǐ　de
大卫：这 是 你 的

　　　　　fángjiān　ma?
　　　　　房间 吗？

Tāngmǔ:　Bù,　zhè　shì　wǒ　dìdi　de　fángjiān.　Wǒ　de
汤姆：不，这 是 我 弟弟 的 房间。我 的

　　　　　fángjiān　zài　duìmiàn.
　　　　　房间 在 对面。

Dàwèi:　Nǐ　de　fángjiān　hěn　liàng.
大卫：你 的 房间 很 亮。

Tāngmǔ: Xièxie. Yǐqián zhè shì wǒ māma de shūfáng,

汤姆：   谢谢。以前，这 是 我 妈妈 的 书房，

dāngshí wǒ hé wǒ dìdi hézhù yī jiān

当时 我 和 我 弟弟 合住 一 间

wòshì. Xiànzài zhè shì wǒ zìjǐ de wòshì.

卧室。现在 这 是 我 自己 的 卧室。

Xiànzài wǒ māma hé wǒ bàba yòng yī jiān

现在 我 妈妈 和 我 爸爸 用 一 间

shūfáng, suǒyǐ wǒ kěyǐ zìjǐ zhù zài zhèr.

书房，所以 我 可以 自己 住 在 这儿。

Dàwèi: Nǐ yīdìng xǐhuān yǒu zìjǐ de fángjiān ba?

大卫：   你 一定 喜欢 有 自己 的 房间 吧?

Tāngmǔ: Duì. Yīnwèi wǒ xǐhuān zhěngqí. Kěshì dìdi hěn luàn.

汤姆：   对。因为 我 喜欢 整齐。可是 弟弟 很 乱。

生词 New Words

	Simplified	Traditional	Pinyin	Part of Speech	English
1.	间	間	jiān	*m.w.*	*for rooms*
2.	卧室	卧室	wòshì	*n.*	bedroom
3.	参观	參觀	cānguān	*v.*	visit (a place)
4.	客厅	客廳	kètīng	*n.*	living room
5.	厨房	廚房	chúfáng	*n.*	kitchen
6.	饭厅	飯廳	fàntīng	*n.*	dining room
7.	书房	書房	shūfáng	*n.*	study
8.	里边	裡邊	lǐbiān	*n.*	inside
9.	卫生间	衛生間	wèishēngjiān	*n*	bathroom
10.	过道	過道	guòdào	*n.*	hallway, corridor

11.	中间	中間	zhōngjiān	*n.*	middle
12.	房间	房間	fángjiān	*n.*	room
13.	哇噻		wāsai	*excl.*	wow
14.	真的		zhēn de	*adv.*	really
15.	啊		a	*par.*	*used at the end of a sentence to express moods*
16.	更		gèng	*adv.*	more, even more (see Language Note 1)
17.	对面	對面	duìmiàn	*n.*	opposite, across from
18.	亮		liàng	*adj.*	bright
19.	台	臺	tái	*m.w.*	*for machines (computers, TVs)*
20.	慢		màn	*adj.*	slow
21.	当时	當時	dāngshí	*adv.*	at that time, back then
22.	合住		hézhù	*v.*	live together, share (a living quarter)
23.	自己		zìjǐ	*n.*	self
24.	乱	亂	luàn	*adj.*	messy, in disorder
25.	整齐	整齊	zhěngqí	*adj.*	tidy, in order

Handwritten annotations: 的 / 假 jiǎ adj fake; 合住 — to share; 当时 — 당시; 时间 shí jiān time

学无止境 EXTEND YOUR KNOWLEDGE

Now you have learned how to say some different rooms in a house in Chinese. Below is a list of other rooms that some houses may have:

méntīng 门厅 *entrance*	zhǔ wòshì 主卧室 *master bedroom*	bìchú 壁橱 *closet*	xǐ yīfáng 洗衣房 *laundry room*
chēkù 车库 *garage*	huāyuán 花园 *garden*	yuànzi 院子 *yard*	yángtái 阳台 *balcony*
xǐ zǎojiān 洗澡间 *bathroom*	cèsuǒ 厕所 *toilet*	chǔcángshì 储藏室 *storage room*	dìxiàshì 地下室 *basement*

Shower/Bath

语言注释 Language Notes

1. The use of 更

更 is an adverb meaning "more." It goes before an adjective. It can be used in comparisons.

更好 better, 更快 faster, 更高兴 happier, 更多 more, 更大 bigger

can go before a emotional verb like 喜欢, not in front of action

2. More measure words

台 is often used with machines.

two computers	两台电脑
one TV set	一台电视（机）

间 is used with rooms.

one study	一间书房
three rooms	三间房间

3. Location words

Location words in Chinese are nouns that indicate spatial location such as front, back, top or bottom. The most commonly used location words are: 前边，后边，左边，右边，上边，下边，里边，外边，中间 and 对面. They are used in the following ways:

1) In a 在 sentence indicating the specifics of a location and position:

Q: 我们的狗在哪儿？
Where is our dog?

A: 我们的狗在桌子（的）上边。
Our dog is on top of the table.

Q: 玛丽的猫在哪儿？
Where is Mary's cat?

A: 玛丽的猫在房子（的）后边。
Mary's cat is behind the house.

2) In a 是 sentence indicating the identity, or the name of a thing, in a particular location:

Q: 桌子（的）上边是什么？
What is that thing on top of the table?

A: 桌子（的）上边？哦，那是我的狗。
On top of the table? Oh, that's my dog.

Q: 教学楼（的）后边是什么？
What is behind the classroom building?

A: 教学楼（的）后边是网球场。
That is the tennis court.

3) In a 有 sentence indicating there is a thing in a particular location (usually new information):

Q: 桌子（的）上边有什么？
What is there on top of the table?

A: 桌子（的）上边有一个电脑。
There is a computer on top of the table.

Q: 教学楼（的）后边有什么？

What is there behind the classroom building?

A: 教学楼（的）后边有网球场。

There is a tennis court behind the classroom building.

Note: when a location word is preceded by another noun, the particle 的 is often omitted. See also Unit 6.1 Language Note 2 for more about location words.

 中国文化一瞥 A Glimpse into Chinese Culture

For more information and activities related to Chinese culture, please go to http://my. cheng-tsui.com/huanying.

1. Read aloud the lyrics of a contemporary folk song from Yunnan Province. Pay special attention to your tones.

Village boys sing this folk song when they go to the mountains with their horses. The song is quite long because the boys describe what they do throughout the year. Here is a sample of the first two months.

Fàng Mǎ Shān Gē

放 马 山 歌

Zhēng yuè fàng mǎ zhēng yuè zhēng,

正 月 放 马 正 月 正，

Gǎn qǐ mǎ lái dēng lù chéng.

赶 起 马 来 登 路 程。

Dà mǎ gǎn lái shān tóu shàng,

大 马 赶 来 山 头 上，

Xiǎo mǎ gǎn lái suí hòu gēn.

小 马 赶 来 随 后 跟。

Èr yuè fàng mǎ bǎi cǎo fā,

二 月 放 马 百 草 发，

Xiǎo	mǎ	chī	cǎo	shēn	shān	lǐ	pǎo.
小	马	吃	草	深	山	里	跑。

Mǎ	wú	yě	cǎo	bù	huì	pàng,
马	无	野	草	不	会	胖，

Cǎo	wú	lù	shuǐ	bù	huì	fā.
草	无	露	水	不	会	发。

Horses are set free to pasture

In the first month of the year,
I start the journey with my horses.
The grown horses are led to the mountains,
The younger horses are following behind.
Horses are set free to pasture,
In the second month of the year, when grasses grow everywhere,
Young horses eat grasses and run deep into the mountains.
Without grass, horses cannot grow,
Without dew, grasses cannot grow.

2. Chinese Proverbs and Idioms

sān	rén	xíng,	bì	yǒu	wǒ	shī
三	人	行，	必	有	我	师。

When three people travel together, at least one of them is my teacher.

zhī	bǐ	zhī	jǐ
知	彼	知	己

estimate correctly one's strength as well as that of one's opponent

你知道吗? **Did you know?**

In the past, most Chinese families had limited space in their living quarters. In some densely populated cities, it was common for a family to live in a room or a small apartment. Therefore, most children had to share their bedroom with their siblings, their grandparents, and sometimes, their parents.

In recent years, it has become quite common for a child to have his or her own bedroom. With the rise of living standards, the housing situation for both rural and urban residents has improved a great deal. Many rural families can afford to build larger and modern houses, whereas urban residents have also moved to bigger and newer apartments. In addition, most Chinese families have fewer children. One child per family is the norm in many parts of China.

After the new generation of Chinese has got used to having their own space, they become more aware of "privacy." Many Chinese parents still do not understand what the big deal is about privacy. It is an old tradition for family members to share everything. The conflict of views sometimes causes misunderstanding between children and their parents. So much has changed so fast in a short period of time in China. The Chinese people are adjusting to the changes as well as to new concepts coming along with the changes.

A traditional–style Chinese building.

6.4 在哪儿买汉语书？
Where to Buy a Chinese Book?

王府井书店

Wangfujing Bookstore in Beijing.

对话一 Dialogue 1

(Maria is preparing for the HSK, a Chinese proficiency test. She wants to know where she can get the test preparation materials).

Mǎlìyà: Tāngmǔ, nǐ zhīdào zài nǎr mǎi duìwài Hànyǔ

玛丽娅：汤姆，你 知道 在 哪儿 买 对外 汉语

jiàokēshū ma?

教科书 吗？

I think   *or Cotastment*

Tāngmǔ: Wo xiǎng, nǐ kěyǐ qù wàiwén shūdiàn huòzhě

汤姆： 我 想，你 可以 去 外文 书店 或者

Dōngfēng Shūdiàn.

东风 书店。

Mǎlìyà: Dōngfēng Shūdiàn zai nǎr?

玛丽娅：东风 书店 在 哪儿？

Tāngmǔ: Zài   Zhōngshān Lù.

汤姆：   在   中山路。 *(road name)*

Mǎlìyà: Zài   Zhōngshān Lù   shénme   dìfāng?

玛丽娅：   在   中山路   什么   地方？   *where*

Tāngmǔ: Zài   yī   gè   yínháng   de   pángbiān.

汤姆：   在   一   个   银行   的   旁边。

Mǎlìyà: Nǎ gè   yínháng?

玛丽娅：   哪个   银行？

Tāngmǔ: Wǒ   wàng   le   yínháng   de   míngzì.   Dōngfēng Shūdiàn

汤姆：   我   忘   了   银行   的   名字。 东风   书店

   de   pángbiān   hé   duìmiàn   yǒu   xǔduō   *restaurant* fàndiàn.

   的   旁边   和   对面   有   许多   饭店。

Mǎlìyà: Xièxie,   wǒ   zhōumò   qù   Dōngfēng Shūdiàn   kànkan.

玛丽娅：   谢谢， 我   周末   去   东风   书店   看看。

王府井 (wángfǔjǐng), a well-known shopping district in Beijing.

对话二 Dialogue 2

(Tom is showing some photos to his mother.)

Tāngmǔ: Māma, nín kàn, zhè shì wǒ he péngyoumen
汤姆: 妈妈，您 看，这 是 我 和 朋友们

de zhàopiàn.
的 照片。

Māma: Zhēn bùcuò! Zhè gè shūdiàn zhēn piàoliàng.
妈妈: 真 不错！这 个 书店 真 漂亮。

Tāngmǔ: Shì a. Zhè jiù shì wǒ cháng cháng qù de
汤姆: 是 啊。这 就 是 我 常 常 去 的

Dōngfēng Shūdiàn.
东风 书店。

Māma: Oh. Nǐ zuǒbiān shì shéi?
妈妈: 哦。你 左边 是 谁？

Tāngmǔ: Wǒ zuǒbiān shì Mǎkè, yòubiān shì Líndá.
汤姆: 我 左边 是 马克，右边 是 琳达。

Māma: Líndá zhēn piàoliàng! Líndá hòubiān de shì shéi?
妈妈: 琳达 真 漂亮！琳达 后边 的 是 谁？

Tāngmǔ: Nà shì Mǎlìyà hé tā gēge Āndōngní. Wǒ
汤姆: 那 是 玛丽娅 和 她 哥哥 安东尼。我

qiánbiān de xiǎoháir shì Mǎlìyà de mèimei Nínà.
前边 的 小孩儿 是 玛丽娅 的 妹妹 妮娜。

生词 New Words

	Simplified	Traditional	Pinyin	Part of Speech	English
1.	对外	對外	duìwài	s.p.	(oriented towards) overseas, abroad
2.	教科书	教科書	jiàokēshū	n.	textbook (formal)
3.	外文		wàiwén	n.	foreign language
4.	书店	書店	shūdiàn	n.	bookstore
5.	或者		huòzhě	conj.	or
6.	银行	銀行	yínháng	n.	bank
7.	饭店	飯店	fàndiàn	n.	restaurant
8.	忘记		wàngjì	v.	forget
9.	照片		zhàopiàn	n.	photo
10.	真不错	真不錯	zhēn bùcuò	s.p.	Really nice!
11.	小孩儿	小孩兒	xiǎoháir	n.	little kid

[handwritten note next to row 5: 还是 used in question]
[handwritten note next to row 5: in statement.]

Proper Nouns

12.	东风	東風	Dōngfēng		East Wind
13.	琳达	琳達	Líndá		Linda

语言注释 Language Notes

1. Time phrase with 以前 (before) and 以后 (after)

In Chinese, a time phrase always goes before the predicate of a sentence. (See Unit 4.5 Language Note 1 for more examples.)

下课以后，我回家了。

After class, I went home.

学生八点以前到学校。
Students arrive at school before eight.

网球比赛以前，我们照了几张照片。
We took a few photos before the tennis match.

2. Location words used to modify other nouns

Location words can be used to modify other nouns, indicating "which one":

你要哪张桌子？
Which table would you like?

我要左边的桌子。
I'd like the one on the left.

哪个人是你的老师？
Which person is your teacher?

右边的人（是我的老师）。
The one on the right (is my teacher).

3. 这就是… (this is [precisely]…)

This expression is often used when someone finally gets to show people what s/he means (usually after several previous attempts to explain it). 就 here is used to intensify the tone, and can be roughly translated into something like "precisely," "exactly."

这就是我常去的饭店。
This is (exactly) the restaurant that I often go to.

这就是我们的礼堂。
Here, this is our auditorium.

这就是我的卧室。
(Precisely), this is my bedroom.

学无止境 EXTEND YOUR KNOWLEDGE

So far you have learned about the different rooms in a house. How about adding a few pieces of furniture in the rooms? Below is a list of commonly used furniture:

书桌	shūzhuō	desk
书架	shūjià	bookshelf
咖啡桌	kāfēizhuō	coffee table
椅子	yǐzi	chair
大沙发	dà shāfā	couch
小沙发	xiǎo shāfā	armchair
台灯	táidēng	lamp

中国文化一瞥 A Glimpse into Chinese Culture

For more information and activities related to Chinese culture, please go to http://my.cheng-tsui.com/huanying.

1. **Read aloud the lyrics of an old Chinese folk song, paying special attention to the tone changes of 一.**

Yàn	Ér	Luò	Dài	Guò
雁	儿	落	带	过

Yī	nián	lǎo	yī	nián,	yī	rì	mò	yī	rì,
一	年	老	一	年，	一	日	没	一	日，

Yī	qiū	yòu	yī	qiū,	yī	bèi	cuī	yī	bèi.
一	秋	又	一	秋，	一	辈	催	一	辈。

Yī	jù	yī	lí	bié,	yī	xǐ	yī	shāng bēi.
一	聚	一	离	别，	一	喜	一	伤 悲。

Yī	tà	yī	shēn	wò,	yī	shēng	yī	mèng lǐ.
一	榻	一	身	卧，	一	生	一	梦 里。

Xún	yī	huǒ	xiāng	shí,	tā	yī	huì,	zán	yī	huì,
寻	一	伙	相	识，	他	一	会，	咱	一	会，

Dōu	yī	bān	xiāng	zhī,	chuī	yī	huí	chàng	yī	huí.
都	一	般	相	知，	吹	一	回，	唱	一	回。

Reflections

Getting older year by year, life passes day by day,

One autumn after another, one generation after another.

Farewell after a meeting, sorrow after joy,

A bed for a person, a dream for a life.

Make a group of friends, he takes some time, I take some time,

We know each other momentarily, play a while, sing a while.

2. Chinese Proverbs and Idioms

xīn	kǒu	rú	yī
心	口	如	一

speak one's mind frankly

rì	jī	yuè	lěi
日	积	月	累

accumulated day by day and month by month

你知道吗? **Did you know?**

Between 1949 and 1979, the Chinese government controlled almost all businesses, including bookstores. During those years, almost every town had a "New China Bookstore" (新华书店 Xīnhuá Shūdiàn), which sold books in Chinese language. In big cities, there was also a "Foreign Language Bookstore" (外文书店 Wàiwén Shūdiàn), where readers could find books in foreign languages. Under strict management, bookstores all over China were selling similar products.

Since the economic reforms in 1979, many more bookstores have emerged. Some are state-owned and some are privately owned. Some cater to the general interest and some are specialized in a specific line of products. Readers can go to a "Music Bookstore" (音乐书店) to get music books, music CDs, and DVDs, to a "Classics Bookstore" (古籍书店 gǔjí shūdiàn) to buy classical works, and to a "Fine Arts Bookstore" (美术书店 měishù shūdiàn) to obtain books on paintings or artists. Some overseas bookstores have also set up branches in China. Although "New China Bookstore" remains the largest bookstore chain, many readers love to go to the "Book City" (书城 Shū Chéng), where you can find almost all of the recent publications. For many Chinese families, going to the "Book City" is a family outing, as the whole family can spend half a day in the Book City. While the parents are busy reading literature, history, and how-to books, small children are lost in the jungle of cartoon books and storybooks.

In recent years, shopping for books online has become another possibility for city residents. After you have selected a book online, you need to give your address to the online bookstore. Within a day or two, someone will come on his bike with the book you have ordered in his hands. He will collect the money for the online bookstore, plus three yuan (about 40 US cents) for the delivery fee. If you are too busy to go to a bookstore, this is certainly a great way to get the latest book, especially since the bus fare to the bookstore is usually more than three yuan!

6.5 请来参加我的晚会
Please Come to My Party

对话一 Dialogue 1

Mǎlìyà:
玛丽娅： ~~Xīngqīwǔ~~ wǎnshàng qī diǎn zài wǒ jiā ~~kāi~~ *host a*
星期五 晚上 七 点 在 我 家 开

Party
wǎnhuì, nǐ xiǎng lái ma?
晚会， 你 想 来 吗？

Kǎilì:
凯丽： Xièxie, wǒ yīdìng qù. Hái yǒu shéi lái cānjiā
谢谢， 我 一定 去。 还 有 谁 来 参加

wǎnhuì?
晚会？

Mǎlìyà:
玛丽娅： Dàwèi hé Tāngmǔ.
大卫 和 汤姆。

Kǎilì:
凯丽： Nǐ jiā zài nǎr?
你 家 在 哪儿？

Mǎlìyà: Lǎoběi Jiē bā bā qī hào.

玛丽娅： 老北 街 八 八 七 号。

Kǎilì: Lǎoběi Jiē shì bù shì yǒu yīxiē shāngdiàn?

凯丽： 老北 街 是 不 是 有 一些 商店？

Mǎlìyà: Duì. Wǒ jiā duìmiàn yǒu yínháng, fàndiàn,

玛丽娅： 对。我 家 对面 有 银行、饭店、

kāfēiguǎn. Wǒ jiā hòubiān yǒu yī gè xiǎo

咖啡馆。我 家 后边 有 一 个 小

gōngyuán.

公园。

Kǎilì: Wǒ xiǎng wǒ yǒu nǐ de diànhuà hàomǎ.

凯丽： 我 想 我 有 你 的 电话 号码。

Nǐ de diànhuà shì bù shì liù sān wǔ

你 的 电话 是 不 是 六 三 五

yī yī èr sān bā?

一 一 二 三 八？

Mǎlìyà: Shì de, yǒu wèntí gěi wǒ dǎ diànhuà.

玛丽娅： 是 的，有 问题 给 我 打 电话。

Kǎilì: Hǎo, zàijiàn.

凯丽： 好，再见。

Mǎlìyà: Zàijiàn.

玛丽娅： 再见。

对话二 Dialogue 2

(Kelly and Tom arrive at Maria's party.)

Mǎlìyà: Huānyíng, huānyíng! Qǐng jìn.

玛丽娅：欢迎，欢迎！请进。

Tāngmǔ: Xièxie!

汤姆：谢谢！

Mǎlìyà: Qǐng zuò ba. Nǐmen yào hē shénme?

玛丽娅：请坐吧。你们要喝什么？

Kǎilì: Kěkǒukělè.

凯丽：可口可乐。

Tāngmǔ: Qǐng gěi wǒ yī bēi bīng shuǐ.

汤姆：请给我一杯冰水。

Mǎlìyà: Hǎo, nǐmen děng deng.

玛丽娅：好，你们等等。

Kǎilì: Tāngmǔ, shǔjià nǐ dǎsuàn qù nǎr?

凯丽：汤姆，暑假你打算去哪儿？

Tāngmǔ: Wǒ yào qù Běijīng kàn yéye nǎinai. Nǐ ne?

汤姆：我要去北京看爷爷奶奶。你呢？

Kǎilì: Wǒ yào huí Měiguó guò shǔjià.

凯丽：我要回美国过暑假。

Tāngmǔ: Nǐ zài Měiguó dǎsuàn zuò shénme?

汤姆：你在美国打算做什么？

Kǎilì: Yóu you yǒng, kàn kan shū, wán wan diànnǎo.

凯丽：游游泳，看看书，玩玩电脑。

Duìle, wǒmen hái yào qù Jiānádà kàn lǎolao.

对了，我们还要去加拿大看姥姥。

Tāngmǔ: Nǐ fùmǔ zhēn hǎo, shǔjià ràng nǐ xiūxi xiūxi.
汤姆： 你 父母 真 好， 暑假 让 你 休息 休息。

Wǒ bàba ràng wǒ shǔjià qù xué shùxué,
我 爸爸 让 我 暑假 去 学 数学、

diànnǎo, wǔshù hé gāngqín.
电脑、 武术 和 钢琴。

Kǎilì: Shénme? Tāmen bù ràng nǐ xiūxi ma?
凯丽： 什么？ 他们 不 让 你 休息 吗？

Tāngmǔ: Tāmen shuō, bù qù xuéxiào shàngkè jiù shì
汤姆： 他们 说， 不 去 学校 上课 就 是

xiūxi.
休息。

Kǎilì: Shì ma? Kàn, Dàwèi lái le.
凯丽： 是 吗？ 看， 大卫 来 了。

Dàwèi: Nǐmen hǎo.
大卫： 你们 好。

Tāngmǔ: Dàwèi, shǔjià nǐ huí Xiānggǎng ma?
汤姆： 大卫， 暑假 你 回 香港 吗？

Dàwèi: Duì, huānyíng nǐmen lái Xiānggǎng wán.
大卫： 对， 欢迎 你们 来 香港 玩。

(Maria brings the drinks to Tom and Kelly.)

Mǎlìyà: Dàwèi, nǐ shuō shénme?
玛丽娅： 大卫， 你 说 什么？

Dàwèi: Wǒ shuō, huānyíng nǐmen lái Xiānggǎng wán.
大卫： 我 说， 欢迎 你们 来 香港 玩。

Mǎlìyà: Tài hǎo le, wǒ yīdìng qù.
玛丽娅： 太 好 了， 我 一定 去。

生词 New Words

	Simplified	Traditional	Pinyin	Part of speech	English
1.	商店		shāngdiàn	n.	shop, store
2.	咖啡馆	咖啡館	kāfēiguǎn	n.	cafe, coffee house
3.	问题	問題	wèntí	n.	question
4.	打电话	打電話	dǎ diànhuà	v.o.	make a phone call
5.	进	進	jìn	v.	enter, come in
6.	喝		hē	v.	drink
7.	等		děng	v.	wait
8.	杯		bēi	m.w.	for cups and glasses
9.	暑假		shǔjià	n.	summer vacation
10.	打算		dǎsuàn	v.	plan
11.	姥姥		lǎolao	n.	maternal grandmother

晚会 wan hui party (handwritten)

Proper Nouns

里 is not used in proper noun / use 有 (handwritten)

13.	可口可乐	可口可樂	Kěkǒukělè	p.n.	Coca-cola
14.	加拿大		Jiānádà	p.n.	Canada

进来 jin lai — when one are inside and someae coming in (handwritten)

进去 — when one is outside and someone is going in is please goin' before ne. (handwritten)

语言注释 Language Notes

1. Different ways to ask a yes/no question

1) Sentence + 吗?

你上汉语课吗?　　　　Do you take a Chinese class?

他很忙吗?　　　　　　Is he busy?

2) Subject + Verb/Adjective 不 Verb/Adjective + (Object)?

你上不上汉语课？ Do you take a Chinese class?

他忙不忙？ Is he busy?

3) Subject + 是不是 + the rest of the sentence?

你是不是上汉语课？ Do you take a Chinese class?

他是不是很忙？ Is he busy?

TAG +
"对吗?"
"好吗?"
like

2. The use of 对了 *(by the way)*

对了 is often used in spoken Chinese, indicating the speaker (1) suddenly remembers something, or (2) wants to change a topic.

suddenly mention

我们明天上午去。对了，上午我要开会，我们下午去吧。

go to a meeting

Let's go tomorrow morning. Oh, no, I have to go to a meeting in the morning. Let's go in the afternoon then.

好，我们下课以后去打网球。对了，你知道马克明天要回美国吗？

OK, let's play tennis after class. By the way, do you know that Mark is going back to the US tomorrow?

3. 给···打电话 and 打电话给···

There are two ways of saying "call someone."

玛丽娅给汤姆打电话。 Maria called Tom.

玛丽娅打电话给汤姆。 Maria called Tom.

中国文化一瞥 **A Glimpse into Chinese Culture**

For more information and activities related to Chinese culture, please go to http://my. cheng-tsui.com/huanying.

1. Read aloud the lyrics of a Chinese children's song.

The following song is from Yunnan Province. Children sing this song while playing a riddle game. They can also create and solve their own riddles spontaneously and sing the riddles to the tune of the song. The following is an example.

Cāi　Yī　Cāi

猜　一　猜

Xiǎo　guāi　guāi　lái　xiǎo　guāi　guāi,
小　乖　乖　来　小　乖　乖，

Wǒ　men　shuō　gěi　nǐ　men　cāi,
我　们　说　给　你　们　猜，

Shén　me　cháng　cháng　zhǎng　shàng　tiān?
什　么　长　长　长　上　天？

Shén　me　chā　zài　shuǐ　zhōng　jiān?
什　么　插　在　水　中　间？

Shén　me　yǒu　tuǐ　bù　zǒu　lù?
什　么　有　腿　不　走　路？

Shén　me　yǒu　zuǐ　bù　chàng　gē?
什　么　有　嘴　不　唱　歌？

Xiǎo　guāi　guāi　yā　me　xiǎo　guāi　guāi,
小　乖　乖　呀　么　小　乖　乖，

Wǒ　men　zhè　jiù　cāi　chū　lái,
我　们　这　就　猜　出　来，

Gāo	lóu	cháng	cháng	zhǎng	shàng	tiān,
高	楼	长	长	长	上	天，

Qiáo	dūn	chā	zài	shuǐ	zhōng	jiān,
桥	墩	插	在	水	中	间，

Bǎn	dèng	yǒu	tuǐ	bù	zǒu	lù,
板	凳	有	腿	不	走	路，

Lǎ	bā	yǒu	zuǐ	bù	chàng	gē.
喇	叭	有	嘴	不	唱	歌。

Take a Guess

Come, come, little friends,

We'll say the riddles and you will guess,

What is high and grows into the sky?

What stands in the water?

What has legs but cannot walk?

What has a mouth but cannot talk?

Come, come, little friends,

We know the answers to your riddles,

A skyscraper grows into the sky,

Piers of a bridge stand in the water,

A stool has legs but cannot walk,

A horn has a mouth but cannot talk.

2. Chinese Proverbs and Idioms

qīng　chē　shú　lù

轻　车　熟　路

do something one knows well

chē　shuǐ　mǎ　lóng

车　水　马　龙

heavy traffic

你知道吗？ **Did you know?**

For most Chinese, a party means a banquet. Families hold banquets to celebrate holidays, weddings, and other special occasions. Friends gather at banquets to celebrate graduation, new employment, promotion, or anything good in life. If it is a formal occasion, a banquet begins with a ceremony of who should enter the banquet room first and where each guest should sit. The most respected guest should enter the room first and sit facing the entrance. To show their politeness, many guests try to sit in the least honorable seat with their back towards the entrance. If it is a family gathering, children occupy these least honorable seats.

During a banquet, many successive courses are brought in. Cold dishes (similar to appetizers) are served first. Depending on how elaborate the banquet is, cold dishes come in an even number of 4, 6, 8 and more. They are followed by hot dishes, which also come in an even number. The number of hot dishes should, at least, match the number of the cold dishes that have been served. When guests have stuffed themselves with these cold and hot dishes of meat, fish, poultry, and vegetables, steamed rice and a soup are brought in. That signals that a banquet is winding down. The last dish, similar to the West, is a desert. The Chinese desert is quite simple. It usually consists of some fruits or a sweet soup.

Before everyone leaves, the guests usually thank the host for a "superb" banquet, whereas the host needs to apologize for the "inferior" quality of the food. This, of course, has nothing to do with the real quality of the food. It is another way to show politeness.

6.6 第六单元复习
Unit 6 Review

课文一 Text 1

(Maria has received an email from her pen pal in China.)

玛丽娅：

你好！

很高兴认识你。我叫小明。我在太原上中学。我们的学校在太原西边，离我家不远，我每天走路去学校。我们的学习很忙。我每天上午八点到下午五点都在学校上课。我们的作业很多，每天晚上我做作业。没有时间看电视，也没有时间玩电脑。我有时候十点半睡觉，有时候十一点睡觉。

我喜欢打篮球。我家后边有一个公园，公园里有一个篮球场。可是星期一到星期五我都没有时间去运动。周末我有时候去打篮球。我家对面有一个书店，这个书店有一些英语书。我的《哈利波特》是在那儿买的。可是我学习太忙，没有时间看。你喜欢《哈利波特》吗？

你的朋友：小明
11月26日

A famous restaurant in Tianjin.

课文二 Text 2

(Tom's mother is telling Tom about the neighborhood she grew up in.)

我们家住在北京的东边。我们家旁边有许多商店。左边是一个小饭店。那个小饭店叫"天津饭店"，主人是天津人。他做的饭很好吃。每天，有许多人去那儿吃饭。我们家右边有一个大商店。里边卖吃的和用的东西。我们家对面有一个小吃店。那儿的小吃非常好吃。每天我去上学以前，都去小吃店买小吃。小吃店的旁边是一个小书店。下课以后，我和朋友常常去那儿看书。在书店工作的是两个老太太。她们很喜欢学生去那儿看书。

离我家不远有一个小公园。每天许多老人去那里运动。公园后边有一个篮球场。因为

我 很 喜欢 打 篮球，所以 常常 去。每天 有 不 少 人 在 篮球场 打 篮球。在 那儿，我 认识 了 一些 <u>新</u> 朋 友，有 男的，也 有 女的；有 中学生，也 有 小学 生 和 大学生。他们 家 都 离 公园 不 远。周末 我们 常常 打 篮球。

Snack food for sale at a night market.

生词 New Words

	Simplified	Traditional	Pinyin	Part of speech	English
1.	到		dào	prep./v.	to, arrive
2.	卖	賣	mài	v.	sell
3.	小吃		xiǎochī	n.	snack food
4.	主人		zhǔrén	n.	owner

Proper Nouns

	Simplified	Traditional	Pinyin	Part of speech	English
5.	太原		Tàiyuán	p.n.	Taiyuan
6.	哈利 波特		Hālì Bōtè	p.n.	Harry Potter

SELF-ASSESSMENT

In Unit 6, you have learned how to describe locations and positions, the layout of a house, and the different buildings in a school. Have you reached the learning goals of Unit 6? After completing the exercises for Unit 6 in your Workbook, fill out the following self-assessment sheet.

Yes/No	*Can you say and do these things in Chinese?*
Y	Tell the names of some major Chinese cities.
N	Tell where some major cities are located in China and in relation to each other.
Y	Tell where in the city/town your school is located.
Y	Describe the layout of your school.
N	Describe the layout of your house.
Y	Describe your neighborhood and the surroundings of your school.
Y	Describe a sequence of events (one event happens before/after another).
N	Talk about your future plans.

Yes/No	*Do you know how to do these things?*
Y	Describe a sequence of events (one event happens before/after another).
Y	Describe completion of an action.
Y	Use different ways to ask a yes/no question.
N	Use three different ways (有、在、是) to describe a location or a position.
Y	Use time phrases 以前 and 以后 in a sentence.
Y	Use location words to modify a noun.

11–13	yes	excellent
7–10	yes	good
0–6	yes	need some work

附录一
Appendix 1

拼音变调和拼写规则 Tone Changes and Pinyin Spelling Rules

I. The Pronunciation of Two Third Tones

There are some special rules for pronouncing Chinese words. In our text, 你好 is written as **nǐ hǎo** but pronounced as **ní hǎo**. This is because when two or more 3rd tones come one after another, the first 3rd tone will be pronounced as a 2nd tone. The last 3rd tone will always be pronounced as a 3rd tone. For example:

nǐ hǎo	(pronounced as **ní hǎo**)
yě hěn hǎo	(pronounced as **yé hén hǎo**)

II. The Pronunciation of 一 and 不

The tones of "一" and "不" change according to the tone of the syllable that follows. The character 一 is pronounced in the fourth tone (**yì**) when followed by 1st, 2nd and 3rd tones, and the second tone (**yí**) when followed by a 4th tone. For example:

yī tiān	(pronounced as **yì tiān**)
yī nián	(pronounced as **yì nián**)
yī diǎn	(pronounced as **yì diǎn**)
yī biàn	(pronounced as **yí biàn**)

Similarly, when 不 is followed by 1st, 2nd and 3rd tones, it is pronounced in the fourth tone (**bù**). When it is followed by a 4th tone, it is pronounced in the second tone (**bú**). In the pronunciation exercises, we show tone changes for the purpose of teaching correct pronunciation. Elsewhere, we write pinyin words with their base tones.

III. Pinyin Spelling Rules: How to Group Pinyin Syllables into Words

In this book, some pinyin words like "Dīng" contain one syllable, while other pinyin words like "Lǎoshī" contain two or more syllables. The *Basic Rules for Hanyu Pinyin Orthography* (《汉语拼音正词法基本规则》[1]) published by the Chinese government specifies 36 rules regarding the standards in pinyin spelling. In general, when a Chinese word (词) that represents an independent meaning contains more than one character, this word should be transliterated as one multi-syllable word in pinyin. For example, the word 学生, meaning "student," should be written in *pinyin* as **xuésheng**, instead of **xué shēng**. In the pinyin system, proper nouns are capitalized, and the first letter of the first word in a sentence should be capitalized.

---

[1] 《中文拼音正词法基本规则》(*Basic Rules for Hanyu Pinyin Orthography*), published and adopted by the Bureau of National Standardization of the People's Republic of China, 1996. See http://www.pinyin.info/ for more information.

附录二
Appendix 2

汉字的笔划、笔顺和部首 Strokes, Stroke Order, and Radicals

I. The Basic Strokes of a Character

Examples:

认 不 中 人 大 冰 口 了 刻 饭 也 我

II. Stroke Order[2]

The strokes of Chinese characters must be written in a certain order. Here are the basic rules for writing characters in the correct order.

Rule	Example
Left before right	一
Top before bottom	三
Top to down	川
Horizontal stroke before intersecting vertical stroke	十
Left-slanted stroke before right-slanted stroke	八

---

[2] For an animated illustration of the stroke orders in Chinese, please go to the following web link: http://en.wikipedia.org/wiki/Stroke_order#Basic_rules_of_stroke_order. If you would like to see the stroke orders of each character that you are learning, here's a fantastic website: http://online.eon.com.hk/.

Rule	Example
Left vertical stroke (usually) before top horizontal stroke	口
Horizontal "support stroke" last	生
Center stroke before wings	水
Left-falling stroke before right-falling stroke	文
(Diagonal right-to-left before left-to-right)	
Outside before inside	向
Bottom enclosing strokes last	国
Minor strokes (often) last	戈

III. The 214 Chinese Radicals*

Radical Number	Radical	Variants	Simplified Radical	Chinese Name	English Name	Stroke Count
1	一			yī	one	1
2	丨			gǔn	line	1
3	丶			zhǔ	dot	1
4	丿	㇏ (fú), ㇀ (yí)		piē	slash	1
5	乙	㇄ (yǐn), ㇆		yì	second	1

*This list of radicals is based on the following sources: http://en.wikipedia.org/wiki/List_of_Kangxi_radicals#1_stroke, http://www.yellowbridge.com/chinese/radicals.php.

Radical Number	Radical	Variants	Simplified Radical	Chinese Name	English Name	Stroke Count
6	亅			jué	hook	1
7	二			èr	two	2
8	亠			tóu	lid	2
9	人	亻		rén	man	2
10	儿			rén	legs	2
11	入			rù	enter	2
12	八	丷		bā	eight	2
13	冂			jiǒng	down box	2
14	冖			mì	over	2
15	冫			bǐng	ice	2
16	几			jǐ	table	2
17	凵			qǔ	open box	2
18	刀	刂		dāo	knife	2
19	力			lì	power	2
20	勹			bāo	wrap	2
21	匕			bǐ	spoon	2
22	匚			fāng	right open box	2
23	匸			xǐ	hiding enclosure	2

Radical Number	Radical	Variants	Simplified Radical	Chinese Name	English Name	Stroke Count
24	十			shí	ten	2
25	卜			bǔ	Mysticism	2
26	卩			jié	seal	2
27	厂			hàn	cliff	2
28	厶			sī	private	2
29	又			yòu	again	2
30	口			kǒu	mouth	3
31	囗			wéi	enclosure	3
32	土			tǔ	earth	3
33	士			shì	scholar	3
34	夂			suī (bottom)	go	3
35	夊			zhi (top)	go slowly	3
36	夕			xì	evening	3
37	大			dà	big	3
38	女			nǚ	woman	3
39	子			zǐ	child	3
40	宀			mián	roof	3
41	寸			cùn	inch	3

Radical Number	Radical	Variants	Simplified Radical	Chinese Name	English Name	Stroke Count
42	小			xiǎo	small	3
43	尢	尣		wāng	lame	3
44	尸			shī	corpse	3
45	屮			chè	sprout	3
46	山			shān	mountain	3
47	川	巛, 巜 (guì)		chuān	river	3
48	工			gōng	work	3
49	己			jǐ	oneself	3
50	巾			jīn	turban	3
51	干			gān	dry	3
52	幺			yāo	short thread	3
53	广			yǎn	dotted cliff	3
54	廴			yǐn	long stride	3
55	廾			gǒng	two hands	3
56	弋			yì	shoot	3
57	弓			gōng	bow	3
58	彐	彑		jì	snout	3

Radical Number	Radical	Variants	Simplified Radical	Chinese Name	English Name	Stroke Count
59	彡			shān	bristle	3
60	彳			chì	step	3
61	心	忄		xīn	heart	4
62	戈			gē	weapon	4
63	戶			hù	door	4
64	手	扌		shǒu	hand	4
65	支			zhī	branch	4
66	攴	攵		pū	rap	4
67	文			wén	script	4
68	斗			dǒu	dipper	4
69	斤			jīn	axe	4
70	方			fāng	square	4
71	无			wú	not	4
72	日			rì	sun	4
73	曰			yuē	say	4
74	月			yuè	moon	4
75	木			mù	tree	4
76	欠			qiàn	lack	4

Radical Number	Radical	Variants	Simplified Radical	Chinese Name	English Name	Stroke Count
77	止			zhǐ	stop	4
78	歹			dǎi	death	4
79	殳			shū	weapon	4
80	毋			mú	do not	4
81	比			bǐ	compare	4
82	毛			máo	fur	4
83	氏			shì	clan	4
84	气			qì	steam	4
85	水	氵		shuǐ	water	4
86	火	灬		huǒ	fire	4
87	爪	爫		zhǎo	claw	4
88	父			fù	father	4
89	爻			yáo	double x	4
90	爿			qiáng	half tree trunk	4
91	片			piàn	slice	4
92	牙			yá	teeth	4
93	牛	牛		niú	cow	4
94	犬	犭		quǎn	dog	4

Radical Number	Radical	Variants	Simplified Radical	Chinese Name	English Name	Stroke Count
95	玄			xuán	profound	5
96	玉	王		yù	jade	5
97	瓜			guā	melon	5
98	瓦			wǎ	tile	5
99	甘			gān	sweet	5
100	生			shēng	life	5
101	用			yòng	use	5
102	田			tián	field	5
103	疋			pǐ	bolt of cloth	5
104	疒			chuáng	sickness	5
105	癶			bò	dotted tent	5
106	白			bái	white	5
107	皮			pí	skin	5
108	皿			mǐn	dish	5
109	目			mù	eye	5
110	矛			máo	spear	5
111	矢			shǐ	arrow	5
112	石			shí	stone	5

Radical Number	Radical	Variants	Simplified Radical	Chinese Name	English Name	Stroke Count
113	示	礻		shì	spirit	5
114	禸			rǒu	track	5
115	禾			hé	grain	5
116	穴			xuè	cave	5
117	立			lì	stand	5
118	竹			zhú	bamboo	6
119	米			mǐ	rice	6
120	糸		纟	mì	silk	6
121	缶			fǒu	jar	6
122	网	罒		wǎng	net	6
123	羊			yáng	sheep	6
124	羽			yǔ	feather	6
125	老			lǎo	old	6
126	而			ér	and	6
127	耒			lěi	plow	6
128	耳			ěr	ear	6
129	聿			yù	brush	6
130	肉			ròu	meat	6

Radical Number	Radical	Variants	Simplified Radical	Chinese Name	English Name	Stroke Count
131	臣			chén	minister	6
132	自			zì	self	6
133	至			zhì	arrive	6
134	臼			jiù	mortar	6
135	舌			shé	tongue	6
136	舛			chuǎn	oppose	6
137	舟			zhōu	boat	6
138	艮			gèn	stopping	6
139	色			sè	color	6
140	艸	艹		cǎo	grass	6
141	虍			hū	tiger	6
142	虫			chóng	insect	6
143	血			xuě	blood	6
144	行			xíng	walk enclosure	6
145	衣	衤		yī	clothes	6
146	襾	西		yà	west	6
147	見		见	jiàn	see	7
148	角			jué	horn	7

Radical Number	Radical	Variants	Simplified Radical	Chinese Name	English Name	Stroke Count
149	言		讠	yán	speech	7
150	谷			gǔ	valley	7
151	豆			dòu	bean	7
152	豕			shǐ	pig	7
153	豸			zhì	badger	7
154	貝		贝	bèi	shell	7
155	赤			chì	red	7
156	走			zǒu	run	7
157	足			zú	foot	7
158	身			shēn	body	7
159	車		车	chē	cart	7
160	辛			xīn	bitter	7
161	辰			chén	morning	7
162	辵	辶		chuò	walk	7
163	邑	阝 (right)		yì	city	7
164	酉			yǒu	wine	7
165	釆			biàn	distinguish	7
166	里			lǐ	village	7

Radical Number	Radical	Variants	Simplified Radical	Chinese Name	English Name	Stroke Count
167	金			jīn	gold	8
168	長		长	cháng	long	8
169	門		门	mén	gate	8
170	阜	阝 (left)		fù	mound	8
171	隶			dài	slave	8
172	佳			zhuī	short tailed bird	8
173	雨			yǔ	rain	8
174	青			qīng	blue	8
175	非			fēi	wrong	8
176	面			miàn	face	9
177	革			gé	leather	9
178	韋		韦	wéi	tanned leather	9
179	韭			jiǔ	leek	9
180	音			yīn	sound	9
181	頁		页	yè	leaf	9
182	風		风	fēng	wind	9
183	飛		飞	fēi	fly	9
184	食	飠	饣	shí	eat	9

Radical Number	Radical	Variants	Simplified Radical	Chinese Name	English Name	Stroke Count
185	首			shǒu	head	9
186	香			xiāng	fragrant	9
187	馬		马	mǎ	horse	10
188	骨			gǔ	bone	10
189	高			gāo	tall	10
190	髟			biāo	hair	10
191	鬥		斗	dòu	fight	10
192	鬯			chàng	sacrificial wine	10
193	鬲			Lì	cauldron	10
194	鬼			guǐ	ghost	10
195	魚		鱼	yú	fish	11
196	鳥		鸟	niǎo	bird	11
197	鹵		卤	lǔ	salt	11
198	鹿			lù	deer	11
199	麥		麦	mài	wheat	11
200	麻			má	hemp	11
201	黃			huáng	yellow	12
202	黍			shǔ	millet	12

Radical Number	Radical	Variants	Simplified Radical	Chinese Name	English Name	Stroke Count
203	黑			hēi	black	12
204	黹			zhǐ	embroidery	12
205	黽		黾	mǐn	frog	13
206	鼎			dǐng	tripod	13
207	鼓			gǔ	drum	13
208	鼠			shǔ	rat	13
209	鼻			bí	nose	14
210	齊		齐	qí	even	14
211	齒		齿	chǐ	tooth	15
212	龍		龙	lóng	dragon	16
213	龜		龟	guī	turtle	16
214	龠			yuè	flute	17

附录三
Appendix 3

对话、课文（繁体字版）Dialogues and Texts in Traditional Characters

Unit 1.2, Dialogue 1

(It is the first day of school. Maria Rossini goes to her Chinese class.)

丁老師：你好！我是丁老師。你呢？
瑪麗婭：您好！我是瑪麗婭。
丁老師：你好！我是丁老師。
湯姆：　您好！我是湯姆。

Unit 1.2, Dialogue 2

(The class is over.)

丁老師：再見。
瑪麗婭：再見。

Unit 1.3, Dialogue 1

(Maria greets Tom.)

瑪麗婭：你好嗎，湯姆？
湯姆：　很好，謝謝。你呢？你怎麼樣？
瑪麗婭：我也挺好的。

Unit 1.3, Dialogue 2

(Tom introduces David to Maria. David is an international student who comes from France.)

湯姆：　(To Maria) 唉，瑪麗婭，你們認識嗎？這是大衛。他也
　　　　是我們班的學生。(To David) 這是我的朋友瑪麗婭。
瑪麗婭：你好，大衛！
大衛：　你好，瑪麗婭！

Unit 1.4, Dialogue 1

(Maria meets Kelly at a lunch table. Kelly is an international student who comes from the U. S.)

瑪麗婭： 你好！我叫瑪麗婭。你叫甚麼名字？

凱麗： 你好！我叫凱麗，我姓斯坦納。

瑪麗婭： 你家住在上海嗎？

凱麗： 不，我家住在杭州。你家住在哪兒？

瑪麗婭： 我家住在上海。

Unit 1.4, Dialogue 2

(The people in Maria's class are introducing themselves.)

瑪麗婭： 你們好！我叫瑪麗婭，姓羅西尼。我家住在
上海。我學習漢語。

湯姆： 大家好！我姓王，叫湯姆。我家也住在上海。

大衛： 我叫大衛格林。我家不住在上海。我家住在香港。
我也學習漢語。

Unit 1.5, Dialogue 1

(Maria and Tom exchange their contact information.)

瑪麗婭： 我家的電話號碼是：6351-1238。你家的電話號碼
是多少？

湯姆： 我家的電話號碼是：3789-6551。

瑪麗婭： 你的電子郵件呢？

湯姆： 我的是：tom@hotmail.com.

瑪麗婭： 謝謝。

Unit 1.5, Dialogue 2

(Tom meets Kelly in the school's cafeteria.)

湯姆： 請問，你是黛安嗎？

凱麗： 不是，我是凱麗。

湯姆： 對不起。

凱麗： 沒關係。你認識大衛嗎？

湯姆： 認識。他是我朋友。我叫湯姆。

凱麗： 認識你很高興。你知道大衛的手機號碼嗎？

湯姆： 知道。1312-254-3366。

凱麗:　　謝謝。

湯姆:　　不客氣。

Unit 1.6, Dialogue 1

瑪麗婭:　你 好!

湯姆:　　你 好!

瑪麗婭:　我 是 瑪麗婭。你 呢?

湯姆:　　我 姓 王, 叫 湯姆。

大衛:　　你們 好! 我 叫 大衛格林。你們 認識 她(tā) 嗎? 她 是 我 朋友 凱麗。

凱麗:　　你們 好! 認識 你們 很 高興。

Unit 1.6, Dialogue 2

丁老師:　請問, 你 叫 甚麼 名字?

凱麗:　　老師 好! 我 叫 凱麗。

丁老師:　你 家 住在 哪兒?

凱麗:　　我 家 住在 杭州。

丁老師:　你 家 的 電話 號碼 是 多少?

凱麗:　　三七二五—六七一九

丁老師:　謝謝! 你的 電子 郵件 是 甚麼?

凱麗:　　是 kaili@sohu.com

Unit 1.6, Text

你們 好! 我 姓 丁, 叫 丁明 (míng)。我 是 你們 的 漢語 老師。認識 你們 很 高興。

　　我 住在 上海。我 的 電話 號碼 是 六三四五–八八九零。我 的 電子 郵件 是 ding@sohu.com.

Unit 2.1, Dialogue 1

(In Maria's Chinese class, students are taking turns to tell each other about their families.)

瑪麗婭:　你 好, 湯姆! 這 是 我 的 一家。我 家 有 五個 人, 爸爸、媽媽、哥哥、妹妹 和 我。我 家 住在 上海。我 爸爸 媽媽 都 在 上海 工作。你 家 呢?

湯姆:　　我 家 有 四個 人, 爸爸、媽媽、弟弟 和 我。我 弟弟 叫 杰米。我 媽媽 在 上海 工作, 我 爸爸 在 舊金山 和 上海 工作。

Unit 2.1, Dialogue 2

(David and Kelly are chatting about their families.)

大衛： 凱麗，你家有幾個人？

凱麗： 我家有五個人：爸爸、媽媽、兩個姐姐和我。

大衛： 你沒有哥哥和弟弟嗎？

凱麗： 沒有。你呢？

大衛： 我有一個哥哥和一個妹妹。他們和我爸爸、媽媽都住在香港。

Unit 2.2, Text

(Maria is talking about her parents.)

我爸爸四十歲。他在一個公司工作。他是經理。他喜歡運動。

我媽媽四十五歲。她是護士。她喜歡聽音樂。他們都很忙。

Unit 2.2, Dialogue

(Maria is looking at a picture of her Chinese friend Xiao Li's family.)

瑪麗婭： 這是你爸爸吧？

小麗： 對。

瑪麗婭： 你爸爸多大啦？

小麗： 他四十六歲。

瑪麗婭： 他在哪兒工作？

小麗： 他在北京的一個電腦公司工作。他是電腦工程師。

瑪麗婭： 你媽媽做甚麼工作？

小麗： 她是上海第一中學的老師。

Unit 2.3, Text

(Maria talks about her siblings.)

我哥哥叫安東尼。他是學生。他上高中。安東尼很聰明。

他 學習 很 用功。他 也 很 喜歡 運動。他 有 許多 朋友。我 妹妹 叫 妮娜。她 上 幼兒園。她 很 可愛。她 養 一只 小貓 和 一 只 小狗。

Unit 2.3, Dialogue

瑪麗婭：你 有 兄弟 姐妹 嗎？

湯姆：　我 有 一個 弟弟，叫 杰米。

瑪麗婭：杰米 多 大 啦？

湯姆：　十 歲。

瑪麗婭：他 喜歡 做 甚麼？

湯姆：　他 喜歡 運動，喜歡 玩 電腦 游戲，也 喜歡 跟 "老虎" 玩。

瑪麗婭：老虎？

湯姆：　杰米 的 狗 叫 "老虎"。

Unit 2.4, Dialogue 1

瑪麗婭：你 家 住 在 上海 市 嗎？

湯姆：　對。

瑪麗婭：上海 甚麼 地方？

湯姆：　黃浦 區 北京 路 1005 號 201 室。你 家 呢？

瑪麗婭：我 家 也 住 在 上海，老 北 街 887號。

Unit 2.4, Dialogue 2

湯姆：　大衛，你 養 寵物 嗎？

大衛：　養。我 養 一只 狗，叫 "八弟"。它 很 聰明。它 知道 我 家 的 地址：香港 十一 街 556號。

Unit 2.5, Dialogue 1

(Tom shows a picture of his grandparents to Maria).

瑪麗婭：他們 是 誰？

湯姆：　他們 是 我 爺爺 奶奶。

瑪麗婭：他們 是 中國人 嗎？

湯姆：　是 的。他們 住 在 北京。

瑪麗婭： 你 爺爺 還 工作 嗎？

湯姆： 不。我 爺爺 奶奶 都 退休 了。可是 爺爺 有 時候 在 健身 房 做 義工。

Unit 2.5, Dialogue 2

(At the International Club, Tom makes a new friend.)

湯姆： 你好！我 叫 湯姆。你 呢？

順愛： 你好！我 是 金順愛。

湯姆： 你 是 哪 國 人？

順愛： 我 是 韓國人。你 呢？

湯姆： 我 是 美國人。

順愛： 你 家 住 在 美國 嗎？

湯姆： 不。我 跟 爸爸、媽媽 和 弟弟 住 在 上海，因為 我 爸爸 在 上海 工作。你 呢？你 家 住 在 上海 嗎？

順愛： 對。我 家 住 在 上海 的 黃浦 區。

Unit 2.6, Text 1

你們 好！我 是 丁明。我 是 漢語 老師。我 家 有 五 個 人，爸 爸、媽媽、弟弟、妹妹 和 我。我 在 上海 工作。我 的 家人 都 住 在 北京。

我 爸爸 是 一 個 公司 的 經理。他 五十五 歲。我 媽媽 是 幼 兒園 老師，她 五十四 歲。我 弟弟 在 美國。他 在 一 個 電腦 公 司 工作。我 妹妹 是 大學生。她 在 大學 學習 音樂。

我們 家 沒有 狗，也 沒有 貓。我 很 喜歡 狗，可是 我 媽媽 不 喜歡。

Unit 2.6, Text 2

我 叫 大衛。我 今年 十四 歲。我 家 有 六 個 人，爸爸、媽媽、兩 個 姐姐、一 個 弟弟 和 我。我們 家 住 在 香港。我 媽媽 是 大學 老師。我 爸爸 在 電話 公司 工作。他 是 客戶 服務 的 經 理。我們 一 家 都 是 法國人。

我 的 兩 個 姐姐 都 在 紐約。一 個 在 那兒 上 大學，一 個 在 那兒 工作。我 姐姐 是 小學 老師。我 弟弟 十三 歲。他 上 中 學。

　　我弟弟和我都喜歡 "八弟"。八弟很聰明,可是許多人不喜歡它,因為它喜歡叫。

Unit 3.1, Dialogue 1

凱麗： 你的生日是幾月幾號?

瑪麗婭：四月二十五號。

凱麗： 今天是四月二十號,星期一。我看看四月二十五號是星期幾……太好了,是星期六!

瑪麗婭：對。

凱麗： 星期六我們沒有課。我請你去看電影,好嗎?

瑪麗婭：太好了。

Unit 3.1, Dialogue 2

(Tom is helping his mother to mark a birthday calendar.)

媽媽： 二月十一號是杰米的生日。三月三十號是你爸爸的生日。六月五號是你的生日。

湯姆： 您的生日是不是十一月九號?

媽媽： 是的。你知道不知道爺爺奶奶的生日?

湯姆： 爺爺的生日我不知道,可是我知道奶奶的生日是八月一號。

媽媽： 那你知道不知道爺爺的生日是哪年呢?

湯姆： 不知道。

媽媽： 我只知道爺爺的生日是一九三三年,但是不知道是幾月幾號。我們去問問爸爸。

Unit 3.2, Dialogue 1

(Before class.)

湯姆： 現在幾點?

瑪麗婭：差五分八點。

湯姆： 今天我們幾點上漢語課?

瑪麗婭：八點十五。

湯姆： 哦。明天也是八點十五分上漢語課嗎?

瑪麗婭：不是。明天是十點二十。

Unit 3.2, Dialogue 2

大衛：   現在 幾點？

瑪麗婭： 兩點 五十分。你 現在 回 宿舍 嗎？

大衛：   不。三點 一刻 我 和 湯姆 去 打 網球。

瑪麗婭： 是 嗎？去 哪兒 打？

大衛：   健身房。你 現在 回家 嗎？

瑪麗婭： 不回。三點半 我 和 凱麗 去 電腦房 做 作業。

大衛：   再見。

瑪麗婭： 再見。

Unit 3.3, Text

(Maria is writing a letter to her pen pal 小明, who lives in Taiyuan, China).

小明：

你 好！

我 叫 瑪麗婭。我 是 美國 人。現在 在 上海 國際 學校 學習。

我們 學校 的 學生 每天 有 很 多 課。我 每天 早上 六點 半 起床。七點半 去 學校。我們 上午 八點 一刻 開始 上課。中午 十二點 在 學校 吃 午飯。下午 兩點 四十五 下課。下課 以 後，我 有時候 做 作業，有時候 和 朋友 去 運動。我 很 喜歡 運 動。晚上 我 學習，看 電視，玩 電腦。我 十點 睡覺。你 的 一天 呢？也 很 忙 嗎？

祝

好！

你 的 朋友：瑪麗婭

10 月 15 日

Unit 3.3, Dialogue

(Maria and Tom are planning to see a movie with Kelly).

瑪麗婭： 今天 晚上 我們 去 看 電影，好 嗎？

湯姆：   甚麼 電影？

瑪麗婭：《超人》。

湯姆：   電影 幾點 開始？

瑪麗婭：六點。

湯姆：　在 哪兒？

瑪麗婭：勝利 電影院。

湯姆：　好，我們 差 十分 六點 在 電影院 見。

Unit 3.4, Dialogue

(Anthony and Maria are talking about their classes.)

安東尼：今天 第一節 你 上 甚麼 課？

瑪麗婭：今天 是 星期三 嗎？

安東尼：對。

瑪麗婭：我 看 看……今天 第一節 我 上 漢語，然後 上 數學、
　　　　歷史、英語、化學 和 體育。你 呢？

安東尼：今天 我 很 忙。有 數學、英語、體育、法語、中國
　　　　歷史、經濟學 和 電腦。

Unit 3.4, Text

(Maria is emailing her Chinese pen pal about her course schedule.)

小明：

　　你 好！

　　這個 學期 我 上 六門 課：漢語、英語、數學、物理、
化學、體育。每 門 課 都 有 作業，所以 我 很 忙。我 喜歡
英語 課 和 漢語 課，不 太 喜歡 物理課，因為 物理 課 的
作業 太 多 了。

　　你 這個 學期 上 幾 門 課？忙 不 忙？你 喜歡 哪門 課？

瑪麗婭

Unit 3.5, Dialogue 1

(Maria and Tom are chatting as they leave Friday's class.)

湯姆：　明天 你 要 做 甚麼？

瑪麗婭：明天 上午 我 學 鋼琴。下午 去 看 張爺爺 和 張 奶奶。

湯姆：　張爺爺 張奶奶 是 誰？

瑪麗婭：他們 是 我們 家 的 好 朋友。

湯姆：　他們 住 在 哪兒？

瑪麗婭：他們 也 住 在 上海。明天 你 做 甚麼？

湯姆：　我 上午 和 爸爸 去 打 網球，下午 去 學 武術。

瑪麗婭：周末 快樂。

湯姆：　周末 快樂。

Unit 3.5, Dialogue 2

(Maria makes a phone call to Kelly on Saturday evening).

瑪麗婭：喂，請問 凱麗 在 嗎？

凱麗：　我 就是。

瑪麗婭：你 好，凱麗。我 是 瑪麗婭。今天 你 有事 嗎？

凱麗：　今天 我 和 爸爸 媽媽 去 吃飯。

瑪麗婭：你 爸爸 媽媽 在 上海 嗎？

凱麗：　對，他們 明天 下午 回 杭州。

瑪麗婭：那 你 明天 呢？

凱麗：　明天 上午 我們 去 教堂。下午 沒有 事。

瑪麗婭：明天 下午 我們 去 公園，好 嗎？

凱麗：　好。幾點 去？

瑪麗婭：明天 下午 一點半。

凱麗：　我們 在 哪兒 見？

瑪麗婭：在 人民 公園 門口，好 嗎？

凱麗：　好，明天 下午 見。

Unit 3.6, Text

我的 妹妹 妮娜 每天 上午 八點 去 幼兒園，下午 三點半 回家。妮娜 在 幼兒園 上 英語課、數學課、音樂課、美術課 和 體育課。她 最 喜歡 體育課。妮娜 在 幼兒園 有 很多 朋友。這個 星期六 妮娜 要 參加 她 朋友 的 生日 晚會。晚會 下午 一點半 開始。妮娜 的 朋友 住 在 杭州，所以 妮娜 和 我 媽媽 上午 要 離開 上海 去 杭州★。

Unit 3.6, Dialogue

大衛：　湯姆，這個 週末 你 要 做 什麼？

湯姆：　星期六 上午 我 和 爸爸 打 網球，下午 去 學 武術。
　　　　星期天 我 要 做 數學 作業 和 歷史 作業。你 呢？

大衛：　我 星期六 和 朋友 去 公園。星期天 上午 去 教堂，
　　　　下午 在 家 看 球，晚上 做 作業。

湯姆：　看 什麼 球?

大衛：　棒球。

湯姆：　你 喜歡 打 棒球 嗎?

大衛：　非常 喜歡。你 呢?

湯姆：　馬馬虎虎。

Unit 4.1, Dialogue 1

(At the school library.)

瑪麗婭：湯姆，那個 藍書包 是 你 的 嗎?

湯姆：　不是。我 的 書包 是 綠色 的，不 是 藍色 的。

瑪麗婭：這個 書包 不 是 你 的，也 不 是 我 的，是 誰 的 呢?

湯姆：　是 不 是 大衛 的? 大衛 有 一個 藍書包。

瑪麗婭：大衛 的 藍書包 是 舊 的，可是 這個 是 新 的。

湯姆：　書包 上 有 沒有 名字?

瑪麗婭：讓 我 看看。有 名字。八弟。

湯姆：　八弟? 那 是 大衛 的 狗。狗 沒有 書包 吧?

Unit 4.1, Dialogue 2

(David runs into the library.)

大衛：　啊，我 的 書包 在 這兒。

湯姆：　這 是 你 的 還是 八弟 的 書包?

大衛：　原來 是 八弟 的，現在 是 我 的。我 的 書包 太 舊 了，
　　　　所以 我 用 八弟 的 書包。

瑪麗婭：狗 也 有 書包 嗎?

大衛：　對。放 狗 的 玩具。

Unit 4.2, Dialogue 1

(Nina watches Maria putting things into her school bag.)

妮娜：　　明天 你 帶 幾 本 課本 去 學校?

瑪麗婭：五 本。你 看，有 數學、漢語、英語、歷史、和 化學。

妮娜：　　你 帶 本子 嗎?

瑪麗婭：帶。我 帶 兩 本 練習本。

妮娜：　你每天帶那麼多書和本子去學校嗎？

瑪麗婭：對。你呢？

妮娜：　我帶一本英語書，一本練習本和一盒蠟筆。

Unit 4.2, Dialogue 2

(After class.)

湯姆：　凱麗，借我一支筆用用，好嗎？

凱麗：　好，你要甚麼顏色的？

湯姆：　紅的。你有嗎？

凱麗：　對不起，我只有藍的和黑的。

湯姆：　誰有紅的？

瑪麗婭：丁老師有。

Unit 4.3, Dialogue 1

(Maria and Kelly are at a stationery store).

瑪麗婭：你要買甚麼？

凱麗：　我要買練習本。

瑪麗婭：練習本在那兒。我們去那兒看看。

凱麗：　這種練習本很好，可是我不喜歡黃的。

瑪麗婭：你喜歡？這兒有綠的、白的、紫的和藍的。

凱麗：　紫色很好看，我買一本紫的。

瑪麗婭：我們去看看筆。我要買鉛筆。

凱麗：　你看，這支圓珠筆是紫的。我買一支。

瑪麗婭：你是不是很喜歡紫色？

凱麗：　是的。

瑪麗婭：這兒有紫色的橡皮和紫色的尺子。你要嗎？

凱麗：　好，我再買一塊紫色的橡皮和一把紫色的尺子。

Unit 4.3, Dialogue 2

瑪麗婭：我們去那兒看看，我要買一個文件夾。

凱麗：　這個文件夾很好看。

瑪麗婭：可是太大了，我要一個小的。

凱麗：　這兒有小的。

瑪麗婭：好，我買一個。你看，這兒有 MP3 播放器。你有 MP3 播放器 嗎？

凱麗：　我有一個。你呢？

瑪麗婭：我 沒有。

Unit 4.4, Dialogue 1

(At the computer lab.)

大衛：　你有漢英 詞典 嗎？

湯姆：　沒有。可是 網上有。你為甚麼不用網上的 詞典？

大衛：　在哪個 網站？

湯姆：　在 http://www.tigernt.com。網上 詞典 很 容易用。

大衛：　謝謝。聽說 現在 網上還有 許多書，非常 方便。

湯姆：　對，我 常常用 網上 詞典，因為我 喜歡上 網 看書。

大衛：　你喜歡看甚麼書？

湯姆：　我最喜歡看 歷史 書。

大衛：　我有一張 光盤。這張 光盤上有很多 歷史書。我 明天給你。

湯姆：　太好了！你的光盤上有世界 歷史書嗎？

大衛：　有世界 歷史，也有中國 歷史、美國 歷史、英國 歷史，還有 電腦 歷史、電影 歷史、電視 歷史。我最 喜歡看 電腦 歷史。

Unit 4.4, Dialogue 2

凱麗：　這是你的 MP3 嗎？這麼小。

瑪麗婭：不是。這是優盤。我用優盤存文件。

凱麗：　我原來用 磁盤存文件，現在用 MP3。

瑪麗婭：你喜歡你的 MP3 嗎？

凱麗：　很喜歡。我用 MP3 聽音樂，也用 MP3 存電腦文件。

Unit 4.5, Dialogue 1

大衛：　星期六我們去人民 公園，好嗎？

瑪麗婭：好。我們去打球，好嗎？

湯姆：　　好啊。你們 有 足球 嗎？

凱麗：　　我們 去 打 籃球 吧！我 有 籃球。

瑪麗婭：好。打 球 以後，我們 去 溜 旱冰，怎么樣？你們 喜歡 溜 旱冰 嗎？

凱麗：　　很 喜歡。明天 我 帶 旱冰 鞋。

湯姆：　　我 也 帶 一 雙。

大衛：　　我 喜歡 玩 滑板。我 帶 我 的 滑板。

湯姆：　　太 好 了，打 籃球 以後，大衛 玩 滑板，我們 三個 溜 旱冰。

Unit 4.5, Dialogue 2

媽媽：　　明天 我們 去 公園 野餐，好 嗎？

杰米：　　太 好 了。我們 要 帶 甚麼？

爸爸：　　午飯。

媽媽：　　還要 帶 四 個 杯子、四 個 盤子、四 把 刀、叉 和 一些 紙巾。

爸爸：　　我們 是 不 是 再 帶 一 個 足球？野餐 以前，我們 踢 足球。

湯姆：　　好。我 和 杰米 一 隊，爸爸 媽媽 一 隊。

杰米：　　我們 帶 "老虎" 去 嗎？

湯姆：　　帶。

杰米：　　"老虎" 也 和 我們 一 隊。

Unit 4.6, Dialogue

瑪麗婭：你 每天 上網 嗎？

湯姆：　　對。

瑪麗婭：在 學校 還是 在 家？

湯姆：　　有時候 在 學校，有時候 在 家。

瑪麗婭：你 上網 做 甚麼？

湯姆：　　看 email，聽 音樂，用 網上 詞典，玩 電腦 游戲。

瑪麗婭：你們 家 用 電話 上網 嗎？

湯姆：　不。我爸爸是電腦工程師,有時候要上網。因為用電話上網不方便,所以他用寬帶。你們家呢?

瑪麗婭：我們也用寬帶。爸爸、媽媽、安東尼和我都上網,用電話上網太不方便了。

Unit 4.6, Text

瑪麗婭帶妮娜去買蠟筆。蠟筆有大盒和小盒的。小盒的蠟筆有八色、十六色、和二十四色,大盒的蠟筆有九十六色。妮娜喜歡大盒的,可是帶大盒的蠟筆去幼兒園不方便,所以瑪麗婭給妮娜買了一盒大的,一盒小的。大的在家用,小的去幼兒園用。妮娜還要買一個鉛筆盒,放她的鉛筆、圓珠筆、橡皮和尺子。

Unit 5.1, Dialogue 1

(大家在瑪麗婭家。)

安東尼：今天晚上我想去看中國電影,你們想去嗎?

湯姆：　甚麼電影?

安東尼：《美麗上海》。

湯姆：　好,我們現在去嗎?

安東尼：不,晚上去。

妮娜：　我也要去。

安東尼：不能帶你去。

妮娜：　為甚麼?

安東尼：因為你是幼兒園的,不能看這個電影。再說,電影八點開始,可是你每天八點半睡覺。

妮娜：　瑪麗婭,今天晚上你可以帶我去看電影嗎?

瑪麗婭：今天晚上我沒空兒,因為我要做作業,明天我可以帶你去看電影。

妮娜：　我們去看《木蘭》,好嗎?

瑪麗婭：好。

Unit 5.1, Dialogue 2

(安東尼去看電影以前，問爸爸要錢。)

安東尼：爸爸，您能給我一點兒錢嗎？今天晚上我要去看電影。

爸爸：　好吧。

安東尼：謝謝爸爸。爸爸，再見。

爸爸：　電影八點開始，現在才六點，你要去哪兒？

安東尼：我和湯姆先去書店，再去電影院。

爸爸：　你幾點回家？

安東尼：十點半。

爸爸：　太晚了吧？

安東尼：《美麗上海》要看兩個小時。

爸爸：　好吧，早去早回。

安東尼：爸爸，再見。

Unit 5.2 , Dialogue 1

（湯姆給瑪麗婭打電話。）

湯姆：　瑪麗婭，你在看電視嗎？法國隊和美國隊正在比賽呢。

瑪麗婭：沒有，我在下載電腦游戲呢。

湯姆：　哪個游戲？

瑪麗婭：Super Mario. 你在看球賽嗎？

湯姆：　對，我也一邊看球，一邊下載音樂呢。

瑪麗婭：甚麼音樂？

湯姆：　U2 的。

瑪麗婭：你為甚麼不買他們的 CD 呢？

湯姆：　CD 上的歌，我有的喜歡，有的不喜歡。在網上，我可以只下載我喜歡的。

瑪麗婭：你去哪個網站下載？

湯姆：　我去音樂網站。

Unit 5.2, Dialogue 2

（下課以後，瑪麗婭和凱麗在說話。）

瑪麗婭：這個星期五晚上學校有鋼琴比賽。

凱麗：　是我們學校學生的鋼琴比賽嗎?

瑪麗婭：不是。是上海幼兒園學生的鋼琴比賽。我妹妹妮娜
　　　　要來參加。

凱麗：　妮娜會彈鋼琴嗎?

瑪麗婭：她正在學習彈鋼琴,會彈一點兒。她的鋼琴老師
　　　　讓她來參加比賽。

凱麗：　你也會彈鋼琴嗎?

瑪麗婭：會。我還會拉小提琴。你呢?

凱麗：　我會彈豎琴。我家的人都很喜歡音樂。我媽媽
　　　　會彈鋼琴,我爸爸會拉大提琴,我姐姐會彈
　　　　吉他。

Unit 5.3, Dialogue 1

（瑪麗婭給湯姆打電話。）

瑪麗婭：喂,湯姆在嗎?

湯姆：　我就是湯姆。

瑪麗婭：你好,湯姆,我是瑪麗婭。我在做數學作業,
　　　　九十八頁上有一個問題我不懂。想問問你。
　　　　你也在做數學作業嗎?

湯姆：　沒有。我在玩電腦游戲呢。

瑪麗婭：甚麼? 你不知道明天有數學考試嗎?

湯姆：　知道,我先玩一會兒,再做作業。

瑪麗婭：你父母讓你玩兒電腦游戲嗎?

湯姆：　每天我可以玩一個小時。

瑪麗婭：那你先玩兒吧,我等一會兒再給你打電話。

Unit 5.3, Dialogue 2

（五點半,湯姆的媽媽回來了。）

媽媽：　湯姆,你在做甚麼?

湯姆：　我在玩電腦游戲。

媽媽： 你應該少玩兒電腦游戲。每天你最多可以玩兒一個
小時。杰米呢？他在做甚麼？

湯姆： 他正在看卡通呢。

媽媽： 他作業做了嗎？

湯姆： 哎呦，您的寶貝杰米每天回了家就做作業。

媽媽： 你應該學習杰米。

湯姆： 應該，應該！我吃了晚飯就做。

媽媽： 今天晚上你想吃甚麼？

湯姆： 我們可以吃餃子嗎？

媽媽： 可以，家里有一些冰餃子，等你爸爸回來了我們
就下餃子吃。

Unit 5.4, Dialogue 1

（瑪麗婭一家周末要去南京旅行。）

妮娜： 瑪麗婭，我們星期六去南京，你帶甚麼？

瑪麗婭：我要帶漢語書。我們星期一有漢語考試，我坐車
的時候，可以看書。

妮娜： 我要帶熊貓和咪咪。你看書的時候，我可以和它
們玩。

瑪麗婭：你可以帶熊貓，不能帶咪咪。咪咪上了車就不高
興。它不喜歡坐車。

妮娜： 為甚麼狗喜歡坐車，貓不喜歡呢？

瑪麗婭：我也不知道，你可以問一問咪咪，它為甚麼不喜歡
坐車。

妮娜： 可是咪咪不會說話。它只會說："咪咪。"

Unit 5.4, Dialogue 2

（在去南京的車上。瑪麗婭的父母坐在前邊，三個孩子坐在後
邊。）

安東尼：媽媽，我們能不能聽音樂？

媽媽： 好啊。你們要聽古典音樂還是流行音樂？

安東尼：我喜歡流行音樂。

瑪麗婭：我也是。

媽媽：　好吧，我們聽流行音樂。

妮娜：　媽媽，我要喝水。

瑪麗婭：這兒有水，你喝吧。

媽媽：　我們可以在前邊停一停嗎？那兒的風景很美，我們可以看一看風景。

瑪麗婭：我餓了。我們去哪兒吃午飯？

爸爸：　你們想吃中餐還是西餐？

瑪麗婭：我想吃中餐。

安東尼：我隨便。

妮娜：　媽媽，我要去廁所。

媽媽：　你可以等一等嗎？

妮娜：　我可以等五分鐘。

安東尼：爸爸，你看，前邊有漢堡王，我們可以在那兒停車。妮娜可以去廁所。

Unit 5.5, Dialogue 1

（下課的時候，瑪麗婭和湯姆在談電視節目。）

瑪麗婭：你喜歡看哪些電視節目？

湯姆：　我喜歡看球，看電影，還喜歡看MTV的音樂節目。你呢？

瑪麗婭：我喜歡看電視劇。也喜歡看新聞，可是我最喜歡看中央電視臺的文藝節目。

湯姆：　你喜歡看旅游節目嗎？

瑪麗婭：非常喜歡。可是安東尼不喜歡。我一看旅游節目，他就喊著要看體育節目。他一喊著要看體育節目，妮娜就說要看卡通片。我看，我們最好一人有一臺電視機。

湯姆：　對。我不喜歡我父母看的電視節目。我媽媽常常看英語節目。我爸爸每天看經濟新聞。最好我有自己的電視機。

Unit 5.5, Dialogue 2

（湯姆在給爺爺打電話。）

湯姆： 爺爺，您好。我是湯姆。

爺爺： 啊，湯姆，你們都好嗎?

湯姆： 我們都很好。爺爺，您和奶奶在做甚麼呢?

爺爺： 我在看報，奶奶在看第五頻道的電視劇。

湯姆： 爺爺，您不喜歡看奶奶的電視劇嗎?

爺爺： 哈哈．．．我喜歡看電視新聞。有時候，看一些老電影。你們那兒也有許多電視節目吧?

湯姆： 對，我們家訂有線電視，可以收到五十多個頻道。

爺爺： 那麼多?

湯姆： 是啊，有新聞頻道、電影頻道、體育頻道，還有英語頻道。

爺爺： 是嗎? 你每天看電視嗎?

湯姆： 每天看，可是看的時間不長。媽媽說，我每天最多能看一個小時。她讓我少看電視，多看書，多運動。

爺爺： 對。你應該多看書，只看電視不看書會笨。你也應該多運動，只看電視不運動會胖。

湯姆： 爺爺，爸爸要和你說話。爺爺，再見。

爺爺： 再見。

Unit 5.6, Text 1

凱麗家的人都非常喜歡音樂。凱麗的爸爸會拉大提琴，她媽媽會彈鋼琴，她姐姐會彈吉他，凱麗會彈豎琴。有時候，他們在一起練習。有的朋友說，凱麗家可以開家庭音樂會。可是凱麗說：“我們不能開，因為我和爸爸媽媽想開古典音樂會，可是姐姐要開流行音樂會。”

　　凱麗的姐姐說：“古典音樂和流行音樂都很好聽。我們可以開一個有古典音樂，也有流行音樂的音樂會。你們可以表演古典音樂，我可以一邊彈吉他一邊唱歌。”

今年 春節 凱麗 家 要 開 一 個 家庭 音樂會。很 多 朋友 會 來 參加。一些 中國 朋友 也 要 來。凱麗 的 姐姐 正在 學 唱 中國 歌 呢。凱麗 正在 練習 彈 中國 音樂。

Unit 5.6, Text 2

大衛 給 湯姆 打 電話 的 時候，湯姆 正在 做 作業。大衛 最近 下 載 了 一 個 電腦 游戲，可是 那個 游戲 有 一些 病毒，那些 病毒 常常 讓 大衛 的 電腦 不能 運行。大衛 想，湯姆 也 常常 下載 音 樂 和 游戲，可以 問 問 他，哪些 游戲 不 應該 下載。湯姆 告訴 大衛，他 應該 去 一 個 網站 下載 去 病毒 的 軟件。那個 軟件 非 常 有用。

湯姆 和 大衛 都 很 喜歡 玩 電腦 游戲，可是 不能 每天 玩。 他們 的 父母 都 讓 他們 多 學習，少 玩 電腦。大衛 告訴 湯姆： "以後，我 要 做 電腦 游戲 工程師，這樣 每天 可以 玩 電腦 游戲。"

湯姆 說："你 做 了 電腦 游戲 工程師，就 要 每天 寫 游戲 軟件，所以 還是 不能 每天 玩 游戲。"

Unit 6.1, Text

請 看 中國 地圖。這 是 北京。北京 是 中國 的 首都，在 中國 的 北部。中國 的 北部 還 有 一 個 大 城市，叫 天津。那 是 上海。 上海 是 中國 最 大 的 城市，在 中國 的 東部。我們 再 來 看一看 中國 的 西部 和 南部。中國 的 西部 有 一 個 很 古老 的 城市，叫 西安。這 是 廣州，在 中國 的 南部。那 是 重慶。重慶 在 中國 的 中部。許多 人 住 在 這些 大 城市 里。

Unit 6.1, Dialogue

(Kelly and David are talking about their weekend plans.)

大衛： 凱麗，這個 周末 你 要 做 甚麼？

凱麗： 我 要 回 杭州 看 父母。你 回家 嗎？

大衛： 我 不 回家。我 家 住 在 香港。太 遠 了。有 長 周末 的 時候，我 再 回家。

凱麗： 你 想 去 杭州 嗎？杭州 在 上海 的 南邊，坐 火車 兩 個 小時，不 太 遠。你 可以 去 我 家 過 周末。

大衛： 真的嗎？不好意思打擾你父母。

凱麗： 不會的。我父母一定會很歡迎你去玩兒。

大衛： 那太好了！聽說杭州很美麗，是嗎？

凱麗： 對。杭州有一個湖，叫西湖。西湖很大。西湖的旁邊有許多小公園，風景非常美麗。我們可以去西湖走走看看。

大衛： 太好了。謝謝你請我去你家過周末。我們星期五還是星期六去？

凱麗： 我們坐星期五下午五點的火車去，好嗎？

大衛： 好。

Unit 6.2, Dialogue 1

(Tom is talking to his grandfather over the phone.)

湯姆： 爺爺，您好！我是湯姆。

爺爺： 湯姆，你好嗎？

湯姆： 我很好。

爺爺： 學習忙不忙？

湯姆： 學習很忙。我還參加了學校的網球隊，星期一和星期三下午要訓練。

爺爺： 你們的學校在哪兒？

湯姆： 在上海的西邊。

爺爺： 離你們家遠嗎？

湯姆： 不遠。我每天走路去學校。

爺爺： 走路好。走路也是一種運動。我每天走路去公園。

Unit 6.2, Dialogue 2

(Tom is telling his grandfather about his school.)

爺爺： 你們的學校大嗎？

湯姆： 不大不小。學校有兩個教學樓，一個圖書館、還有餐廳、籃球場甚麼的。

爺爺： 你的教室在哪個教學樓？

湯姆： 我的教室在第一教學樓。

爺爺： 學校 有 網球場 嗎?

湯姆： 有。網球場 在 教學樓 右邊。教學樓 前邊 是 籃球場，
左邊 是 圖書館。

爺爺： 學生 餐廳 在 哪兒?

湯姆： 學生 餐廳 在 教學樓 後邊。

爺爺： 你 每天 在 學校 餐廳 吃 午飯 嗎?

湯姆： 有時候 在 學校 餐廳 吃，有時候 在 學校 外邊 吃。

Unit 6.3, Dialogue 1

(Maria is in Hangzhou for the weekend. She is visiting Kelly's home.)

瑪麗婭： 凱麗，你 家 的 客廳 真 漂亮! 。你們 有 幾 間 臥室?

凱麗： 三 間。來，我 帶 你 參觀 參觀 吧。這 是 客廳。這 是
我們 的 廚房 和 飯廳。飯廳 旁邊 是 我 父母 的 書房。
客廳 的 左邊 是 我 父母 的 臥室，里邊 有 一 個 衛生
間。我 和 姐姐 的 臥室 在 過道 的 這邊。我們 倆 的 臥
室 中間 也 有 一 個 衛生間。

瑪麗婭： 哇噻，你 家 的 房子 真 大!

凱麗： 是 啊。走，我們 去 我 的 房間 吧。

瑪麗婭： 哎呦，你 的 房間 也 夠 大 的。

凱麗： 我 姐姐 的 房間 更 大。她 的 房間 就 在 對面。你 想 去
書房 看看 嗎?

瑪麗婭： 好啊! 你們 家 的 書房 里 有 這么 多 書! 還有 兩臺
電腦 呢。

凱麗： 這臺 電腦 是 爸爸 的，那臺 是 媽媽、姐姐 和 我 的。

瑪麗婭： 你 不用 你 爸爸 的 電腦 嗎?

凱麗： 不用。他 的 電腦 太 慢 了。

Unit 6.3, Dialogue 2

(David is visiting Tom's home.)

大衛： 這 是 你 的 房間 嗎?

湯姆： 不，這 是 我 弟弟 的 房間。我 的 房間 在 對面。

大衛： 你 的 房間 很 亮。

湯姆： 謝謝。以前，這是我媽媽的書房，當時我和我弟弟合住一間臥室。現在這是我自己的臥室。現在我媽媽和我爸爸用一間書房，所以我可以自己住在這兒。

大衛： 你一定喜歡有自己的房間吧？

湯姆： 對。因為我喜歡整齊。可是弟弟很亂。

Unit 6.4, Dialogue 1

(Maria is preparing for the HSK, a Chinese proficiency test. She wants to know where she can get the test preparation materials).

瑪麗婭： 湯姆，你知道在哪兒買對外漢語教科書嗎？

湯姆： 我想，你可以去外文書店或者東風書店。

瑪麗婭： 東風書店在哪兒？

湯姆： 在中山路。

瑪麗婭： 在中山路甚麼地方？

湯姆： 在一個銀行的旁邊。

瑪麗婭： 哪個銀行？

湯姆： 我忘了銀行的名字。東風書店的旁邊和對面有許多飯店。

瑪麗婭： 謝謝，我周末去東風書店看看。

Unit 6.4, Dialogue 2

(Tom is showing some photos to his mother.)

湯姆： 媽媽，您看，這是我和朋友們的照片。

媽媽： 真不錯！這個書店真漂亮。

湯姆： 是啊。這就是我常常去的東風書店。

媽媽： 哦。你左邊是誰？

湯姆： 我左邊是馬克，右邊是琳達。

媽媽： 琳達真漂亮！琳達後邊的是誰？

湯姆： 那是瑪麗婭和她哥哥安東尼。我前邊的小孩兒是瑪麗婭的妹妹妮娜。

Unit 6.5, Dialogue 1

瑪麗婭：星期五晚上七點在我家開晚會，你想來嗎？
凱麗：謝謝，我一定去。還有誰來參加晚會？
瑪麗婭：大衛和湯姆。
凱麗：你家在哪兒？
瑪麗婭：老北街八八七號。
凱麗：老北街是不是有一些商店？
瑪麗婭：對。我家對面有銀行、飯店、咖啡館。我家後邊有一個小公園。
凱麗：我想我有你的電話號碼。你的電話是不是六三五一一二三八？
瑪麗婭：是的，有問題給我打電話。
凱麗：好，再見。
瑪麗婭：再見。

Unit 6.5, Dialogue 2

(Kelly and Tom arrive at Maria's party.)

瑪麗婭：歡迎，歡迎！請進。
湯姆：謝謝！
瑪麗婭：請坐吧。你們要喝甚麼？
凱麗：可口可樂。
湯姆：請給我一杯冰水。
瑪麗婭：好，你們等等。
凱麗：湯姆，暑假你打算去哪兒？
湯姆：我要去北京看爺爺奶奶。你呢？
凱麗：我要回美國過暑假。
湯姆：你在美國打算做甚麼？
凱麗：游游泳，看看書，玩玩電腦。對了，我們還要去加拿大看姥姥。
湯姆：你父母真好，暑假讓你休息休息。我爸爸讓我暑假去學數學、電腦、武術和鋼琴。
凱麗：甚麼？他們不讓你休息嗎？
湯姆：他們說，不去學校上課就是休息。

凱麗：　是嗎？看，大衛來了。

大衛：　你們好。

湯姆：　大衛，暑假你回香港嗎？

大衛：　對，歡迎你們來香港玩。

(Maria brings the drinks to Tom and Kelly.)

瑪麗婭：大衛，你說甚麼？

大衛：　我說，歡迎你們來香港玩。

瑪麗婭：太好了，我一定去。

Unit 6.6, Text 1

(Maria has received an email from her pen pal in China.)

瑪麗婭：

你好！

很高興認識你。我叫小明。我在太原上中學。我們的學校在太原西邊，離我家不遠，我每天走路去學校。我們的學習很忙。我每天上午八點到下午五點都在學校上課。我們的作業很多，每天晚上我做作業。沒有時間看電視，也沒有時間玩電腦。我有時候十點半睡覺，有時候十一點睡覺。

我喜歡打籃球。我家後邊有一個公園，公園裡有一個籃球場。可是星期一到星期五我都沒有時間去運動。周末我有時候去打籃球。我家對面有一個書店，這個書店有一些英語書。我的《哈利波特》是在那兒買的。可是我學習太忙，沒有時間看。你喜歡《哈利波特》嗎？

你的朋友：小明

11月26日

Unit 6.6, Text 2

(Tom's mother is telling Tom about the neighborhood she grew up in.)

我們家住在北京的東邊。我們家旁邊有許多商店。左邊是一個小飯店。那個小飯店叫"天津飯店"，主人是天津人。他做的飯很好吃。每天，有許多人去那兒吃飯。我們家右邊有一個大商店。里邊賣吃的和用的東西。我們家對面有一個小吃店。那兒的小吃非常好吃。每天我去上學以前，都去小吃店買小吃。小吃店的旁邊是一個小書店。下課以後，我和朋友常常去那兒看書。在書店工作的是兩個老太太。她們很喜歡學生去那兒看書。

離我家不遠有一個小公園。每天許多老人去那里運動。公園後邊有一個籃球場。因為我很喜歡打籃球，所以常常去。每天有不少人在籃球場打籃球。在那兒，我認識了一些新朋友，有男的，也有女的；有中學生，也有小學生和大學生。他們家都離公園不遠。周末我們常常打籃球。

生词索引
Vocabulary Index

This list contains vocabulary found in each lesson's New Words and Extend Your Knowledge (EYK) sections. Words from Extend Your Knowledge are shown in color because they are supplementary and not required for students to memorize. For proper nouns, see the Proper Nouns Index.

Simplified	Traditional	Pinyin	English	Lesson
A				
啊		a	*a mood particle*	4.5
唉		āi	hey	1.3
B				
吧		ba	*a modal particle*	2.2
八		bā	eight	1.6
八月		bāyuè	August	3.1 EYK
把		bǎ	*a measure word for a handful*	4.3
爸爸		bàba	dad, father	2.1
白(色)		bái(sè)	white (color)	4.3
班		bān	class (a group of students meeting regularly in a course)	1.3
版主		bǎnzhǔ	webmaster	4.4 EYK
办公楼	辦公樓	bàngōnglóu	office building	6.2 EYK
半		bàn	half	3.2
半夜		bànyè	midnight	3.3 EYK
棒球		bàngqiú	baseball	3.6
报		bào	newspaper	5.5

Simplified	Traditional	Pinyin	English	Lesson
杯		bēi	*a measure word for cups and glasses*	6.5
杯子		bēizi	cup	4.5
北部		běibù	north, northern part	6.1
本		běn	*a measure word for books, notebooks*	4.2
本子		běnzi	notebook	4.2
比赛	比賽	bǐsài	(sports) match, competition	5.2
笔	筆	bǐ	pen	4.2
壁橱	壁櫥	bìchú	closet	6.3 EYK
表演		biǎoyǎn	perform, performance	5.6
冰		bīng	frozen, ice	5.3
病毒		bìngdú	virus	5.6
不		bù	no, not	1.4
不好意思		bùhǎoyìsī	feel ill at ease, feel indebted	6.1
不客气		bù kèqi	don't be polite, you are welcome	1.5

C

Simplified	Traditional	Pinyin	English	Lesson
才		cái	only	5.1
参观	參觀	cānguān	visit (a place)	6.3
参加	參加	cānjiā	attend, participate	3.6
餐厅	餐廳	cāntīng	restaurant, cafeteria	6.2
仓鼠	倉鼠	cāngshǔ	hamster	2.3 EYK
操场	操場	cāochǎng	exercise field; playground	6.2 EYK
厕所	廁所	cèsuǒ	bathroom, washroom, toilet	5.4, 6.3 EYK
叉		chā	fork	4.5
差		chà	lack, short of	3.2
长	長	cháng	long	6.1
常常		chángcháng	often	4.4

Simplified	Traditional	Pinyin	English	Lesson
唱		chàng	sing	5.6
车	車	chē	vehicle	5.4
车库	車庫	chēkù	garage	6.3 EYK
橙(色)		chéng(sè)	orange	4.1 EYK
城市		chéngshì	city	6.1
吃		chī	eat	3.3
尺(子)		chǐ(zi)	ruler	4.3
宠物	寵物	chǒngwù	pets	2.4
初中		chūzhōng	middle school	3.4 EYK
厨房	廚房	chúfáng	kitchen	6.3
储藏室	儲藏室	chǔcángshì	storage room	6.3 EYK
春节	春節	chūnjié	Spring Festival	5.6
词典	詞典	cídiǎn	dictionary	4.4
磁盘	磁盤	cípán	floppy diskette	4.4
聪明	聰明	cōngmíng	intelligent, clever	2.3
存		cún	store, save	4.4

D

Simplified	Traditional	Pinyin	English	Lesson
打		dǎ	play	3.2
打的		dǎ dī	take a cab (colloquial)	6.1 EYK
打电话	打電話	dǎ diànhuà	make a phone call	6.5
打球		dǎqiú	play ball	4.5
打扰	打擾	dǎrǎo	disturb	6.1
打算		dǎsuàn	plan	6.5
大		dà	big	4.3
大家		dàjiā	everybody, everyone	1.4
大门	大門	dàmén	main entrance	6.2 EYK
大沙发	大沙發	dà shāfā	couch	6.4 EYK
大提琴		dàtíqín	cello	5.2
大学	大學	dàxué	university, college	3.4 EYK
大学生	大學生	dàxuésheng	university, college student	2.6

Simplified	Traditional	Pinyin	English	Lesson
带		dài	take, take along	4.2
单元	單元	dānyuán	apartment	2.4 EYK
当时	當時	dāngshí	at that time, back then	6.3
刀		dāo	knife	4.5
到		dào	to, arrive	6.6
的		de	*possessive particle*	1.3
等		děng	wait	5.4; 6.5
地方		dìfāng	place	2.4
地图	地圖	dìtú	map	6.1
地下室		dìxiàshì	basement	6.3 EYK
地址		dìzhǐ	address	2.4
弟弟		dìdi	younger brother	2.1
第		dì	*prefix used to form ordinal numbers*	2.2; 5.5
第……节	第……節	dì…jié	number of a class period	3.4
点		diǎn	o'clock	3.2
电话	電話	diànhuà	telephone	1.5
电脑	電腦	diànnǎo	computer	2.2
电脑房	電腦房	diànnǎofáng	computer lab	3.2
电脑室	電腦室	diànnǎoshì	computer lab	6.2 EYK
电视	電視	diànshì	TV	3.3
电视机	電視機	diànshìjī	TV set	5.5
电视剧	電視劇	diànshìjù	TV drama	5.5
电视台	電視臺	diànshìtái	TV station	5.5
电影	電影	diànyǐng	movie	3.1
电影院	電影院	diànyǐngyuàn	cinema	3.3
电子邮件	電子郵件	diànzi yóujiàn	e-mail address	1.5
订	訂	dìng	subscribe	5.5
东部	東部	dōngbù	east, eastern part	6.1
都		dōu	all	2.1
独立房	獨立房	dúlìfáng	single family house	2.4 EYK
队	隊	duì	team	4.5

Simplified	Traditional	Pinyin	English	Lesson
对	對	duì	right, correct	2.2
对不起	對不起	duìbùqǐ	I am sorry	1.5
对面	對面	duìmiàn	opposite, across from	6.3
对外	對外	duìwài	(oriented towards) overseas, abroad	6.4
多		duō	many	4.2
多大		duō dà	how old …	2.2
多少		duōshao	how many/what's the number	1.5

E

饿	餓	è	hungry	5.4
二		èr	two	1.6
二月		èryuè	February	3.1 EYK

F

法官		fǎguān	judge	2.2 EYK
饭店	飯店	fàndiàn	restaurant	6.4
饭厅	飯廳	fàntīng	dining room	6.3
方便		fāngbiàn	convenient	4.4
房地产商	房地產商	fángdìchǎn shāng	real estate agent	2.2 EYK
房间	房間	fángjiān	room	6.3
放		fàng	put, place	4.1
非常		fēicháng	very, extremely	3.6
分		fēn	minute	3.2
分钟	分鐘	fēnzhōng	minute	5.4
粉(色)		fěn(sè)	pink (cosmetic powder color)	4.1 EYK
风景	風景	fēngjǐng	scenery	5.4
服务		fúwù	service	2.6
服务员	服務員	fúwùyuán	waiter/service people	2.2 EYK
父母		fùmǔ	parents	5.3

Simplified	Traditional	Pinyin	English	Lesson
G				
钢琴	鋼琴	gāngqín	piano	3.5
高兴	高興	gāoxìng	glad	1.5
高中		gāozhōng	high school	2.3, 3.4 EYK
哥哥		gēge	elder brother	2.1
歌		gē	song	5.2
个	個	gè	*a measure word for people and some other nouns*	2.1
给	給	gěi	give, to	4.4
跟		gēn	together with, with	2.3
更		gèng	more, even more	6.3
工程师	工程師	gōngchéngshī	engineer	2.2
工作		gōngzuò	work	2.1
公司		gōngsī	company	2.2
公司职员	公司職員	gōngsī zhíyuán	office worker	2.2 EYK
狗		gǒu	dog	2.3
古典		gǔdiǎn	classical	5.4
古老		gǔlǎo	ancient	6.1
光盘	光盤	guāngpán	CD, DVD	4.4
国	國	guó	country	2.5
国际	國際	guójì	international	3.3
过	過	guò	spend, celebrate	6.1
过道	過道	guòdào	hallway, corridor	6.3
H				
还	還	hái	still, also	2.5
喊		hǎn	yell out, shout	5.5
汉语老师	漢語老師	Hànyǔ lǎoshī	Chinese teacher	1.6
好		hǎo	well, good, fine	1.2
号	號	hào	date (in spoken Chinese)	3.1

Simplified	Traditional	Pinyin	English	Lesson
号码	號碼	hàomǎ	(telephone or street) number	1.5
喝		hē	drink	6.5
合住		hézhù	live together, share (a living quarter)	6.3
和		hé	and (only links two nouns or noun phrases)	2.1
盒		hé	box, (can be used as a measure word)	4.2
黑(色)		hēi(sè)	black (color)	4.2
很		hěn	very	1.3
红(色)	紅(色)	hóng	red (color)	4.2
后边	後邊	hòubiān	back, behind	6.2
后天	後天	hòutiān	the day after tomorrow	3.2 EYK
湖		hú	lake	6.1
互联网	互聯網	hùliánwǎng	World Wide Web	4.4 EYK
护士	護士	hùshì	nurse	2.2
花园	花園	huāyuán	garden	6.3 EYK
花园房	花園房	huāyuánfáng	house with a garden	2.4 EYK
滑板		huábǎn	skateboard	4.5
化学	化學	huàxué	chemistry	3.4
话	話	huà	spoken language, words	5.4
欢迎	歡迎	huānyíng	welcome	6.1
黄(色)		huáng(sè)	yellow (color)	4.3
灰(色)		huī(sè)	grey	4.1 EYK
回		huí	go back to	3.2
回来	回來	huílái	return, come back	5.3
会	會	huì	know how to, be likely to	5.2
会员	會員	huìyuán	member	2.6 EYK
会员卡	會員卡	huìyuánkǎ	membership card	2.6 EYK
火车	火車	huǒchē	train	6.1
或者		huòzhě	or	6.4

Simplified	Traditional	Pinyin	English	Lesson
J				
吉他		jítā	guitar	5.2
几	幾	jǐ	how many (for a number less than 10)	2.1
几	幾	jǐ	which (month, week, day, etc.)	3.1
家		jiā	family	1.4
家人		jiārén	family members	2.6
家庭		jiātíng	family	2.4
间	間	jiān	*a measure word for rooms*	6.3
见	見	jiàn	meet	3.3
健身房		jiànshēnfáng	gym	2.5
饺子	餃子	jiǎozi	dumpling	5.3
叫		jiào	given name is, full name is	1.4
叫		jiào	bark, yelp	2.6
教导处	教導處	jiàodǎochù	dean's office	6.2 EYK
教科书	教科書	jiàokēshū	textbook (formal)	6.4
教室		jiàoshì	classroom	6.2
教堂		jiàotáng	church	3.5
教学	教學	jiàoxué	teaching	6.2
街		jiē	street	2.4
节目	節目	jiémù	(entertainment) program	5.5
姐姐		jiějie	elder sister	2.1
借		jiè	borrow, lend	4.2
今年		jīnnián	this year	2.6
今天		jīntiān	today	3.1
金鱼	金魚	jīnyú	goldfish	2.3 EYK
进	進	jìn	enter, come in	6.5
经济分析员	經濟分析員	jīngjì fēnxīyuán	financial analyst	2.2 EYK
经济学	經濟學	jīngjìxué	economics	3.4
经理	經理	jīnglǐ	manager	2.2

Simplified	Traditional	Pinyin	English	Lesson
警察		jǐngchá	police officer	2.2 EYK
九		jiǔ	nine	1.6
九月		jiǔyuè	September	3.1 EYK
久仰		jiǔyǎng	I've been admiring you for a long time.	1.5 EYK
旧	舊	jiù	old	4.1
就		jiù	then, precisely, just	5.3
俱乐部	俱樂部	jū lè bù	club	2.6 EYK

K

Simplified	Traditional	Pinyin	English	Lesson
咖啡馆	咖啡館	kāfēiguǎn	cafe, coffee house	6.5
咖啡桌		kāfēizhuō	coffee table	6.4 EYK
卡通		kǎtōng	cartoon	5.3
卡通片		kǎtōngpiàn	cartoon film	5.5
开	開	kāi	hold (a meeting, party, conference, etc.)	5.6
开始	開始	kāishǐ	start, begin	3.3
看		kàn	watch, look, see	3.1
考试	考試	kǎoshì	test, exam	5.3
可爱	可愛	kě'ài	lovely, cute	2.3
可是		kěshì	but, however	2.5
可以		kěyǐ	may	5.1
刻		kè	quarter (of an hour)	3.2
客户		kèhù	client, customer	2.6
客厅	客廳	kètīng	living room	6.3
课	課	kè	class	3.1
课本	課本	kèběn	textbook	4.2
课程表	課程表	kèchéngbiǎo	course schedule	3.4
块	塊	kuài	a measure word for pieces	4.3
快乐	快樂	kuàilè	happy	3.5
宽带	寬带	kuāndài	broadband	4.6

Simplified	Traditional	Pinyin	English	Lesson
L				
啦		la	*a particle to indicate change of a situation/state*	2.2
拉		lā	play (violin, viola, cello...)	5.2
蜡笔	蠟筆	làbǐ	crayon	4.2
蓝(色)	藍(色)	lán(sè)	blue (color)	4.1
篮球	籃球	lánqiú	basketball	4.5
篮球场	籃球場	lánqiúchǎng	basketball court	6.2
老虎		lǎohǔ	tiger	2.3
姥姥		lǎolao	maternal grandmother	6.5
老师	老師	lǎoshī	teacher	1.2
了		le	*a particle to indicate change of a situation/state*	2.5
离	離	lí	from, off, away	6.2
离开	離開	líkāi	leave	3.6
礼拜二	禮拜二	lǐbàièr	Tuesday	3.1 EYK
礼拜六	禮拜六	lǐbàiliù	Saturday	3.1 EYK
礼拜日	禮拜日	lǐbàirì	Sunday	3.1 EYK
礼拜三	禮拜三	lǐbàisān	Wednesday	3.1 EYK
礼拜四	禮拜四	lǐbàisì	Thursday	3.1 EYK
礼拜天	禮拜天	lǐbàitiān	Sunday	3.1 EYK
礼拜五	禮拜五	lǐbàiwǔ	Friday	3.1 EYK
礼拜一	禮拜一	lǐbàiyī	Monday	3.1 EYK
礼堂	禮堂	lǐtáng	auditorium	6.2 EYK
里边	裡邊	lǐbiān	inside	6.3
历史	歷史	lìshǐ	history	3.4
连体别墅	連體別墅	liántǐ biéshù	townhouse	2.4 EYK
练习	練習	liànxí	practice	5.6
练习本	練習本	liànxíběn	notebook	4.2
两	兩	liǎng	two (of ..., followed by a measure word)	2.1

Simplified	Traditional	Pinyin	English	Lesson
亮		liàng	bright	6.3
凌晨		língchén	after midnight (1–4 a.m.)	3.3 EYK
零		líng	zero	1.6
溜旱冰		liū hànbīng	roller skate	4.5
流行		liúxíng	popular	5.4
六		liù	six	1.6
六月		liùyuè	June	3.1 EYK
楼	樓	lóu	story, building	2.4 EYK, 6.2
路		lù	road	2.4
旅行		lǚxíng	travel	5.4
旅游	旅遊	lǚyóu	travel, tourism	5.5
绿(色)	綠(色)	lǜ(sè)	green (color)	4.1
律师	律師	lǜshī	lawyer	2.2 EYK
乱	亂	luàn	messy, in disorder	6.3

M

Simplified	Traditional	Pinyin	English	Lesson
吗	嗎	ma	*a modal particle used in a question*	1.3
妈妈	媽媽	māma	mom, mother	2.1
马	馬	mǎ	horse	2.3 EYK
马马虎虎		mǎmahǔhu	so-so	3.6
买	買	mǎi	buy	4.3
卖	賣	mài	sell	6.6
慢		màn	slow	6.3
忙		máng	busy	2.2
猫	貓	māo	cat	2.3
没		méi	do not (have)	2.1
没关系	沒關係	méiguānxi	that's alright all right, no problem	1.5
没空儿	沒空兒	méikòngr	do not have free time	5.1

Simplified	Traditional	Pinyin	English	Lesson
每天		měitiān	every day	3.3
美		měi	beautiful	5.4
美丽	美麗	měilì	beautiful	5.1
美术	美術	měishù	fine arts	3.6
妹妹		mèimei	younger sister	2.1
门	門	mén	*a measure word for an academic course*	3.4
门	門	mén	gate/door	2.4 EYK
门口	門口	ménkǒu	gate, entrance	3.5
门厅	門廳	méntīng	entrance	6.3 EYK
咪咪		mīmī	meow	5.4
米(色)		mǐ(sè)	beige (rice color)	4.1 EYK
免费下载	免費下載	miǎnfèi xiàzài	free download	4.4 EYK
名字		míngzi	name	1.4
明天		míngtiān	tomorrow	3.2
MP3播放器		MP sān bōfàngqì	MP3 player	4.3

N

Simplified	Traditional	Pinyin	English	Lesson
那么	那麼	nàme	so	4.2
那儿	那兒	nàr	there	2.6
哪儿	哪兒	nǎr	where	1.4
奶奶		nǎinai	(paternal) grandmother	2.5
南边	南邊	nánbiān	south	6.1
南部		nánbù	south, southern part	6.1
呢		ne	*a modal particle used in a tag question*	1.2
能		néng	have the ability to, can	5.1
你		nǐ	you	1.2
你们	你們	nǐmen	you (plural)	1.3
年		nián	year	3.1
年龄	年齡	niánlíng	age	2.6 EYK

Simplified	Traditional	Pinyin	English	Lesson
鸟	鳥	niǎo	bird	2.3 EYK
您		nín	you (respectful form)	1.2

O

Simplified	Traditional	Pinyin	English	Lesson
哦		ò	oh	3.2

P

Simplified	Traditional	Pinyin	English	Lesson
盘子	盤子	pánzi	plate	4.5
旁边	旁邊	pángbiān	side, next to	6.1
胖		pàng	fat, overweight	5.5
朋友		péngyou	friend	1.3
频道	頻道	píndào	(TV) channel	5.5

Q

Simplified	Traditional	Pinyin	English	Lesson
七		qī	seven	1.6
七月		qīyuè	July	3.1 EYK
骑摩托车	騎摩托車	qí mótuóchē	ride a motorcycle	6.1 EYK
骑脚踏车	騎腳踏車	qí jiǎotàchē	ride a bike (Taiwan)	6.1 EYK
骑自行车	騎自行車	qí zìxíngchē	ride a bike	6.1 EYK
起床		qǐchuáng	get up	3.3
铅笔	鉛筆	qiānbǐ	pencil	4.3
铅笔盒	鉛筆盒	qiānbǐhé	pencil box	4.6
前边	前邊	qiánbiān	front	5.4
前天		qiántiān	the day before yesterday	3.2 EYK
钱	錢	qián	money	5.1
青蛙		qīngwā	frog	2.3 EYK
请问	請問	qǐngwèn	excuse me	1.5
球赛	球賽	qiúsài	ball game	5.2
区	區	qū	district	2.4
去		qù	go	3.1
去		qù	eliminate	5.6

Simplified	Traditional	Pinyin	English	Lesson
R				
然后	然後	ránhòu	afterwards	3.4
让	讓	ràng	let, allow	4.1
人		rén	people, person	2.1
认识	認識	rènshi	know (to recognize)	1.3
日		rì	date (in written Chinese); day	3.1
容易		róngyì	easy	4.4
软件	軟件	ruǎnjiàn	software	5.6
S				
三		sān	three	1.6
三月		sānyuè	March	3.1 EYK
商店		shāngdiàn	shop, store	6.5
商人		shāngrén	businessperson	2.2 EYK
上		shàng	attend (school)	2.3
上		shàng	on	4.1
上个星期	上個星期	shànggè xīngqī	last week	3.2 EYK
上个月	上個月	shànggè yuè	last month	3.2 EYK
上课	上課	shàng kè	have class	3.2
上网	上網	shàng wǎng	go online	4.4
上午		shàngwǔ	morning (8-11a.m.)	3.3, 3.5
少		shǎo	less, few	5.5
蛇		shé	snake	2.3 EYK
谁	誰	shéi, shuí	who, whom	2.5
什么	甚麼	shénme	what	1.4
生日		shēngrì	birthday	3.1
省		shěng	province	6.1 EYK
十		shí	ten	1.6
十二月		shí'èryuè	December	3.1 EYK
十一月		shí'yīyuè	November	3.1 EYK

Simplified	Traditional	Pinyin	English	Lesson
十月		shíyuè	October	3.1 EYK
时候	時候	shíhòu	time	5.4
实验室	實驗室	shíyànshì	laboratory	6.2 EYK
世界		shìjiè	world	4.4
市		shì	city	2.4
事		shì	matters, business	3.5
是		shì	am, are, is (to be)	1.2
室		shì	room, apartment	2.4
收到		shōudào	receive	5.5
手机	手機	shǒujī	cell phone	1.5
首都		shǒudū	capital	6.1
售货员	售貨員	shòuhuòyuán	store clerk	2.2 EYK
书	書	shū	book	4.2
书包	書包	shūbāo	school bag	4.1
书店	書店	shūdiàn	bookstore	6.4
书房	書房	shūfáng	study	6.3
书架	書架	shūjià	book shelf	6.4 EYK
书桌	書桌	shūzhuō	desk	6.4 EYK
暑假		shǔjià	summer vacation	6.5
竖琴	豎琴	shùqín	harp	5.2
数学	數學	shùxué	mathematics	3.4
双	雙	shuāng	*a measure word for a pair*	4.5
水		shuǐ	water	5.4
睡觉	睡覺	shuìjiào	sleep, go to bed	3.3
说	說	shuō	speak, say	5.4
四		sì	four	1.6
四月		sìyuè	April	3.1 EYK
宿舍		sùshè	dormitory	3.2
岁	歲	suì	years old (in age)	2.2
随便	隨便	suíbiàn	anything will do; easy-going	5.4
所以		suǒyǐ	therefore	3.4

Simplified	Traditional	Pinyin	English	Lesson
T				
它		tā	it	2.4
他		tā	he/him	1.3
她		tā	she/her	1.6
台	臺	tái	*a measure word for machines (computers, TVs)*	6.3
台灯	檯燈	táidēng	lamp	6.4 EYK
太好了		tài hǎo le	great	3.1
弹	彈	tán	play (piano, guitar)	5.2
特别行政区	特別行政區	tèbié xíngzhèngqū	special administrative region	6.1 EYK
踢		tī	kick	4.5
体育	體育	tǐyù	physical education	3.4
体育馆	體育館	tǐyùguǎn	gymnasium	6.2 EYK
天		tiān	day	3.3
听	聽	tīng	listen	2.2
听说	聽說	tīngshuō	it is said	4.4
停		tíng	stop	5.4
挺…的		tǐng … de	quite …	1.3
同学	同學	tóngxué	classmate	3.4 EYK
推销员	推銷員	tuīxiāoyuán	salesperson (for products)	2.2 EYK
退休		tuìxiū	retire	2.5
W				
哇噻		wāsai	wow	6.3
外边	外邊	wàibiān	outside	6.2
外文		wàiwén	foreign language	6.4
玩		wán	play	2.3
玩具		wánjù	toy	4.1
晚		wǎn	late	5.1
晚上		wǎnshàng	evening, night	3.3
晚饭	晚飯	wǎnfàn	dinner	3.3 EYK, 5.3

Simplified	Traditional	Pinyin	English	Lesson
晚会	晚會	wǎnhuì	party	3.6
网吧	網吧	wǎngbā	Internet café	4.4 EYK
网球	網球	wǎngqiú	tennis	3.2
网球场	網球場	wǎngqiúchǎng	tennis court	6.2
网上	網上	wǎngshàng	online	4.4
网上聊天	網上聊天	wǎngshàng liáotiān	online chat	4.4 EYK
网上 聊天室	網上 聊天室	wǎngshàng liáotiān shì	Internet chat room	4.4 EYK
网页	網頁	wǎngyè	web page	4.4 EYK
网站	網站	wǎngzhàn	website, web address	4.4
网址	網址	wǎngzhǐ	web address	4.4 EYK
忘		wàng	forget	6.4
卫生间	衛生間	wèishēngjiān	bathroom	6.3
为什么	為甚麼	wèishénme	why	4.4
喂		wèi	hello (in a phone call)	3.5
文件		wénjiàn	file	4.4
文件夹	文件夾	wénjiànjiā	file folder	4.3
文具		wénjù	stationery	4.3
文艺	文藝	wényì	arts and culture	5.5
问	問	wèn	ask	3.1
问题	問題	wèntí	question	6.5
我		wǒ	I, me	1.2
我们	我們	wǒmen	we, us	1.3
卧室	臥室	wòshì	bedroom	6.3
乌龟	烏龜	wūguī	turtle	2.3 EYK
五		wǔ	five	1.6
午饭	午飯	wǔfàn	lunch	3.3
五月		wǔyuè	May	3.1 EYK
武术	武術	wǔshù	martial arts	3.5
物理		wùlǐ	physics	3.4

Simplified	Traditional	Pinyin	English	Lesson
X				
西边	西邊	xībiān	west side	6.2
西部		xībù	west, western part	6.1
西餐		Xīcān	Western food	5.4
蜥蜴		xīyì	lizard	2.3 EYK
洗衣房		xǐyīfáng	laundry room	6.3 EYK
洗澡间	洗澡間	xǐzǎojiān	bathroom	6.3 EYK
喜欢	喜歡	xǐhuān	like	2.2
下饺子		xià jiǎozi	cook dumplings	5.3
下个星期	下個星期	xiàgè xīngqī	next week	3.2 EYK
下个月	下個月	xiàgè yuè	next month	3.2 EYK
下课	下課	xiàkè	get out of class	3.3
下午		xiàwǔ	afternoon (1-5 p.m.)	3.3, 3.5
下载	下載	xiàzǎi	download	5.2
先…再…		xiān...zài...	first...then...	5.1
现在	现在	xiànzài	now, right now	3.2
想		xiǎng	would like to, want, intend	5.1
橡皮		xiàngpí	eraser	4.3
小		xiǎo	young, small	2.3
小吃		xiǎochī	snack food	6.6
小孩儿	小孩兒	xiǎoháir	little kid	6.4
小区	小區	xiǎoqū	enclosed residential area, neighborhood community	2.4
小沙发	小沙發	xiǎo shāfā	armchair	6.4
小时	小時	xiǎoshí	hour	5.1
小提琴		xiǎotíqín	violin	5.2
小学	小學	xiǎoxué	primary school	3.4 EYK
校长办公室	校長辦公室	xiàozhǎng bàngōngshì	principal's office	6.2
鞋		xié	shoe	4.5
谢谢	謝謝	xièxie	thank you, thanks	1.3

Simplified	Traditional	Pinyin	English	Lesson
新		xīn	new	4.1
新闻	新聞	xīnwén	news	5.5
星期二		xīngqīèr	Tuesday	3.1
星期六		xīngqīliù	Saturday	3.1
星期日		xīngqīrì	Sunday	3.1
星期三		xīngqīsān	Wednesday	3.1
星期四		xīngqīsì	Thursday	3.1
星期天		xīngqītiān	Sunday	3.1
星期五		xīngqīwǔ	Friday	3.1
星期一		xīngqīyī	Monday	3.1
姓		xìng	surname, surname is	1.4
姓名		xìng míng	name (of a person)	2.6
幸会	幸會	xìnghuì	pleased to meet you (polite, formal expression)	1.5
兄弟姐妹		xiōngdì jiěmèi	siblings, brothers and sisters	2.3
熊猫	熊貓	xióngmāo	panda	5.4
许多	許多	xǔduō	many	2.3
学期	學期	xuéqī	semester	3.4
学生	學生	xuésheng	student	1.3
学生活动中心	學生活動	xuésheng huódòng zhōngxīn	student activity center	6.2
学生宿舍		xuésheng sùshè	student dorm	6.2
学习	學習	xuéxí	study, learn	1.4
学校	學校	xuéxiào	school	3.3
训练	訓練	xùnliàn	train, training	6.2

Y

研究生院		yánjiùshēng yuàn	graduate school	3.4 EYK
颜色	顏色	yánsè	color	4.2
演员	演員	yǎnyuán	actor	2.2 EYK
羊		yáng	sheep	2.3 EYK

Simplified	Traditional	Pinyin	English	Lesson
阳台	陽台	yángtái	balcony	6.3 EYK
养	養	yǎng	raise, nurture	2.3
		yāo/yī	one	1.6
一				
要		yào	want, plan	3.5
爷爷	爺爺	yéye	(paternal) grandfather	2.5
也		yě	also	1.3
野餐		yěcān	picnic	4.5
夜宵		yèxiāo	late night snack	3.3 EYK
一边…	一邊…	yībiān...	at the same time, while	5.2
一边…	一邊…	yībiān...		
一点	一點	yīdiǎn	a little, some	5.1
一定		yīdìng	definitely	6.1
一会儿	一會兒	yīhuìr	a little while	5.3
一些		yīxiē	some, several	5.6
一月		yīyuè	January	3.1 EYK
医生	醫生	yīshēng	doctor	2.2 EYK
以后	以後	yǐhòu	after	3.3
以前		yǐqián	before	4.5
椅子		yǐzi	chair	6.4 EYK
义工	義工	yìgōng	volunteer	2.5
因特网	因特網	yīntèwǎng	Internet	4.4 EYK
因为	因為	yīnwèi	because	2.5
音乐	音樂	yīnyuè	music	2.2
银行	銀行	yínháng	bank	6.4
应该	應該	yīnggāi	should, ought to	5.3
用		yòng	use	4.1
用功		yònggōng	diligent, hard-working	2.3
优盘	優盤	yōupán	USB flash drive	4.4
游戏	遊戲	yóuxì	game	2.3
游泳池		yóuyǒngchí	swimming pool	6.2 EYK
有		yǒu	have, there is, there are	2.1

Simplified	Traditional	Pinyin	English	Lesson
有的		yǒude	some	5.2
有事		yǒu shì	occupied; have something to do	3.5
有时候	有時候	yǒushíhou	sometimes	2.5
有线电视	有線電視	yǒuxiàn diànshì	cable TV	5.5
有效期		yǒuxiàoqī	valid period	2.6 EYK
右边	右邊	yòubiān	right (side)	6.2
幼儿园	幼兒園	yòu'éryuán	kindergarten	2.3, 3.4 EYK
原来	原來	yuánlái	originally	4.1
圆珠笔	圓珠筆	yuánzhūbǐ	ballpoint pen	4.3
远	遠	yuǎn	far	6.1
院子		yuànzi	yard	6.3 EYK
月		yuè	month	3.1
运动	運動	yùndòng	sports	2.2
运行	運行	yùnxíng	run, operate, operation	5.6
Z				
在		zài	in, at	1.4
再		zài	also, again	4.5
再见	再見	zàijiàn	good bye	1.2
再说	再說	zàishuō	moreover, in addition	5.1
早		zǎo	early	5.1
早饭	早飯	zǎofàn	breakfast	3.3 EYK
早上/早晨		zǎoshàng/zǎochen	morning (before 8 a.m.)	3.3 EYK
怎么	怎麼	zěnme	how come...	5.3
怎么样	怎麼樣	zěnmeyàng	how (is it)?	1.3
张	張	zhāng	*a measure word for flat objects*	4.4
照片		zhàopiàn	photo	6.4
着	著	zhe	*a particle indicating accompanying action*	5.5

Simplified	Traditional	Pinyin	English	Lesson
这	這	zhè	this	1.3
这个星期	這個星期	zhège xīngqī	this week	3.2 EYK
这个月	這個月	zhège yuè	this month	3.2 EYK
这儿	這兒	zhèr	here	4.1
这些	這些	zhèxiē	these	6.1
真		zhēn	really	6.3
真不错	真不錯	zhēn bùcuò	Really nice!	6.4
整齐	整齊	zhěngqí	tidy, in order	6.3
正		zhèng	*an adverb indicating an action in progress*	5.2
只	隻	zhī	*a measure word for certain animals such as dogs and cats*	2.3
支		zhī	*a measure word for pens*	4.2
知道		zhīdào	to know (a fact)	1.5
直辖市	直轄市	zhíxiáshì	municipality	6.1 EYK
只		zhǐ	only	3.1
纸巾	紙巾	zhǐjīn	paper napkin	4.5
至		zhì	until	2.6 EYK
中部		zhōngbù	middle, the central part	6.1
中餐		zhōngcān	Chinese food	5.4
中间	中間	zhōngjiān	middle	6.3
中午		zhōngwǔ	noon	3.3
中学	中學	zhōngxué	secondary school	2.2, 3.4 EYK
中央		zhōngyāng	central	5.5
种	種	zhǒng	type, kind	4.3
周二		zhōu'èr	Tuesday	3.1 EYK
周六		zhōuliù	Saturday	3.1 EYK
周末	週末	zhōumò	weekend	3.5
周日		zhōurì	Sunday	3.1 EYK
周三		zhōusān	Wednesday	3.1 EYK

Simplified	Traditional	Pinyin	English	Lesson
周四		zhōusì	Thursday	3.1 EYK
周五		zhōuwǔ	Friday	3.1 EYK
周一		zhōuyī	Monday	3.1 EYK
住		zhù	live	1.4
主人		zhǔrén	owner	6.6
主人卧室	主人臥室	zhǔrén wòshì	master bedroom	6.3 EYK
祝		zhù	wish	3.3
紫(色)		zǐ(sè)	purple (color)	4.3
自己		zìjǐ	self	6.3
自治区	自治區	zìzhìqū	autonomous region	6.1 EYK
棕(色)		zōng(sè)	brown	4.1 EYK
走路		zǒu lù	walk	6.2
足球		zúqiú	soccer (in the U.S.), football	4.5
最		zuì	most	4.4
昨天		zuótiān	yesterday	3.2 EYK
左边	左邊	zuǒbiān	left (side)	6.2
作业	作業	zuòyè	homework	3.2
坐		zuò	ride, sit	5.4
坐出租汽车	坐出租汽車	zuò chūzū qìchē	travel by taxi	6.1 EYK
坐船		zuòchuán	travel by boat	6.1 EYK
坐电车	坐電車	zuò diànchē	travel by trolley	6.1 EYK
坐地铁	坐地鐵	zuò dìtiě	travel by subway	6.1 EYK
坐飞机	坐飛機	zuò fēijī	travel by plane	6.1 EYK
坐公车	坐公車	zuo gōngchē	travel by bus (Taiwan)	6.1 EYK
坐公共汽车	坐公共汽車	zuò gōnggòng qìchē	travel by bus	6.1 EYK
坐计程车	坐計程車	zuò jìchéng chē	travel by taxi (Taiwan)	6.1 EYK
做		zuò	do, work	2.2

专有名词索引
Proper Nouns Index

This list contains proper nouns from each lesson's New Words and Extend Your Knowledge sections.

Simplified	Traditional	Pinyin	English	Lesson
A				
埃及		Āijí	Egypt	2.5 EYK
澳拜客		Àobàikè	Outback Steak House	5.4 EYK
B				
八弟		Bādì	Buddy	2.4
巴西		Bāxī	Brazil	2.4 EYK
北京		Běijīng	Beijing	2.2
百事可乐	百事可樂	Bǎishǐ Kělè	Pepsi-Cola	5.4 EYK
棒约翰	棒約翰	Bàng Yuēhàn	Papa John's	5.4 EYK
必胜客	必勝客	Bìshèngkè	Pizza Hut	5.4 EYK
C				
超人		Chāo Rén	Superman	3.3
重庆	重慶	Chóngqìng	Chongqing	6.1
D				
大卫	大衛	Dàwèi	David	1.3
黛安		Dài'ān	Diane	1.5
德国	德國	Déguó	Germany	2.5 EYK
德语/德文	德語/德文	Déyǔ/Déwén	German (language)	1.4 EYK

Simplified	Traditional	Pinyin	English	Lesson
丁		Dīng	a Chinese surname	1.2
丁明		Dīng Míng	a person's name	2.6
东风	東風	Dōngfēng	East Wind (name of a bookstore)	6.4

E

俄国	俄國	Éguó	Russia	2.5 EYK
俄语/俄文	俄語/俄文	Éyǔ/Éwén	Russian (language)	1.4 EYK

F

法国	法國	Fǎguó	France	5.2, 2.5 EYK
法语	法語	Fǎyǔ	French (language)	3.4
菲律宾	菲律賓	Fēilùbīn	the Philippines	2.5 EYK

G

格林		Gélín	Green	1.4
广州	廣州	Guǎngzhōu	Guangzhou	6.1

H

哈利 波特		Hālì Bōtè	Harry Potter	6.6
韩国	韓國	Hánguó	Korea	2.5 EYK
韩国人	韓國人	Hánguórén	Korean	2.5
汉堡王	漢堡王	Hànbǎowáng	Burger King	5.4
汉语	漢語	Hànyǔ	Chinese (language)	1.4
杭州		Hángzhōu	Hangzhou (a city near Shanghai)	1.4
黄浦		Huángpǔ	a district in Shanghai	2.4

J

加拿大		Jiānádà	Canada	2.5 EYK, 6.5
杰米	傑米	Jiémǐ	Jimmy	2.1

Simplified	Traditional	Pinyin	English	Lesson
金顺爱	金順愛	Jīn Shùn'ài	a person's name	2.5
旧金山	舊金山	Jiùjīnshān	San Francisco	2.1

K

凯丽	凱麗	Kǎilì	Kelly	1.4
可口可乐	可口可樂	Kěkǒukělè	Coca-Cola	5.4 EYK, 6.5
肯德基		Kěndéjī	Kentucky Fried Chicken	5.4 EYK

L

拉丁语/	拉丁語/	Lādīngyǔ/	Latin	1.4 EYK
拉丁文	拉丁文	Lādīngwén		
琳达	琳達	Líndá	Linda	6.4
罗西尼	羅西尼	Luóxīní	Rossini	1.4

M

马来西亚	馬來西亞	Mǎláixīyà	Malaysia	2.5 EYK
玛丽娅	瑪麗婭	Mǎlìyà	Maria	1.2
麦当劳	麥當勞	Màidāngláo	McDonald's	5.4 EYK
美国	美國	Měiguó	the United States	2.5, 2.5 EYK
美国人	美國人	Měiguórén	American	2.5
墨西哥		Mòxīgē	Mexico	2.5 EYK
木兰	木蘭	Mù Lán	Mu Lan	5.1

N

南京		Nánjīng	Nanjing	5.4
妮娜		Nínà	Nina	2.3
纽约	紐約	Niǔyuē	New York	2.6

Q

七喜		Qīxǐ	Seven-Up	5.4 EYK

Simplified	Traditional	Pinyin	English	Lesson
R				
人民公园	人民公園	Rénmín Gōngyuán	People's Park	3.5
日本		Rìběn	Japan	2.5 EYK
日语/日文	日語	Rìyǔ/Rìwén	Japanese (language)	1.4 EYK
S				
上海		Shànghǎi	Shanghai	1.4
胜利 电影院	勝利 電影院	Shènglì Diànyǐngyuàn	Victory Movie Theater	3.3
斯坦纳	斯坦納	Sītǎnnà	Steiner	1.4
T				
太原		Tàiyuán	Taiyuan	6.6
汤姆	湯姆	Tāngmǔ	Tom	1.2
天津		Tiānjīn	Tianjin	6.1
W				
王		Wáng	a Chinese surname	1.4
X				
西安		Xī'ān	Xi'an	6.1
西班牙语/西班牙文	西班牙語/西班牙文	Xībānyáyǔ/Xībānyáwén	Spanish (language)	1.4; 2.5 EYK
西湖		Xīhú	West Lake	6.1
小丽	小麗	Xiǎolì	a person's name	2.2
香港		Xiānggǎng	Hong Kong	1.4
新加坡		Xīnjiāpō	Singapore	2.5
星巴克		Xīngbākè	Starbucks	5.4
星期五餐厅		Xīngqīwǔ Cāntīng	T.G.I. Friday's	5.4 EYK

Simplified	Traditional	Pinyin	English	Lesson
Y				
意大利		Yìdàlì	Italy	2.5 EYK
意大利语/ 意大利文	意大利語/ 意大利文	Yìdàlìyǔ/ Yìdàlìwén	Italian (language)	1.4 EYK
印度	印度	Yìndù	India	2.5 EYK
印度尼西亚	印度尼西亞	Yìndùníxīyà	Indonesia	2.5 EYK
英国	英國	Yīngguó	The United Kingdom	2.5 EYK
英语	英語	Yīngyǔ	English (language)	3.4
越南		Yuènán	Vietnam	2.5 EYK
Z				
中国	中國	Zhōngguó	China	2.5 EYK
中国人	中國人	Zhōngguórén	Chinese	2.5
中文		Zhōngwén	Chinese (written language)	1.4
中央 电视台	中央 電視臺	Zhōngyāng Diànshìtái	CCTV (China Central Television)	5.5

语言注释索引
Language Notes Index

Credits

Grateful acknowledgment is made for use of the following photos:

Unit 1

23. Learning to write Chinese characters: Ronghui Shen.

24. Map of China: Public domain photo courtesy of The United States Central Intelligence Agency's World Factbook.

Unit 2

82. Three cousins: Ronghui Shen.

86. A residential community in Shanghai: Ronghui Shen.

90. The Marble Boat at the Summer Palace, Beijing: Public domain photo courtesy of Wikipedia®.

99. Shanghai's Pudong District. Public domain photo courtesy of Wikipedia®.

Unit 3

141. A preschool in Shanghai: Ronghui Shen.

151. Piano: Public domain photo courtesy of Wikipedia®.

152. Shaolin wushu: Public domain photo courtesy of Wikipedia®.

Unit 4

175. Chinese emperors: Public domain photo courtesy of Wikipedia®.

Unit 5

217. Mu Lan: Public domain photo courtesy of Wikipedia®.

236. Public domain photo courtesy of Wikipedia®.

234. Erhu: Public domain photo courtesy of Wikipedia®.

234. A man plays the Chinese 笙 (shēng) on the Thames River: Public domain photo courtesy of Wikipedia®.

242. An Internet café in Xinjiang: Public domain photo courtesy of Wikipedia®.

About the Authors

Dr. Jiaying Howard is Dean of the Immersion School at a language institute in Monterey, California. Previously, she was Professor of Chinese and Director of the Chinese Studies Program at the Monterey Institute of International Studies. She has more than two decades of experience in teaching Chinese as a foreign language, curriculum development, and teacher training. She has published many articles and books, including several Chinese language textbooks.

Ms. Lanting Xu has been a Chinese language teacher at the Bellarmine College Preparatory in San Jose, California for nine years. She is an active member of the Chinese Language Teachers Association of California and served as an AP® Chinese Exam Scoring Leader. Ms. Xu has also taught at Harvard University, the Monterey Institute of International Studies, and Kenyon College.